Double Rainbow at Full Moon

A Novel by

B.A.K. Sim

Agio ✤
PUBLISHING HOUSE

Agio
PUBLISHING HOUSE

151 Howe Street, Victoria BC Canada V8V 4K5

For rights information and bulk orders,
please contact the publishers through
www.agiopublishing.com

Double Rainbow at Full Moon
ISBN 978-1-897435-90-8 (trade paperback)
ISBN 978-1-897435-91-8 (ebook)

Cataloguing information available from
Library and Archives Canada.
Printed on acid-free paper.
Agio Publishing House is a socially responsible
company, measuring success on a
triple-bottom-line basis.
10 9 8 7 6 5 4 3 2 1 d

This novel is a dramatization based on a true story of what happened in Zimbabwe and brought this beautiful country down during the period 2007 and 2008 with flashbacks to events years earlier. Although all political figures and geographical sites are presented under their real names, many characters have been disguised under veiled appearances and fictive names for their own protection.

DEDICATION

This book is dedicated to my husband, Edward,
who inspired me tremendously in his struggle
for survival, and for his determination and willpower
in a desperate situation. I value his vast knowledge of Africa
and his tremendous insight, without which
this book could not have been written.

ACKNOWLEDGEMENTS

This book would not have come about without the deep friendships in Zimbabwe that only grew stronger concurrently with the deepening political crisis. Special thanks to the Sisters of the Convent and to the Fathers and Brothers of the Dominican and the Franciscan Order for their everlasting support.

I am also grateful to the persons who went through my first tentative literary steps and encouraged me to continue. First of all, to my sister Sonja in Denmark, who knew Zimbabwe from her own life there for three years, and to Lina Kantor, who wisely advised me to first write the story in my mother tongue.

To the people of Zimbabwe who suffered so much, never lost hope and always believed in change and kept their dignity. They taught me a basic lesson in life: that good manners have nothing to do with degrees and wealth, but are the connection to your ancestors and your past; and that is what you must value in life. Also they taught me forgiveness. Thank you to Chris Chetsanga, Professor Emeritus in Biochemistry, and his wife Carolyn for explaining certain phrases in the Shona language.

It took me four years to write this book. I first wrote it in Danish. I spent another year translating it into English. In this regard I am deeply indebted to my nephew Esben and his wife Vibeke for sending me the two huge dictionaries by Hermann Vinterberg and C.A. Bodelsen.

When I first came to Canada I had no computer, but Dr. Zig Hancyk without hesitation gave me his old one, and that gesture certainly speeded up the process. Through it all, our faithful black poodle, Simba, always lying next to me in my office when I wrote, developed from being a small puppy into a full-grown dog.

Margaret Spark did the preliminary proofreading, and gave me encouragement to get the book published. Just when I thought everything was perfect, Suzanne Baker James discovered that I had far too many commas, as I was using the Danish grammar rules.

A final vote of thanks to Bruce Batchelor for doing thorough editing and advising to write a prologue and an epilogue. Marsha Batchelor designed a lovely cover, capturing exactly the image I'd seen in my dreams.

TABLE OF CONTENTS

	Prologue	i
CHAPTER 1	Home, Sweet Home	1
CHAPTER 2	By Hook or By Crook	14
CHAPTER 3	Candlelight and Moonlight	28
CHAPTER 4	Fight for Bread	40
CHAPTER 5	The Party Must Go On!	46
CHAPTER 6	Help Thy Neighbour	53
CHAPTER 7	Rest in Peace	66
CHAPTER 8	The Chinoyi Dentist	75
CHAPTER 9	Charity	80
CHAPTER 10	The Piano Teacher	86
CHAPTER 11	Double Rainbow	94
CHAPTER 12	Living in Fear	101
CHAPTER 13	A Season Without Money	116
CHAPTER 14	The End of an Era	129
CHAPTER 15	Hardship and Injustice	136
CHAPTER 16	Exploited	151
CHAPTER 17	Frustrations	166
CHAPTER 18	The Legend	178
CHAPTER 19	Priests and Politics	192
CHAPTER 20	Millions, Billions & Trillions	200
CHAPTER 21	Canadian Evacuation	208
CHAPTER 22	All Kinds of Crooks	215
CHAPTER 23	Election	228
CHAPTER 24	Revenge of the Vote	237
CHAPTER 25	Bad News	250
CHAPTER 26	The Flight	258
	Epilogue	268
	About the Author	275

There is a season for everything, a time for every occupation under heaven:

A time for giving birth, a time for dying; a time for planting, a time for uprooting what has been planted.

A time for killing, a time for healing; a time for knocking down, a time for building.

A time for tears, a time for laughter, a time for mourning, a time for dancing.

A time for throwing stones away, a time for gathering them up; a time for embracing, a time to refrain from embracing.

A time for searching, a time for losing; a time for keeping, a time for throwing away.

A time for tearing, a time for sewing; a time for keeping silent, a time for speaking.

A time for loving, a time for hating; a time for war, a time for peace.

—ECCLESIASTES 3:1-8

PROLOGUE

She had walked for miles on the winding path from the village, hips swinging and pivoting in a regular rhythm like a pendulum. A barefooted *pickanin* followed in her footsteps, sometimes playfully in front and sometimes lagging behind. The woman had a worn pair of running shoes on her wide feet and moved with the smoothness of a gazelle strutting steadily along. Every move was programmed from her strong thigh muscles. On top of her short curly hair she balanced a suitcase keeping her head steady as a rock. She was full of grace and beauty despite her strong bones and muscular body frame. With no wind blowing one could only hear the sound of the grasshoppers and the cicadas singing in concert.

As she approached the intersection with the asphalted road, she noticed a shiny blue car pulling over with two white people in it. She stopped in awe and soon became aware that something had changed. The silence had been broken by screeching tires on the hot asphalt. The noise of sirens and ululation of police cars, building rapidly in intensity, had drowned out the singing of the insects. Abruptly, six outriders thundered up at very high speed and the rider on the front motorcycle braked to a skidding, swerving halt, positioning himself to prevent any cross traffic passing through the intersection. That same routine would be repeated; come to a halt and then catch up later. Like a pride of lions they rode on their thunderous bikes creating a deafening noise in the quiet setting. A high-speed black car appeared after the bikers carrying men in grey who disguised themselves behind dark sunglasses. They were all trained bodyguards and part of the security team. They paved the way for the bulletproof and armour-plated vehicle designed to protect the dignitaries that followed close behind them. A military truck followed, with soldiers in the back holding their machine guns at ready; finger on the trigger, aiming at a few bystanders near the intersection. At the tail of the procession was an ambulance fully equipped in case of emergency should a fatality occur or even an assassination attempt.

The woman who came in from the bush did not wait to see the whole procession. Her heart had started pumping out extra blood to give her muscles more oxygen when her glance locked with one of the soldiers. The reaction was instant and she could not break away; she became as mesmerized as if she was staring into the eyes of a lion. With an enormous determination she managed to unfix her gaze and then break free. She grabbed the pickanin by the hand so violently that the child came right off the ground and then disappeared into the same direction they had come from without ever dropping the suitcase from her head. Soon the tall elephant grass camouflaged her colourful clothing as her sweat ran cold and merged with the smell of burnt wood and the dry yellow vegetation in the bush around her. She paid no heed to the concert of the grasshoppers and the cicadas.

Little did she understand that this rapid display of brute power was a common day occurrence; the regular motorcade of President Mugabe executing his duties.

CHAPTER 1

HOME, SWEET HOME

I am back in Africa and full of ecstasy. This is my home. I breathe in deeply and slowly and it tickles my nostrils, as the air enters the secret places deep down in the lungs and the stomach. Finally I breathe it all out again. The desire to preserve this moment in time is so strong that first everything is deleted. To make sense of it all in its precursory state is what has left me in this chaos. It is like time and space are at a standstill, and only at a slow pace are the voices of nature allowed to fill the air with all its fragrances. This moment of solitude is so precious. Like the slow journey, where the soul is not left behind. The African winter is almost over; it is late August of 2007 and we are approaching spring and the rainy season. The air is bone-dry from the winter drought that has left us with parched land.

Inside the house, the tiled floors are icy cold. Although we are living at an altitude of 1500 metres, you hardly notice it, as our capital Harare is placed on a big plateau and the strong sun is always shining from a cloudless sky. The coolness of the air is only felt a few hours after sunset, when darkness falls. Our days are short during the dry season, but now they begin to get longer, but only by about one hour. The light northern nights of my native Denmark are unknown here; darkness comes suddenly and without warning. The evenings and the nights are pitch-dark, but numerous stars are scattered across and light up the heavens, which seem closer to us.

The Jacaranda trees are longing to burst, but are waiting for a little more humidity in the air. The fine fernlike leaves are still mostly green, but high up in the treetops there are clusters of flower buds and soon its headgear will look like a huge purple umbrella. The lawn looks dry and the big flowerpots in the courtyard with petunia and vivid purplish-red geraniums are thirsty for water. As I no longer have permanent staff I grab the hosepipe myself and immediately feel rewarded to be the plants' saviour. The pots are placed in groups, after Rolanda told me that it is out with lonely soldiers in a row in South

Africa, and we do try to follow up on the trends from there. In one corner of the garden, under the golden evergreen called *Joburg Gold*, I see thick clusters of clivia along the edge of the grass. The elephant ears have crestfallen huge leaves the size of rhubarb, but the minute they get water, they straighten up right away and turn their palm-like leaves towards the sky. The poinsettia bush, where a little grey song-bird sits on one of its branches swinging back and forth, definitely needs pruning. The bird is not grey all over, but has a black head with a crown. I decide not to disturb it, but to postpone the pruning. Jetlag and melancholy disappear as the duties call.

Back inside, I begin to sort out the washing and feel quite relieved there is no power cut. It's a simple task to wash in the automatic Speed Queen and dry the clothes in the dryer. Clyde's shirts take only 20 minutes, as they don't need ironing if they are only semi-dry. Far worse when you have power cuts and do the whole wash in the bath-tub and hang it out to dry in the sun, then you have to iron everything because of the putze flies. When you have servants, they iron every item with knife-edge creases.

Clyde and I moved to this romantic little townhouse in Belgravia a few months before our odyssey to America and Canada. As it is in close proximity to the Parirenyatwa Hospital and the Trauma Centre, we hardly have any power cuts. The neighbourhood consists of weathered old manor houses, which have had several facelifts in the latter years, as many of them are now used as offices by embassies and other international organizations. Their uniformed guards stand outside the big pillars of stately entry gates, saluting every time the big SUVs and Pajeros drive in and out. The new African farmers have also acquired these Pajeros, to such an extent that they are now called Pajero-farmers.

Washing dishes is no work at all in the new shiny metallic dish-washer, Defy's Dishmaid, which I have named *Mercy* after Clyde's first maid on Montgomery Road, where he was living when we met 16 years ago. Mercy is so super-silent that I sometimes have to double check if she is working, and already she is an endangered species, no longer found on the market. Surely we bought the last automatic dishwasher in Zimbabwe. The old Whirlpool that I inherited when my sister left Africa broke down after many years of hard labour, when we were packing our suitcases for Manhattan's snowy winter. Being totally addicted to this mechanical wonder Clyde and I immediately went to Makro to replace it. They had everything from fridges to stoves to microwaves, but we failed to see any dishwashers.

There was this Makro-guy sitting high up in his crane offloading supplies to the various shelves. Clyde asked him, "Where do I find dishwashers?"

"Row No. 7," answered the crane driver competently and we moved on and found the right section, but there were no dishwashers. All the shelves were small and full of textiles. Finally the crane driver came out of his crane and pointed his index finger like a missile towards a stack of dish cloths and hanging table wipers.

Clyde held both hands together like a loudspeaker repeating, "I want a machine to wash dishes, like a machine for washing clothes!"

"Ah," sniffed the Makro stock worker, officious in his impeccable green uniform. "There is no such machine." And whilst he shook his head and his short-trimmed Afro hair, you could almost read his denigrating thoughts about aliens who can't even wash plates with a cloth.

Wasting no more time, Clyde drove full speed in the blue Mercedes, flying over potholes and uneven asphalt. He went behind Mukuvisi Woodlands to take a shortcut to Jaggers Wholesale along Chishawasha Road, making an almost hazardous parking, and running with Olympic speed ahead of me into the department with kitchen appliances. And there she was: Mercy, between the automatic washing machines, even advertised as one. Inside on the racks she had complete instruction manuals, but as far as I could see in these surroundings she might as well have had her C.V. in Chinese. She was in the wrong place at the wrong time and not in demand. Therefore she still carried the old price tag. Clyde quickly realized this wonder-woman was priceless and half of what we would have paid in South Africa, so he paid up front and made sure he got a receipt. The next day she was collected in the blue bakkie, safely tied with blankets and thick ropes.

Amidst these myriad thoughts I hear Anisha's voice over the noisy intercom. She is passing by with some frozen homemade samosas.

Her husband Mohamed has given her a new shiny Swedish Volvo as a birthday present. She is wearing a modern Punjab with sari borderlines and as she gets out the car, her bangles jingle. She wrinkles her sweet little nose pierced with a diamond and kisses me on both cheeks. Like many Indian women her bum is beginning to get wider and her upper arms are too tight inside the sleeves. Although she looks like one of them, Anisha is not a real Muslim Indian, not at all born like that. She is wife No. 2 to Mohamed and her real name was Joan, but with Mohamed's mother still in charge of her son's house, this infidel daughter-in-law has, in the strictest manner, been trained from scratch with an exotic result.

"You must have been shocked when you came back?" Although formed as a question, she says it as a statement.

"Perhaps not really shocked," I explain to Anisha, and then I go on to thank her a million times for the samosas, and return to the subject of the political instability. "You see, the economy has gone that direction since the down slope in 2000 when we had the first petrol crisis. When they removed the three zeroes from the money a year ago, we knew that we would soon be back to where we started. It never became normal again."

Anisha nods agreeingly, "Now you cannot live for less than 150 million a month, so all the time we are forced to make more money."

As I am preparing to brew the tea, we are interrupted by the intercom system. It is Hilton, who runs our plastic factory. As he drives in I am pleased to see that he has still got the silver-grey Mitsubishi Colt that we bought for him when his metal-blue Holden Trooper was stolen. It was an *inside job*, as they say here when our own servants and watchman are involved. They had sawn through the gear safety lock and the iron chains on the Trooper, so his new Mitsubishi has a South African anti-hijack system to stop the thieves from driving very far before the car stops by itself.

"Must have been a shock for you to come back," says Hilton. "We cannot even get meat anymore. It is like the petrol, everything you have to buy on the black market. Baby food for Josh, we go down south to buy it and nappies and all the other stuff." His low flat dialect has a distinct South African pronunciation from the Boers with the strong emphasis on the E's, so when he says *left*, it sounds as if he says *lift*. His appearance and his face is as square as his pronunciation, a bit like a Russian.

I hear my own voice almost joyful: "But it is better with less meat. Clyde and I are semi-vegetarians." And that is true, because when Clyde last year was diagnosed with an almost incurable disease, our whole life changed dramatically and so did our lifestyle.

Every Wednesday our two garden boys come to our gate to clean out our place. They do gardening for all 14 houses in the complex and the common area. Rafael lives in the servant quarter with his wife and children, but Givemore comes every morning on his bicycle, as he lives somewhere else. Despite the fact that Rafael gets many titbits from many of the house owners, his face is not as round as before we left. Givemore is still skin and bones; most likely the *Big A*, as they call it here, when they talk about AIDS. We gave them half of the bonus before we left and the rest they should have now. As Clyde says, "If you give them the whole bonus to begin with, they do bugger-all while we are gone!"

"*Gogogoi!*" They knock on the garden gate, which I unlock.

"*Mangwanani, Madam.*" They exchange the polite morning greetings in the tribal Shona language, to which I answer back, "*Mangwanani*. How are you?" After we have shaken hands, they clap their palms and fingers together as men do; in reply I clap my hands and turn and cup one hand across the other as women do.

"We are here, if *Madam* is here," to which I answer, "I am here."

After a while with a few more polite remarks, I ask, "How much do you now earn per month?"

"One point eight, *Madam*," says Givemore. After that I give each of them a stack of money, equal to one month's pay, well aware that neither of them can exist from the meagre salary that they get on a monthly basis.

"Bodie, where are your keys?" I hear the sound of Clyde's commandeering voice from the parking area. With assistance from Hilton he is putting a new battery in my light green Mercedes. It is a big model E260, which Clyde bought from Tim Coghlan when he left Africa. Clyde has always had an impeccable taste in cars – something

I never prioritized before, but Clyde has taught me that good cars are *safe* cars. So now I also drive these heavyweights.

The first car Clyde gave me was a crème coloured Mercedes SLC, a very heavy sports model that had an acceleration as if you were on your way into outer space. The gear was manual and gave me the first true sense of driving pleasure. Besides I liked that pretty metal curtain in the back windows. As the years went by I even started to remember some of the many models and their identification numbers, as Clyde kept repeating them endlessly and he was always very enthusiastic about the new models being marketed. One day he extended the car park with a convertible 1935 Rolls Royce in a *racing green* colour. It looked ever so pretty in the garage, but I never got the chance to be taken for a drive in it, despite having acquired flowing robes à *la Gatsby*. Clyde was just too busy with the production in the factory, golf tournaments and fishing trips to Lake Kariba.

Clyde drives a metallic blue Mercedes, a model SEL 400. Not that it means much to me, but after Princess Diana was killed in a SEL 400 limousine, now almost 10 years ago in Paris, I remember that particular model very well. He is so typically boyish with his love for cars, yachts, sport and poker. My own prestige is more centred around the home, the Persian rugs and the old paintings. I like to call it *discreet class*. But after we shipped a whole container off a year ago, with our most precious belongings, there is little to show off in the little townhouse. Only a single Persian rug warms the tile floor and the walls seem nude with a few reproductions. A small sofa ensemble in golden velvet is against one wall and two big peach-coloured leather recliners are against the other wall. The big German Hannover piano is squashed in between one of the recliners and the veranda door and makes the room look warm. Despite its simplicity I adore this little townhouse, so safely tucked away between other houses; in fact only the automatic gate leads out to the street, which is a cul-de-sac. The area around us is artistic with coffee bars and exhibits, and under the shady trees in the avenues the African girls sit and braid each other's hair.

It felt great to have my own car again, although at first I was totally confused returning to the left side of the road, but routine comes back so quickly. It is that good feeling of knowing it all, although it cuts both ways, from the potholes to the traffic lights that don't work, or those you have to double check even when they work, because they are so dirty that you just cannot determine the colour. Also some of the lights don't work properly and there is a green – or a red light – on both sides! The general give-way where one yields to traffic from the right is another trap, so one must use the eyes in the back of your head to make sure that nothing will be a surprise, while being aware that hesitation will get you hijacked.

The road signs had already disappeared before we left, not just the metal ones but also the wooden ones that were painted in replacement. The first signs in metal were in extremely high demand when more and more coffin handles were needed due to the increasing number of AIDS-related deaths. The thieves found it easy to dispose of the metal signs to small home industries, which would melt the metal into coffin handles. I have one big advantage here: I know this town inside and out, as I have lived in several neighbourhoods. I do not need signs anymore. I am home again and I watch the early spring, as I did 20 years ago when I first set foot in Zimbabwe.

We have spring when the other world has autumn; our seasons are different. Back then we had no high walls in Harare, we lived in botanical gardens with swimming pools and servants' quarters in the back gardens. We used to laugh at our neighbours in Zambia who slept behind Berlin Walls covered with iron spikes and pieces of broken glass, or they had electric fencing like jails. The diplomats and NGOs went for small-arms courses prior to their expatriation. That was when Zimbabwe was heaven and Zambia was hell.

When Clyde and I renovated the house on Montgomery Road, it became a stately manor with a long avenue of Australian brush cherries, and as they grew tall they became more like trees than bushes, surrounded by four acres of parkland. Clyde named the house *Haven on Earth* and explained to me that it meant a safe harbour on Earth. At the electroplating plant at the factory he had a fine brass sign made, which he hung up on the heavy black iron gate, and when I found out what they were able to produce I asked them to copy the Danish Christmas angels and produce them in brass. So no wonder the name was always misunderstood, as guests and people passing by all thought it was *Heaven on Earth* with all the flying angels. That was until they stole the brass sign and we all started to look like Zambia. In the end Clyde had to sleep with *Dirty Harry* next to his bed, *a .38 Special.*

AT AVONDALE SHOPPING CENTRE I have a choice between two supermarkets, OK and Bon Marché, but most of their shelves are empty. On each shelf is displayed a sign *"Only one per customer!"* Those shelves must have had the most essential goods, such as cooking oil, sugar or their staple grain called *mealie meal.* The vegetables are in a decomposed state; they are more fresh and crisp from the street vendors or the hawkers among the parked cars. I have no problem buying from them, especially if they bring home-grown veggies from their *kamusha*, but it is rare now with the petrol crisis. Usually their goods originate from the supermarkets; a telltale sign is the clingwrap around them, and it happens a lot that they work in tandem with the supermarket, or they simply buy up all the stock there, to walk a few hundred metres to resell it.

When I feel very courageous, I go out to Mbare Market, which is a poverty stricken area 10 km outside town, but one needs escort by a male companion. Mbare was the first centralised area connected with the industry, and the primitive shanties had the highest population density in town. But they have fresh vegetables and many other articles for sale at much lower prices.

All are trying to survive since the government ordered that all prices should be reduced to half. Every time inflation reaches a level where no one can cope, which is also when the computers are unable to follow suit, a couple of zeroes are deleted. This is the method that is being used here to adjust the financial market. In the process many retailers went broke as they did not have the means to buy new stock.

Many foreigners here call the local whites *Rhodies*, with a silent contempt because many of them still live in the past reflecting with arrogance on their past efficiency and importance. Although they were able to fill the corn silos and the shelves in the supermarkets, there was the other side of the coin too. The Rhodies love their supermarkets, while I from my time in India do just fine with street vendors. With dried beans and with only a few vegetables I can create the most nourishing curry dishes. There is lots of fruit to choose from for Clyde. For many years I have actually avoided these supermarket products in the middle aisles, and when I go to a restaurant I can feel quite unwell when I see the Rhodies help themselves to 1200 grams of beef steak, served with chips that have been fried 4 or 5 times in the same oil. Both the Africans and the Rhodies love their barbecue over open fire, and they call it *Braai*. They sear the outside of the meat till it is almost black and serve it with their special sausage called *Boerwors*.

At Silver Glory in Kensington I find butter for 1.5 million dollars. I buy 2 packages straight away. In Green Park I find more butter for only 1.2 million. It dawns on me that the bonus of 1.8 million that I paid to the garden boys hardly covers anything, although they live differently from us and do not put butter on their bread. Like most Africans, they stick their long fingers deep down into the soft part of the bread and pull out the white parts, until only the shell is left. Now they also eat the shell.

I no longer dare to go downtown, at least not alone, as it has been taken over by gangs of robbers. It is now years since I have strolled in the inner city and visited the elegant *Barbour's* or *Meikles,* or sat at the Paris Café behind Beverley's for an outside coffee. A jeweller's shop was involved in the robbery of gold chains from passersby, who had their chains torn right off by street robbers – the store's role came to light when one victim later recognized her own jewellery behind the glass inside the jeweller's shop and alerted police to the conspiracy between shop and the robbers. Now none of the shops get any new items for sale.

The Italian *Sandros* has also closed his restaurant, which used to be a popular place for lunch and dinner, and was one of the few places at night that had entertainment. Now we frequent the places outside Harare, and the cultural life downtown has died, apart from the still-popular *Reps Theatre* on 2nd Street Extension which, despite all odds, still delivers shows that were popular 30 years ago.

When Clyde arrives home from the factory in Ardbennie the phones immediately start ringing, both the mobile and the house telephones, the latter having a noticeably high-pitched tone which makes it difficult to hear the conversation. We are unable to phone abroad as we are cut off from the rest of the world, and British Airways will no longer be flying to Harare after next month.

Clyde says I must get used to the monetary system again, because without the black market we cannot exist. He has a heavy box in the trunk of the car, which I somewhat struggle to carry inside, as Clyde cannot lift. Now the whole lounge is full of bundles of money. Although some new notes have been printed with a higher value, it does not do much good, because the printing itself has contributed to new inflation, and very soon we shall again be carrying heavy suitcases, boxes and pillow covers, when we transport money. Forget plastic bags, if you were to find any, because they would not be strong enough. The inflation is now 10,000 per cent per month. I get so sick and tired of money, and the weight of it. One day I will surely suffer a slipped disc from this venture.

"Think about our sailboat!" says Clyde with bright eyes. His complexion is better and he is not as tired, but although his weight is almost back to where it was, the disease has left its marks. Clyde was never a heavyweight; he is very finely built and he never had any reserves, apart from his beer belly, when he was taken ill. His body became wasted by the disease and his face was ravaged with suffering. As his hair grew back, it became snow white. It was like he just lost his youth in a flash.

"That big brick is brown and is 200,000 each, which makes it 100 million," Clyde rattles off, like some bank clerk, and throws a brick-sized bundle of bills onto the table.

"Wait, wait!" I shout, "What if I have to change less? How many bundles in each brick? Is it always the same?"

"There are 5 bundles in each brick." Clyde moves the fingers the same way he operates a screwdriver.

"But that bundle there is not blue, it is green!" I exclaim while noticing Clyde getting irritated.

"It is *BLUE*, I tell you, the green one is that bundle here with

50,000 and that brick there is therefore 25 million." I hear the Master's voice. There is nothing to argue about and I am staring calmly at the piles of bricks, totally convinced that all men are colour blind. It is not worth arguing; they are always right.

"What about these small ones here for 10,000?" I ask, to move on.

Clyde is unable to sit longer and gets up to press the remote for the television. "It's all the same principle with the bundles. So that brick is only 5 million each."

"And the rate?" I ask. "Is it still 450,000 for yankee-doodles?"

Clyde shakes his head and suggests another code, "Bush money is *Us*, you and me. Pound sterling is *Jock*. You remember Jock, who went to Britain. And Euro is *You*. You shouldn't need more than that. So if I say '1,000 to *US*,' then you know what I mean!"

It takes me a little while before I understand his logic, but then it occurs to me that he thinks of President Bush, when he talks about American dollars – he is not talking about the African bush. To avoid more questions from my side he adds, "You get Jock by doubling up, and the Euro you get by multiplying with 1.35."

In Zimbabwe we have used code language since way back, but talking about strawberries and potatoes like the Rhodies do is just too naïve. The last couple of years the code language has expanded remarkably and covers anything from pasta to vitamins. Or *plastic tubing*, as sister Nancy likes to say, when she imitates Clyde's terminology from plastics. This I tried to explain to my Danish Uncle Gert, when I explained, "Let us call it something *relevant*, something to do with the factory, so if you need supplies, ask for *screws!*" Old Gert, who is now 84 years old, took a long look at me and made the typical gesture of lowering his head, so that his face would come quite close and made this remark, "I *like your screwing business!*" Then he laughed.

During his younger years Gert was both in Sri Lanka and later Nigeria, but I did not know him then. He is what you in Africa call *extended family* and not really related to me, but as his surname Hjorthede matched my place of birth, he is like family. Besides, he is born in Jutland like me. Being extended family, it is safe for us to help him when needed. It would actually be expected from us in Africa.

There was this other Dane who used code words. He was a major general and sent out by the Danish military. He always emphasized that he was sent out on a peace mission but quite early after he had settled down in Zimbabwe, he started feeling the political change.

The major general was a short man, but what he lacked in height, he made up for with a conspicuous Maharaja-beard and horn-rimmed spectacles, which presented a personality to be reckoned with. Unfortunately, he underestimated the velocity of progress in Africa and would perhaps have been less hasty had he known this continent better. Early on he warned the wife, "If I say *Karen Blixen*, you must immediately start packing!" This is now many years ago, when he saw it was a situation of emergency. No sooner said than done, he phones his wife at home, and when she answers the phone and hears the words *Karen Blixen*, the line goes dead. But she knew it was the voice of her husband and she began immediately to pack their belongings. One hour later the major general returned home and without explanation he took their two Ridgeback dogs into the jeep and drove off to the veterinary to have them put down. Their departure went off so quietly that for a long time the official invitations kept coming and many thought they were just overseas.

Since the oil crisis and the farm invasions, the black market grew like the hyacinth creepers in Lake Chivero, the artificial lake that supplies Harare with water. The national bank maintained their official rates, which today are 30,000 to 1 US dollar, so if you go to the bank and exchange money, as a tourist or a missionary or a diplomat, you will only get a fraction of the value, with deduction of bank expenses. The rate will neither cover food nor other living expenses, such as petrol. This artificial rate makes it easier for the government to "pay back" the foreign debt, and at the same time the affluent rich, such as government ministers and indigenous businessmen, can go to the bank and get foreign currency at this incredibly low rate of only 30,000. When they later sell the forex (foreign exchange), they quickly become millionaires in yankee-doodles. So regardless of the attack by the Governor of the Reserve Bank on the black market, it is purely rhetoric. Nobody believes that cock-and-bull story, because the government insiders themselves feed and nourish the black market and become rich from it. Our inflation is the highest in the world and restaurants, doctors, vets, manufacturers, hairdressers, hotels and not to forget street vendors, must every week adjust the prices. The petrol stations no longer have any petrol, everything is bought black market, but we see more cars than ever before. We are going round and round in this eternal cycle, which we are unable to stop, as if on a runaway horse.

For years we have heard the warnings that we are on the way to the bottom, but it is like we are in a bottomless pit. Besides, we cannot just get off and *follow the law*, because then we cannot survive and pay for the food, nor produce anything at the factory. Some of the products we have to import, and many raw materials such as for the plastics, are not found in Zimbabwe. When I look back I remember we had milestones and clear boundaries; we knew how far we would go. Now we are forced to transcend barriers every day. It has become a way of life and we have forgotten where is the limit, because constantly we move our boundary posts. It happens so gradually that you get used to it without any drama, because when you are in the eye of the storm; the decisions are made without hesitation. Besides, there are so many decisions to make and you forget how far it was you would go.

The imagination is strong during times of war and survival. Never have I seen so many people wheelchair-bound or walking on crutches, and big babies with thick diapers. Surely they are stuffed with yankee-doodles, diamonds or gold! It's a world outside Clyde's and my reach, but we are taking part in the worship around the golden calf and the dance is on. One day we may win the big prize, because we are smarter than the farmers.

"The same will not happen to us," says Clyde. "This time something BIG will happen."

I take comfort in the thought that we have an emergency plan.

CHAPTER 2

BY HOOK OR BY CROOK

On our flight back to Africa we were spared the extra miles going via New York to London. The Air Canada flight was unable to take off from Montreal Airport. As we were all seated and ready for take-off, they announced over the loudspeaker that the engines had combustion problems. The air hostess spoke first, but then the Captain confirmed that everyone had to get off, and at that point Clyde and I looked at each other in low spirits, knowing that we would have no chance of catching our connecting flight with British Airways from London to Harare. However, when Air Canada took on the blame and put us on one of their direct flights to London, we felt extremely lucky. Due to the many empty seats, both Clyde and I could occupy three seats each and, when the armrests came up, they were easily constructed into a small bed. It was an unusual luxury to fly with so few passengers, it seldom happens anymore, and then not in the high season. We cancelled dinner as we'd already had a Chinese meal at the airport, paid for by Air Canada. *Just go to sleep and wake up for breakfast before landing.* I looked out and thought to myself, it is really true: *Every cloud has a silver lining.*

In London's Heathrow Airport we had booked a room at Novotel, a smartly designed hotel with skylights and the colour purple in abundance. The room was comfortable and I noticed with satisfaction that the bed was the big European Queen size, which is 10 cm wider than its equivalent in North America. The bathroom had modern wooden floors. Clyde wanted a real English breakfast, as the breakfast on the flight did not satisfy his extra appetite stemming from months on steroids.

"Shouldn't we check if the Baron has arrived?" I enquired. "Just in case?"

But suddenly Clyde was completely exhausted and just left the restaurant without even giving his room number. I went over to re-

14

ception and they confirmed that the Baron had arrived. Then I left a message that we would be resting and only meet for dinner later.

We call him the Baron, because his real name is in fact Baron Matepa. He had confirmed to Clyde that he was in possession of 500,000 American dollars, which was the reason this meeting in London would take place. With the new law that will soon be presented in Zimbabwe's Parliament, we will be forced to surrender 51% of our shares in the company – Africans must own a majority in all local companies. When this meeting had been proposed, Clyde and I just looked at each other and said with one voice, "*500,000 is better than nothing!*" But not a penny less, we pledged, because it might be all we were ever going to get.

In total agreement on our strategy, we greeted the Baron formally at dinner. He placed himself on the same side as Clyde and therefore sat facing me. He was impeccably dressed in a dark pin-striped suit and he greeted me with a rather sullen look, as is custom in the Shona culture, as he addressed me as *Ma'am*, like I was the British Queen. I saw him turning his knees out to both sides to have more space on the small chair. He is fat and has almost shaved off the kinky Afro-hair, which is common for them to do before the hot season starts in Zimbabwe.

I was wearing my black trouser suit and stood out with the thick gold chain that has a single diamond in it. All my Arabian bangles were jingling and on my fingers were several glittering diamond rings. I had taken up the bangle fashion years ago from my Arabic and Indian sisters, whereas the many rings had come later, when I copied the white South Africans. The Shona women normally don't wear jewellery, as their Gospel preaches against it here. I felt rather good with myself.

The Baron tried to avoid the issue and started giving a longer speech about how we had to trust each other in order to work for our mutual benefit. He had first-hand knowledge about a gigantic order from the Zimbabwean government for scotch carts for the new African farmers, and the profit from this production could then go towards buying our factory. Clyde explained that we were talking about ox-drawn carts, and it was then that I realized that we were going back to the Middle Ages in Zimbabwe's agricultural sector!

"But what about our down payment of 500,000 US? Do you have the money here in London?" I asked him to get straight to the point.

"That is where we have a problem," explained the Baron. "But to begin with, I can pay 250,000 and then the rest in local money." He even presented this offer looking proud, as if it was a good proposal.

"Now listen very carefully, my dear Baron," I leaned discreetly towards him, avoiding raising my voice, "We wouldn't even dream about giving you travel expenses to London if the 500,000 were not guaranteed. Your new proposal has no basis for negotiation, and you know as well as I know that the Zimbabwe dollar is of no value. But not to worry, let us instead enjoy the evening and forget all about the sale of the business."

Clyde, who until now had been quiet, tried to pour oil on troubled waters and explained, "My wife should have had the down payment of 500,000, because she transferred that amount of money to invest in Zimbabwe. The next 500,000 should likewise be paid offshore, but here we can of course give a longer term. But I totally agree with my wife that we have nothing further to negotiate, if the first 500,000 doesn't even exist!"

All three of us only had water with the dinner, which was very light. None of us wanted coffee. We needed all the sleep we could get before the long flight tomorrow. I raised my hand towards the Baron and apologized, as Clyde was tired and needed to rest.

"*Ma'am*," the Baron looked at me like a beggar, "you must give me this chance and I shall never disappoint you. Before the end of November I shall finance the 500,000. Let this meeting be the start of our co-operation."

"No problem," said Clyde. "Now we are no longer in a hurry to sell the factory. I am declared free of cancer and will soon be back to my old self. See you at the Airport!" All three of us then exchanged the many handshakes that are custom in Zimbabwe.

But back in the hotel room Clyde showed his irritation, "I just knew it. He has no money and he thinks he can be given the factory."

Clyde has had a factory for many years, out on the sandy soils in

Ardbennie, where no farmer can grow any crops. First he rented a piece of land at Kelvin Road in Granite Side together with five other tenants. He started buying up every property as it came up for sale and after a couple of years he owned all five properties. However, they were all spread out and it was not practical for Clyde's new goals of large-scale production, so he sold it after seven years and bought instead the land in Ardbennie. He had the old rickety shack knocked down and built a double-story factory building and offices. As the years went by, he became surrounded by neighbouring industries. Soon the whole area was identified as the industrial area. Clyde's business grew and grew and he kept expanding with new companies.

BACK IN HARARE THE BARON returns, more keen than ever before and he takes Clyde with him to a meeting in the national bank that is here called Reserve Bank. He meets high-ranking representatives from the Ministry of Agriculture and engineers from both the ministry and the bank. They asked many questions and Clyde has new hope.

"They want to order 2,000 ox-drawn carts to begin with, but they will need far more." He grabs the calculating machine and continues, "You need 3,000 sheets of angle iron 50 by 50. The first idiots are out because they only quoted for 71 million. That wouldn't cover anything and certainly not inflation, so they are now out of the picture. They all asked so many questions, especially the engineers, and they were very impressed. The Baron doesn't understand all those things."

Normally, I am an incurable optimist, but with Clyde's plans there have been many disappointments and it has left its mark. I remember when he was the obvious candidate to choose for producing the election boxes for the government. He had slaved all the Christmas holidays manufacturing a look-through sample box in plastic. Although there were only 27,000 constituencies, the order would be for 40,000. "I don't give a damn, we all know they stuff the papers in many of the ballot boxes in order to win. But I am a businessman, not a politician!" Clyde declared cynically. But as he had delivered the template to the government and was awaiting this big order, nothing happened, because Clyde's template had been given to the Chinese who got the order for 40,000 election boxes and had them produced in China.

"I just hope that it is not the same as with the election boxes. Perhaps they just want you to design the scotch carts and then they end up producing them in China?" I put my doubts forward very carefully.

"I don't think so." Clyde looks deep in thought for a moment. Then he continues, "I will make sure that they pay for 2,000 scotch carts beforehand. Then they can't just walk away, and every time they want more ox carts they will have to pay in advance. We charge 350 million Zimbabwean dollars for each cart and that should cover angle iron, steel plates, wheel tires and the shafts." Clyde punches in some numbers on the calculating machine and asks, "How many zeroes in trillions, love?" I write it down for him: 1 million has 6 zeroes, 1 billion has a thousand million and 1 trillion is one thousand billion. Thank God I noted it down from the pink financial Gazette.

"I think it is OK, they have given us carte blanche to exchange on the black market so that we can import the tires and the angle iron and they will make sure that ZESA doesn't stop our electricity supply to the factory." I can see that Clyde is feeling up to it and gets high as if from a Dry Martini.

Over the week-end Clyde flies to Johannesburg with the Baron, but when he returns I am shocked to hear that he almost had a heart attack. It happened when the cabin pressure suddenly dropped and he felt as if his chest was going to explode.

"You must not fly anymore, Clyde," I say it with a firm conviction and start planning ahead. "When we leave from here, it will be by ship and by train!" Clyde nods in approval.

All our many efforts to sell that factory: every time we believed in the lucky star – or wheel. Last time it was Gillian Sibanda, who managed to persuade us to drive 1,000 km down to Polokwame, the new African name for Pietersburg in South Africa. He had access to an offshore account which paid 200,000 US dollars, and furthermore he had signed a piece of paper that he would write that amount off, if the difference of 1,800,000 was not paid within 6 months. A white lawyer, who knew him from his time in Kwekwe, had written a contract between Sibanda and us and he was convinced that all four parties (himself included) would end up very satisfied, because it goes without saying that the lawyer should have a commission of the sale, paid outside of Zimbabwe.

Our meeting took place at the Holiday Inn in the hotel lobby and as Clyde drives like a racer driver, we were there first. Looking out of the window I noticed a fiery red Twincab and saw presumably Sibanda get out together with an African woman in a colourful dress. Clyde had previously explained that Sibanda was running a regular service over the Beitbridge border post carrying several kilos of gold.

"I am dead certain about this one," Clyde hissed, adding, "and don't you forget our code phrase: *The Eagle has landed.*"

Sibanda looked very young and sporty wearing a white T-shirt and running shoes. He had muscles like a weightlifter and I thought: *You need to be strong to carry so much gold!* There was a bar in the lobby and Clyde asked after a few polite remarks what they wanted to drink. They both wanted coca-cola.

It was a couple of days before Christmas Eve and we knew the traffic could be a nightmare, so right after Clyde and Gillian Sibanda had gone through the proposal to a contract made out by the lawyers in Harare, we made ready for our departure. *But the meeting had been totally unproblematic.* I could not point out anything in particular, nothing had happened to make me worry, but maybe that was the whole reason. I felt doubtful about the whole venture and worried. Would you not have discussed more in detail, studied the running of the factory, the stocks, the valuable machinery and had some *negotiation* first? But perhaps it was all contained in the contract. Or as Clyde used to say, "It is different when you negotiate with Africans."

CLYDE DID NOT WASTE ANY time, but found a bank in Polokwame where he could deposit some foreign cheques. He opened all the secret compartments which the vehicle had plenty of; full of inside pockets like a man's jacket. Another reason for Clyde being so fond of Mercedes cars I suspect because inside they are equipped with se-

cret panels and endless possibilities for transporting smuggled goods
or *money.* "Volvo cars are not bad either," Clyde once confided in me.

Soon thereafter we saw a 2-kilometre-long line of cars moving
slowly towards Beitbridge. Over the radio it was announced that we
could expect a long delay as the custom staff on duty had been fired
over a corruption case at the border post. Although we had nothing
to declare we decided to drive instead back to Zimbabwe through
Botswana, as I reminded Clyde that our friends, Avis and Zeb always
chose that route when they went to Cape Town.

"Good thinking!" said Clyde and quickly found the road that
would take us to Botswana. At first it was really exciting and we entered Botswana without any problems. I recognized all the road signs
with the clear blue arrows and thought they must have been donated
by Danish foreign aid, as they were the same signs as in Denmark.

We passed through the desert with dry palm trees and arrived finally at the border post between Botswana and Zimbabwe. At first
we were surprised to see kilometres of cars and people lined up already long before the border crossing. Most of them were Africans
and many women were among them. You could see they were traders,
carrying huge bundles in bags or goods stuffed into the big chequered
plastic bags with a zipper. Many of them held one child by the hand
and had another smaller child traditionally wrapped in a towel behind
the mother's back. As we passed them in the big blue Mercedes towards the frontier post, we now saw that the entry was closed and we
had to turn around when we came to a high lattice gate.

"What is happening here?" we asked the group of people waiting.

"There is only *one* person working, *Madam,*" they explained, "and
we have been ordered to wait in line."

In the beginning Clyde and I also lined up, but as we never got
any closer, it became insufferable in the heat. Therefore we decided
to take turns and rest in the air-conditioned car, but we made sure at
all times that one of us was waiting in line. As the situation did not
improve, the crowd of people started showing signs of impatience
and the children were crying. Everybody was hungry and thirsty. We
had no toilet facilities, but the men urinated in a long deep ditch with
cement at the bottom. It was along that same ditch we were lining up.

Suddenly the army arrived in open trucks. "They are loaded with batons and AK 47s", exclaimed Clyde with boyish admiration. Shortly after I went to get a rest in the Mercedes and when I exited, I failed to locate Clyde. I returned to a group of three Africans from Bulawayo, as we had been reserving space lining up for one another the whole day. The army commander started shouting at me that I could not stand there. I politely explained to him that I had been standing there since 10 o'clock in the morning. Now it was evening and now it was dark.

"So, why were you not on your spot?" the commander's voice was quite threatening.

"Because I was resting in the Mercedes," I answered him, and pointed towards the vehicle.

After he turned and looked, his whole expression changed. His threatening manner turned into anger and for a moment he looked just like Clyde when he gets a fit, and then he barked at me to take the last end of the line. The three Africans from Bulawayo tried to help me and confirmed that we all kept places for one another, which in fact we had done the whole day. This only made the soldier more aggressive and his complexion became almost grey as he exclaimed in a voice full of contempt, *"You just defend her because she is white!"*

Now I felt it was all too much, that he would turn his anger towards my new friends and I started to lecture him about human rights, then about the Vienna Convention and last about being racist, because nobody could deny it was racism to call me *WHITE!* Like the shorter catechism I gabbled off all the phrases.

In the end he backed off although snorting with scorn, "You sleep in a Mercedes when you should be standing in line and you say it is your *right!*" Shaking his head he walked away looking slightly confused.

At that moment I found Clyde very close to me and he was deathly pale. "Bodie, you are crazy. He could have shot you! That's what they normally do in such a situation. Didn't you see the AK-47 slung over his shoulder?"

His voice sounded admonitory. But I was too upset over the soldier's audacity, and besides I was certainly not going to admit to

Clyde that I had no idea what such weapons look like. The valid reason for not ever panicking: why panic over something you don't even know about. Like getting scared over a spider if you don't know it is a poisonous one. Only long after did I fully grasp that my life had been in real danger.

In the end we crossed the frontier post and entered Zimbabwe, but on the other side there was the same chaos and crowd of people. However, there was a totally different atmosphere, the customs staff were friendly and had set up extra tables outside the building to cope with the situation. Also there were no soldiers. After midnight we got through and around 2 o'clock that same night we arrived in pitch darkness at Churchill Arms Hotel in Bulawayo. Never had I been so happy to see that beautiful hotel in Tudor style. That nightmare was over.

THREE DAYS LATER, I CUT out some newspaper articles from our daily, *The Herald*. They were all about Sibanda.

"Bodie, can I see those cuttings?" asked Clyde and began reading aloud: "Look, he was arrested with 11 kilograms of gold worth over 19 billion, and he was raided at a Harare hotel where he was staying when police detectives from the CID Gold Squad found him in possession of one bar of gold in his briefcase. Another seven bars and two buttons were allegedly recovered underneath the front seat of his car." Reading this, Clyde was shaking his head with a gesture of despair, but he continued with hardly any lip movement, "I guarantee you, that is our money!"

"Really? Does it mean we forget all about selling the factory to him?" I asked and had already accepted the outcome.

"No, that's not what I mean. Besides it won't be him rotting in jail. It will be his cousin Elvis."

But be there gold bars or no gold bars, Sibanda never lived up to his promises and in the end we returned his deposit to an offshore account. It was simply too risky for us to remind him about the contract.

Sibanda was only one of many in the line of buyers interested in buying the factory. Clyde had also a lot of faith in Oscar Kaukonde, a clever sculptor, who had several exhibitions abroad. On Cripps Road, which is the road leading to Harare International Airport, he had a whole park with many variants of small and big stone sculptures. Clyde told me we were talking about big sums of money here, as Oscar sold sculptures to many countries in Europe, especially to Germany and Holland, and he was paid in Euro. Apart from this he still carried on trading in diamonds originating from a river close to his *kamusha*. That is what they call the village where they are born and where many relatives of several generations live together. Oscar Kaukonde was born in the area near the Birchenough Bridge and he always used to walk around and collect stone, which he would later sculpt.

One day he found some black rocklike formations of stone and at first he was unsure if it was really diamonds, but in Holland they had paid him quite a fortune for the find, despite the fact that he had not yet sculpted or polished it. Now the sculpture park was a camouflage for the diamond trade and there was a big demand for his work of art. He constantly freighted huge stone sculptures and black stones to Holland. For them it was attractive that his gem stones had nothing to do with blood diamonds, as they came from his place of birth and not from the war in Congo. Members in his clan had received such stones from participating in the war there as soldiers, and those stones were hard to sell.

Although I have not accompanied Clyde to the Birchenough Bridge and not with my own eyes seen the black stones, I am quite certain of this, because Clyde is a shrewd businessman and he regards Oscar Kaukunde a reliable person and does not leave out the prospect of him wanting to buy the factory in order to have a totally legal business on the outside, for the benefit of the whole family.

Clyde has also made acquaintance with several aristocrats, although some of them are more gentry than nobility, with long German names such as van Hoogstraten, Rautenbach and Bredenkampf, but he says it is a clan surrounding President Mugabe and they are dangerous to deal with, also not trustworthy. I have advised Clyde to keep a long distance to them, being aware of at least Mr. Bredenkampf being into dirty business such as arms dealing. Despite all of this, Clyde still has to try all options; it is in his nature.

"Of course it is by hook or by crook," Clyde assures me with his poker smile and reminds me, "If one day I say *The Eagle has landed*, you must immediately start packing!"

Paradise Lost started about seven years ago around millennium, when we returned from our holiday home in Cape Town and the oil crisis hit us. As the crisis became permanent, we started to look then at the possibilities of selling the factory. A couple of years later we received this letter in Cape Town, sent to our fax machine:

Sir,

Allow me to introduce myself and my brother, Patrick and Paul Mwale of the Democratic Republic of Congo. Our Father was the Congolese Governor to France. He died 6 months ago, before the recent peace talks that were held in South Africa. Our Father worked for the Government since the Mobuto-regime. He was in possession of US dollars 1,500,000 in cash together with other wealth, which he kept hidden in his personal vault. It is a kind of safe built as a tool box and totally fireproof. This vault was built into the wall in one of our Father's houses and he used to store in it a considerable amount of money.

My brother Paul and I collected the safe in question with the wealth mentioned at the hiding place before our Father died. Both the people of Congo and especially the Government wanted to lay hands on it, but due to our Father's international connections and his high status he succeeded in fleeing to Zimbabwe as a refugee under the United Nations together with his family. He chose Zimbabwe because he had a white partner there, which he always called "Mr. Client." He used to deal with our Father in diamonds, that is how we knew him, because he regularly travelled to Congo for his official business. Unfortunately, he had to leave for England because of the land reform programme that is currently taking place in Zimbabwe. He left last year in February, 2001.

But allow me to come to the heart of the matter, how we got the contact to you. The contact originated from this guy called Jean

Pierre, who lived in France most of his life, but came to Congo as well as Zimbabwe in connection with orders for office furniture for the Government. I have understood that your company produced furniture destined for both Congo and Zimbabwe through the Finance Ministry and the Ministry of Agriculture.

In memory of our Father it is therefore our wish that the amount mentioned above be invested in a good way and we would like to buy part of your company, but in such a way that there would be no suspicion. Therefore the shares should first remain in your name and the sum in the vault of a total of 1,500,000 American Dollars would be transferred to your overseas account. In the meantime me and my brother would take on the roles as your normal employees.

Hopefully, this letter will lead to an Agreement, where we may discuss your percentage for your efforts. To the outside we shall pretend that you were a friend of our Father and therefore feel responsible for us.

We trust that your homecoming is in the near future, so that the vault may be handed over safely. This is a deep secret between us.

Thanking you, I remain,
Yours faithfully,
Patrick

Clyde had shown me the letter and would not leave out the possibility of a new life in luxury. One day when I arrived home after shopping I found Clyde out in the scullery together with two young short Africans. They were both slim and dressed in modern sporty clothes and looked like students. Clyde asked for the steam iron and pulled out the ironing board. Next to the folding table I noticed a toolbox. It was open and it looked as if it was full of burnt paper. Clyde waved me away with a gesture that said *Go away*, but a few minutes later I heard him cry out loud, "Jesus, it *is* US dollars!"

When the two young men had left, Clyde explained me that it was Patrick and Paul from Congo and that the toolbox was that vault, which had been built into the wall in their father's house in Congo. Due to the political situation the American intelligence agency CIA had dropped several toolboxes from aeroplanes during the war in Congo in order to pay the rebel forces and their allies. To make sure that the money did not come in the wrong hands they had invented a system, whereby the notes would first have to be painted over with a certain chemical, before the transformation took place and it became a true version of the American dollar. Without this chemical process the money would just look like the burnt paper I had seen in the box, but Clyde had with his own eyes verified that after the chemical had been applied, it turned into a real American dollar note.

On this background Clyde intended to help the two Congolese, because after all it seemed genuine enough. He had lent them a small sum of money in American dollars and promised to keep the safe in a secure place. That safe place was our wine cellar with a secret entry.

The whole situation was driving me crazy and I slept badly that night.

"Clyde, what if they are just charlatans or real crooks?" I asked the next day.

Clyde answered quickly and almost relieved, "I have thought about it, Bodie. I should never have lent them money or received that safe."

"Did you lend them money?" My voice sounded worried.

"Only 4,000 Bush money," said Clyde irritated. "They said they couldn't buy the chemical without foreign currency."

"I think I know what they are doing. They just put ashes on a few notes, which are real American dollars, then they put on the chemical and iron it all off with the steam iron. Exactly like when I clean the table cloth from dripping of wax after candlelight dinners," I said it very carefully and did not dare to look at Clyde.

He only answered after he had made a short telephone call. Then he said, "I have just spoken to Patrick and I said to him that I don't want to be involved. I will meet him at an address near the Montegu Shopping Centre tonight. He will then return the amount in American dollars and get his *safe* back."

Clyde wandered in and out completely restless and threw the ring to the dogs. Then he came back inside. "Bodie, go and get Dirty Harry! You are coming with me!"

He chose the blue bakkie to keep a low profile. I sat on the passenger seat next to him and held the cold pistol in my hand. It was covered with a red and white chequered tablecloth from the garden table, so nobody would take notice while we were driving. It was the plan that I should pull the tablecloth to one side when Patrick came over to the car.

As we arrived at a run-down old house with a low garden gate, Clyde hooted twice lightly. At first I saw absolutely nothing, as there were no lights and it was pitch-dark, but suddenly an African appeared. In his canvas running shoes with rubber soles his steps were silent. Only when he came right up to the open car window where Clyde sat, did I see him and I quickly pulled the tablecloth away. He glanced over to my side and saw the pistol in my lap. His white teeth and the white around his eyeballs were the only contrasts in the darkness.

"Hi, Patrick," Clyde said cheerfully and stood out and handed over the safe. I saw Patrick give him a stack of notes and then they waved goodbye to each other.

Shortly after this experience there was an article in the daily newspaper about a court case against a Congolese gentleman, whose name was entirely different from the name Patrick gave us. But a renowned local businessman had gone to the authorities, because he had *lent* 40,000 American dollars to this conman. The way he was tricked was identical to our own experience, leaving us in no doubt that it was the same conman that had tried to cheat Clyde. Several businessmen of high standing had been conned with the same story, but each time the story had been changed to fit the individual. All had lost big sums of money and it was some sort of a miracle that Clyde had received all of his 4,000 American dollars back.

CHAPTER 3

CANDLELIGHT AND MOONLIGHT

As we are in the twilight of the Gods, Clyde and I are in the same boat. We need desperately to believe in something. Right now we believe in the Baron and the scotch carts. Clyde is also referring to these Medieval ox-drawn carts as scotch carts. The Reserve Bank has paid in advance half of the amount for 2,000 scotch carts in local currency and each cart is priced at 350 million. With a rate of exchange of 350,000 to the US dollar it will give us a good profit, despite the fact that we shall have to import tires and angle iron from South Africa. Clyde says we also have to buy ball bearings and rims as well as the wooden poles to which the draught animal is harnessed.

"But it is pure profit, if we do it in a hurry," Clyde says, voice a deadly hiss, whilst galloping off. Because everything depends on how fast we can do it, or we are eaten up by inflation.

The telephones are ringing both in the factory and at home in our little townhouse in the complex, and when the ordinary lines are out of order, I hear the tune of Abba's famous song *Money, Money, Money* which Clyde has chosen for his ringing tone on the cell phone. They all seem to have cell phones now at the factory and are constantly phoning one another: the Baron and Clyde, Hilton and Clyde, Clyde and O'Connor. O'Connor is our administrative director at the factory.

Every night Clyde and I are completely exhausted and we go to bed before nine. Only for five minutes does Clyde check on who is winning in cricket and golf, but he soon turns off the TV with the remote control and whispers with his lips touching mine, "*One fine day...*" He knows how much I love that special phrase from Madame Butterfly.

Before dawn, at 4 o'clock, before the early birds have started to sing, we hear a big bang. It is the power that has gone, which is unusual here in the embassy area and near the Parirenyatwa Hospital. But in these times one cannot expect to go scot-free. We doze off again until the telephone starts ringing at 7 o'clock. It is Hilton. There is no electricity in the factory.

That same day as the power went and our suburb was plunged into darkness, we had arranged to meet Johnny Katsande and Vania to eat Chinese at China Garden on Rowland Square. We meet at the restaurant, which is situated on a side road off Prince Edward Street towards town and when passing I thought, *this is easy to remember. You go straight from Kensington Shopping Centre, then just one street before North Road or Josiah Tongogara Avenue, as it has been called now for many years.* I note the wooden sign painted in red Chinese colours, as I take note of everything these days, where one can no longer rely on maps, traffic lights and road signs.

As a matter of fact I take note of many details of the surroundings and how everything is deteriorating by the day, or disappearing. Clyde's descriptions are completely useless, as he always refers to some *masculine* sign. Like the other day when I had to find the building where I could pay our telephone bill and he explained, "Darling, you just drive straight on Lomagundi Road and you cannot miss it when you see the tower on the left side."

I looked both to the left and to the right and imagined something looking like an old ruin from a castle, but I saw neither tower nor steeple. The only thing I saw and which I eventually figured out must be *the tower* was an extremely ugly metal construction pointing right up in the sky. Perhaps it was a radio tower? Or a cell phone tower? But strange how men always look at things pointing high up, something like water towers or corn silos, whereas I would notice a beautiful palm tree or some pretty windows on a house right next to it, or some wrought-iron lattice, formed like hearts or diamonds. Those ones made only for security and looking like prison doors I probably wouldn't even notice.

After the curved road on Rowland Square we see a burnt car that was never removed. Wonder what happened here? There must have been a terrible accident.

There is light around the restaurant, which was once a beautiful villa with a big garden. Apparently we are in a different zone, because there is no power cut here and no noise from generators. We walk through the garden and the flowerbeds that are decorated with bricks around them on a narrow passageway. The Chinese have worked hard since we were here last, and there are now two waterfalls to enjoy. At the entrance door they have hung some heavy look-through plastic flaps, which they used in the old days in the bakeries in Copenhagen, when they needed to keep all the bees away from the Danish pastries.

A moment later Vania grabs me from behind. She has very beautiful features, and although I know she is from Eastern Europe, she could be from anywhere. She is tall and thin like me. Her face is elegantly marked by high cheekbones, but for the first time I see that she is looking stressed out. It shows in her eyes that life is now hard. Her body does not have the slightest indication of child-bearing, although she had a few. Her high heels accentuate a pair of slim and well-shaped legs.

Johnny has the typical African smile with big white teeth and his warm embrace is good and makes me feel so safe, as his long arms draws me close to his still overweight body. He is towering over me as he is very tall and he looks very modern in blue jeans and a smart shirt, buttoned up at the top, where a couple of gold chains shine in the night.

As always we enjoy an evening of friendship with Johnny and Vania and we drink too much wine, as we both brought a bottle to the restaurant. Johnny has a very good sense of humour and the evening is filled with both laughter and joking about.

After the dinner at Rowland Square we thought at the time that the power failure was a temporary problem, but that is not the case. It has now become as serious as when we rented a house on Harry Pichanick Drive, after we had sold the mansion on Montgomery Road. Our little townhouse was bought for exactly this reason, as we thought the power would not be cut off in that area, where the big Parirenyatwa Hospital is. But we are all plunged into darkness and these institutions are no longer protected. I hear the most horrifying stories about patients dying due to blackouts. Acute surgery is postponed and monitoring equipment, alarm systems and other high tech procedures are no longer functioning.

Clyde continues paying the extra contract workers, although not being able to make full use of them with the continued power failure, as he expects to solve the problem and find out from ZESA, the Zimbabwe Electricity Supply Authority, what has happened. He contacts a number of people at that power authority during the following days and gets different explanations about the problem. One spokesperson says the fault is caused by the rain that fell Tuesday, and another that there is a fault on the 33 kV high-voltage cable supplying the substations feeding the areas. Only as we start threatening that they will have to deal with Reserve Bank, if they don't reconnect the power to the factory, do we find out the real problem. The more high-ranking folks inform us that the problem is not due to load shedding or procedural or technical errors, nor is it due to the rain that fell on Tuesday. It is simply because the authorities in Mozambique have turned the key when they were never paid. First it was South Africa, then Zambia and now Mozambique.

Yesterday I really got worried about the meat in the deep freezer. Meat that I had tracked down like it was some big safari hunt. I have ostrich, chicken and rolled pork as well as T-bone steaks. But Clyde assures me in a very confident voice, sounding like a scientist, "It will not defrost in three days if you avoid opening the door." Yet he does make alternative arrangements today with a small generator that has been loaded on top of the blue bakkie. The generator belongs to Hilton. I am sprawled across the kitchen counter towards the hatch trying to reach the plug behind the huge combi-fridge. The light comes on in the fridge, but that is all; it does not cool.

"The generator is too small," says Clyde after a while when it does not start to cool. "Tomorrow I shall bring home the big generator."

The townhouse next door is empty, but every day I see a uniformed maid go in and out. During the day she often sits under the big fig tree and in between she helps the two garden boys to remove the weeds from the cobblestones. One day I ask her if she might have extra time to help me. She avoids looking at me and therefore gets that sullen look which is supposed to be polite in the Shona-way as she replies, "I shall first have to ask Master."

"But of course. My husband can also talk to him; they know each other," I answer cheerfully.

Her name is Salome and she tells me it means *to be sent*. All names in Shona have a special meaning. Now Salome comes twice a

week and helps with cleaning and ironing. Only the first week do we
have power. The second week there is a power cut, so she is unable to
vacuum-clean and iron. Salome is not worried about not vacuuming.
She prefers to beat the carpets free of dust, polish the tiled floors and
dust everywhere with a mop. It occurred to me that it will take a long
time to train her to clean the Danish way; she prefers the African-
English way with plenty of polishing and less soap and water. Her efforts remind me of a dry shampoo. Nobody in Denmark would dream
of polishing the floor tiles, it is also too dangerous.

Salome starts with strong force to remove all furniture outside into
the courtyard and the veranda. The loose carpets she places in the sun.
Because it does not matter anymore I say nothing. She works so hard
for such a small body. In between she limps on one leg, and she tells
me that is because she once had an accident on a motorbike. She is
not young anymore but very energetic, and her long arms are never
empty. They always carry a broom. Her afro-hair is hidden beneath
the uniform cap. Her uniform is covered with a pinafore.

The blue bakkie from the factory drives in with builder Gabriel
and the garden boy Givemore in the back of the truck. Buster, who
is our handyman at the factory and in charge of many responsibili-
ties concerning production, is steering the bakkie and parks outside
the garage door. As Buster exits the car, he greets me warmly in the
Shona-manner and I notice that he has taken up Clyde's fashion with
black trousers and black shirt. His behaviour is full of confidence
and pride, but not arrogant. The generator is as heavy as the big steel
safe and looks like a small locomotive, especially as Buster instructs
Givemore to start the engine with the iron handle on one side. Coal-
black smoke pumps up through the chimney, as the handle is turned
faster and faster. The locomotive starts and the light in the fridge is
turned on. After half an hour I feel quite relieved that it starts cooling
inside the fridge.

I try to forget the noise from the generator and start playing the
piano, but it is very difficult to concentrate with all that noise. There
is also noise coming from the neighbouring mansions and it is so
loud that one cannot hear the birds. Other irritating racket is carried
through the treetops all the way from Bon Marché Supermarket.

Clyde has arranged my two gas heaters in the garage as a mini kitchen on top of the heavy money safe that weighs a thousand kilos. It is Clyde's experience that heavy items are rarely stolen in Africa. That was the reason for him producing the heavy iron gates, when we lived in *Haven on Earth* with the result that when we started having power cuts, you would need more than one man to push the gate manually.

"And did we ever have a robbery?" asked Clyde.

"No, but I could never leave the house if the servants were out and I felt locked up like in a prison," I said.

"You were the *princess in the tower* and I knew you were safe," laughed Clyde.

In order to hide that there is a steel safe in my garage kitchen, I have placed a red and white checkered table cloth over it and then put a smaller oil cloth on top of the table cloth. It is a good camouflage, and next to it is an extra fridge and a big garbage bin in plastic. The bin is like the safe, full of bricks of local Zimbabwe dollars. Quite naturally I now waltz between the real kitchen and my garage kitchen through the little courtyard. Every time I collect money I bring a wicker basket with me and carry it over one arm and a checkered dish cloth is covering the bricks. Because I once learned that if you have to hide something – for a good reason, of course – you must do it openly. I remember my father's stories from the Second World War, when he on several occasions had to hide both Jews and Russians in the haystack. The women transported the secret messages in an open bicycle basket or in the luggage carrier behind full of parcels to take away any suspicion. "And stick to the truth!" my father always said. "Otherwise you won't remember."

Suddenly I hear somebody knocking on the garden gate. As I look out of the window, I see a most familiar kind face surrounded by a starched veil. "Hi, Sister Perpetua!"

Somebody must have let her in, probably Rafael, because our intercom system is not working when there is no power. She is looking very stressed and has no time for coffee. But can I handle 300 million? In a businesslike manner she inquires about the rate of exchange and I give her the information. I disappear into the garage with the wicker basket over my arm and return with the dishcloth over the contents.

"Here comes *madam* with the eggs!" says Perpetua with a big laugh and I laugh too because it sounds as funny in German as it does in Danish. In English it really does not mean anything, says Clyde.

We talk a little about the desperate situation resulting in all of us living like criminals just because of one man. I agree with her and assure her that it is always the same in these countries. "When I was in India, I always had my car trunk full of whiskey; otherwise it was impossible to carry out my job."

Inside in the lounge Clyde has had a kind of a mini-generator installed, because he can't live without his TV. But the TV only sheds light in the lounge and I feel uncomfortable cooking by candlelight. Therefore we go out for dinner more these days, unless I have prepared a dinner ahead, which only has to be heated up.

The situation is so serious in the twilight city that the government in the end finds the foreign currency – *forex*, everyone calls it – necessary to pay its bills, and then there is light again. Just when the Catholic nuns had given us a stack of extra thick altar candles. First we get light in the townhouse, but it comes later at the factory, because ZESA is unaware of the agreement we have with the Reserve Bank about special treatment and no power cuts. In the end the Baron and Clyde manage to get the message across that they have to make an exemption with the load shedding, as long as we are producing scotch carts.

Clyde has in the meantime tried to use the manpower for other purposes and the production is ready to burst, as soon as the power comes back on. The ovens have been rebuilt and extended to enable the carts to get in from another angle, when they have to be painted. The angle iron that the Baron has procured is discarded, as it is rubbish. It is even full of rust that has been painted over. Clearly he has got it for nothing and I am shocked to hear that it would have made the workers really ill working with it. They had tried to hide the defects by painting the bars in a rusty red colour, but nothing went unnoticed during Clyde's inspection. When the power returns at full blast, we all feel like we have pushed a locomotive and everybody is full of adrenaline and strength.

Clyde's agent in South Africa is a folk singer and his name is Matthew Beyer. He phones every other day to get instructions, as Clyde can't phone out of the country. The telephone system is collapsing.

One day Matthew drives from Johannesburg to Harare and plays at the Restaurant Aló Aló, situated in the Alliánce Francais building. During his trip he sticks to routine and stays at the *Lion and Elephant* motel with its typical thatched houses called *rondavels*. We have booked a table for 10 persons and enjoy Leslie's gourmet meal, which is somewhat of a miracle these days, considering how difficult it is just to procure a chicken.

Matthew sings from his new album, *Love Songs and What Have You,* and we buy the disc to support a good cause, the SPCA, which is the animal welfare association in Harare. It is the highest priority in Matthew's life. He would give his life for them, whether tame or wild. His rusty deep voice stemming from a long pub life makes it sound very erotic. As he sings *Stand By Me* and *Headed For a Fall,* they all applaud him in the restaurant. The songs are performed in a bit of slow-motion giving the evening a touch of melancholic romance, mirroring our situation in Zimbabwe today. All around I see young pretty women smoking their cigarettes.

The bill is only 26 million despite all of us having had both starter and dessert. Still, Clyde did not bring enough money, but I had the foresight to bring along a few bricks in a plastic bag. From the many transactions I was fully aware of the rapid inflation. My customers make sure that I am constantly updated, and doing all the household shopping has given me a further insight into the whole situation and the prices of commodities.

IN THE WARM EVENING TWO Catholic nuns come to visit. It is Sister Nancy and Sister Rit. The latter I call *Sweet Rit*. They are very recognizable in their habits as they get down from the high steps of the wine-coloured Holden Trooper. We now live close to one another, as the Convent is in town, close to the Presidential Palace. Despite the lovely weather we decide to sit indoors, because the night has sharp ears. Clyde immediately opens a good bottle of red wine. It is a Cabernet Savignon from Robertson's Winery in South Africa. We are celebrating the ox cart production. The two middle-aged nuns are dressed in their formal habits with the starched veil in black and white, but despite the identical habits, they are very different; only the many years of friendship have made them look alike. Sister Nancy will always have that typical Irish nature and her energetic personality makes her very tolerant towards Clyde and his mischiefs. Sweet Rit has a soft side to her, but she has strong leadership qualities like most Germans have.

We no longer feel shy towards them – whether they wear habits or not. Perhaps more when they are dressed in normal clothes. They did that during a holiday to our townhouse in Cape Town and on a fishing trip to Lake Kariba. They even wore Bermuda shorts! The first time I saw them without the veil was quite a shocking experience. To see them with normal haircuts and graying hair was like seeing them *naked*.

"Did you hear about the strike?" asks Sister Nancy, businesslike, and turns towards Clyde, as if he is the business guru. She is referring to the strike in South Africa.

"Yes, we shall probably have to import tires from Korea now," says Clyde. He is obsessed: I envision a big O on his forehead, which means *ox carts*. Meanwhile he is rotating a very advanced bottle opener from Canada looking somewhat like an instrument of torture, and manoeuvring both the Cabernet Sauvignon and balancing four wine glasses between his fingers, instead of using the tray. He reminds me of an octopus.

He speaks to us through the hatch and then sashays through the arch. Then he drops the glasses with a heavy hand on the glazed tile table and fills one of them for Sister Nancy. He pours right up to the rim.

"Not so much for me!" warns Sweet Rit, whilst pulling her grey skirt farther down to cover the knees.

We all raise our glasses and we clink all four together as is the custom in Zimbabwe. "Congratulations with the scotch cart production. *Makorokoto!*" They say it in one voice and repeat congratulation in Shona. They also call the ox-driven carts scotch carts, because they have read about them in the press.

Shortly after, "Have you heart from Gert?"

"Yes," I say. "He is coming with Lizzie this time as planned. I must see what party I can make for them in this little house. It will not be quite the same."

"I am sure it will be just as cosy," assures Sweet Rit. "Perhaps more so when we are not so many people."

Her words take me back down memory lane, recalling all the luncheons and dinner parties we have hosted every time Gert and Lizzie came. He had himself a tradition for curry luncheons, where we were always invited together with the nuns and some Swiss friends, Edgar and Tut. He knew them way back from his young days in Nigeria. He is also close to Avis and Zeb, but they are not invited anymore together with the Swiss, as they had become estranged after a peculiar incident.

It so happened that Avis and Zeb's daughter Colette came to Edgar and Tut's holiday home in Tuscany, Italy.

"Can you imagine," said Tut, "we did *so* much for Colette, because Avis had told us that she was deeply interested in the world of art. Therefore we made all the plans for her, mapping it all out and planning the whole trip. But later when collecting her, we learned that she had done absolutely nothing according to the plans. She was only interested in finding out if David was circumcised in Michelangelo's picture. Yes, and then the *Hermès scarf.* She was more interested in getting that silly square scarf, which is not even Italian."

As with many things in life, it is not the big adversities that cause division; sometimes it is that trivial incidence, *un banalité.* But after this episode Tut and Edgar cannot stay in the same room with Avis and Zeb. On the other hand, when you know the Swiss people, you can easily imagine they took great pains to plan the venture for the young Colette.

Gert married Lizzie in his young days, after she had been Miss Denmark, and he brought her to Nigeria, but the marriage did not last; it ended in divorce. However, their disagreements over the years developed into a warm friendship, which they never had when they were married to one another. And then, of course, the fact that neither of them had any luck finding a new partner and as Lizzie said, "Since we both never found one, we might as well stay friends!"

Eventually they started to travel together and went to Zimbabwe numerous times during the months when the Danish weather was intolerable. They were surrounded by a staff of 10 people in the farmhouse in Ruwa, where they enjoyed every moment being waited upon and spoilt. The staff is much bigger than we are used to in Zimbabwe, but they were comparing with their status in Nigeria and found it quite adequate.

All of us are friends like one big family clan. Clyde and I see both the nuns and Gert and Lizzie. Then we mix with Tut and Edgar and Avis and Zeb, but we never make the mistake of inviting the two couples together.

For many years Clyde has delivered school furniture to the Convent, beds to the hospital in Masvingo, and beds and desks to the Emerald Hill Children's Home.

Friday afternoon Clyde asks me if I want to see the new production at the factory. "Of course," I say happily and get ready immediately. We no longer close early on Fridays; even the week-ends are busy and the plastic factory runs a night shift.

From far away I can hear a deafening noise coming from the sawmill and the resounding stroke of the hammers in the new department where they are producing ox carts. The sparks are flying around the many welders working there, and the bluish light gives the impression of a cave dwelling full of ghosts. They are all in their welding gear and look like rough motor bikers, faces hidden behind helmets. Just looking at these masked men is both mysterious and fearful. In between they yank open the helmets when they have to check the work.

Clyde has organized different stages of the productions and made several jigs, and trained the workers individually for each unit. Besides our own welders he has also hired welders from two other factories in Ardbennie. Our big trucks, painted in blue and orange logo colours, zoom back and forth between McDermaid and Ardbennie Welding Company to collect steel plates which they have bent and moulded, almost like when you make a model aeroplane, and 50 x 50 mm angle iron boxed for the axle. The insufferable scraping sounds, which I feel to the marrow when they load products into the truck, tell me one thing for sure: we are not dealing with products in paper or carton, but iron and steel, heavy metal as only *real* men can work with. Men who are not put off with a wee bit of noise pollution and do not complain about trifles.

Another jig illustrates the cartload on the ox-drawn cart. Clyde looks at me and reads the admiration in my eyes. Rather proudly he shows me the U-bolts and the pole to be inserted, when the donkeys or the cows shall pull the load. There is no doubt in my mind that this is a fantastic project and I am completely astonished over the enormity of it all and feel the tears coming to my eyes. Where has Clyde got all that knowledge from? To totally change from the production of hospital equipment and school furniture, and in a few days produce agricultural machinery instead. Now I understand why he became ill. He does not sit down two minutes. He flies around constantly with that soft folding rule that is hanging in his leather belt and checks on all measurements by the millimetre. Some of the angle iron is immediately discarded due to irregularities. Clyde then shows the welders how to check the right angle. You do it by turning them upside down to see that they stand completely straight and there is no wobbling, or they fall over.

The Baron was here yesterday with representatives from the Reserve Bank and the Ministry of Agriculture. They were worried whether we really were producing or we had just lined our pockets with the prepayment.

"They were very impressed," says Clyde with enthusiasm in his voice and bright eyes. He loves this challenge and continues, self-assured, "By the way, we have already got the next order for 4,000 scotch carts and they understand that it will now cost 650 million each cart with this inflation. We will also get better conditions to work under, as they will prepay the full amount. If we hurry up, it will make us rich."

CHAPTER 4

FIGHT FOR BREAD

The following morning I go shopping to see what possibilities I have to make a party when Gert and Lizzie come. It becomes more difficult every day, because there is no meat on the shelves, only endless rows of nitrate-filled *Colcom* sausages, and everything from pig ears to pig's trotters. I avoid that as long as there are fruits and vegetables. There is no longer milk, eggs or bread. I decide to drive to my old neighbourhood in Chisipite, where the Lewisam butcher is located. Along the road I see the beautiful Jacaranda-trees in full bloom. Unexpectedly, I find ostrich meat from the butcher's cold counter and I grab four packets. That is all I can buy as I have to pay in cash, and there is a strict limit as to how much cash you can draw in the bank, no matter how much you have deposited in the account. In the distance I hear a faint drumbeat. They are drumming for rain.

Next morning I start lining up early outside Bon Marché Supermarket in Avondale, as I am told there is bread. It is close to where I live and the queue is not too long, but still it takes a long time before it is my turn. As I finally arrive at the counter, where the assistant baker is handing out the bread, he says to me, "Sorry, Madam, bread is finished, but, if you wait, there is soon coming a new tray!"

I stand glued to the counter and the line of many Africans standing behind me grows steadily, as the rumour spreads quickly when there is bread available.

Suddenly, a whole army of policemen arrive. They are dressed in blue and brown uniforms and they start giving commands in order to get in front of the line. I keep standing. They command, "You must *all* leave the shop!"

The Africans start very slowly to move towards the exit, but they are arguing in anguish. A small thin African remains standing next to me. The blue uniform now speaks directly to me, "Everybody must line up outside!"

My voice is very firm as I reply, "I have been standing in line for

a very long time and now it is *my* turn!" Then I just ignore him. From
my side vision I see him walk across to his colleagues to have a conference in his local Shona language.

After a long time they shout, "Everybody OUT!" With arms ges-
ticulating they direct the many Africans outside the building.

I remain standing and the little African moves a little closer to my
side and looks as if he is my houseboy. The voices in uniform get
louder and louder and now they bark out their threats. "We are closing
shop. All managers must leave!"

Meanwhile the baking team is working full speed as if they are on
a piece-work contract. They are so concentrated that they hardly hear
the commands of the police, or perhaps they are just ignoring them
like me.

Now another policeman walks towards me. He is wearing gold-
rimmed glasses and the colour of his uniform indicates that he is of a
higher rank. It is a brown uniform.

"Excuse me, Madam, you must go outside!" He looks at me from
the side and I slowly turn to face him. I give him the look that is more
powerful than words and run him a once-over, taking in every detail.

I wait a long time before I lean a little closer towards him and in a
very low voice I reprimand him like a school teacher: "It is both im-
moral and illegal to abuse your uniform!"

He is now rejected and I place my elbows on the counter in the
position I had before his intrusion. The little African does not budge
an inch from my side and moves closer to me. We are now alone in
the shop together with the police corps and a single attendant from
the bakery.

Outside, a 200-metre-long row of a mixed population has formed,
spanning in years from child to adult to old people. Men and women
all huddled together, but most of the women carry a load on their
backs, rocking gently the little creature muffled up in a big towel
on her back and the little legs spread out on her hips. The towel is
fitted tightly under the baby's bum and tied in front at the mother's
waist. They stand in the merciless heat of the sun and little do they
know that it might be in vain, because there is not enough bread for
everybody, even if they might be permitted to line up again inside.

They are desperate now without their staple grain of mealie meal. The bread at least gives them the illusion of a meal. This miserable white Zimbabwe bread of poor nutritional value, without wheat germ, over-processed and so full of substitutes that it cannot even be cut, ends up all in crumbs because they have had to mix the flour with maize meal. Even the flies and the insects are not tempted to eat it. Which reminds me, I must start baking again, but first I need to get more flour from South Africa. Unfortunately, it is not part of the African culture to bake bread, like the Arabs and the Indians, who can make flat bread on a stone.

"Here you are, Madam, a nice and fresh bread for you!" I am awak-ened from my dream and feel that it has been a worthwhile experience, especially as I am rewarded with that big warm African smile from the shop attendant. The little thin African next to me also receives his bread. At first he looks dumbfounded, but soon after his whole expression changes and he looks as if he struck gold. Then he grabs the bakery assistant's hand and then my hand and he is grinning from ear to ear. These smiles are so rare now. The faces begin to look stiff, the cheeks hollow and the eyes have a haunted look. The people also don't chatter anymore or slam the palms together when they line up.

Out in the parking lot I am received with a round of applause, as I walk towards my car with the bread in my hand, like some celebrity. They like that you can stand up for yourself, especially where the police are concerned.

Life is much easier when you are in harmony. My harmony is barometric and goes up and down with Clyde's mood swings, ever-changing, depending on the frustrations he has at the factory. To out-siders he is always charming and lively at parties, flirting right, left and centre with both sexes, but always sitting far away from me. At home in our little townhouse he is a dumb animal, sitting glued to the peach-coloured leather recliner with the remote control in his hand. But like a dog just waiting for the slightest invitation to jump up, I interpret every little occurrence as an appeal. Therefore, I think that Clyde is opening the Chilean red wine so that we can be intimate, but after I raise my crystal glass and begin to chatter, I am dismissed with a wave of his hand, "I am watching TV!"

This morning I summoned up my courage and mentioned to Clyde my feelings about his silence, but all he said was, "I am trying to spare my voice, so it will heal more quickly. Sorry about that."

"Yes, very well. But where is the logic?" I ask. "If you were quiet when we are out, I could understand. But you are extremely lively. I wish we could have it like Mano and ZsaZsa. They always sit together and laugh together, no matter whom they are with."

I had stopped then and there, because it was to be expected that it would take time for him to heal. It had all been very traumatic, being diagnosed with the disease. The treatment to get rid of it was extremely unpleasant to say the least, and one wondered if the whole thing had affected him in one way or another. After the keyhole examination in New York he was clearing his throat constantly, and it had been very difficult to get him off the steroids. Besides, one lung had been damaged and burnt during radiation treatment in Johannesburg in South Africa. Finally, the overtaxing of his whole system in connection with the order for the ox-carts certainly was not good for his health, but not under any circumstances would he lose out on the chance to earn such a big sum of money, which would normally take years to earn. So I resign and take shelter in my book.

Salome is sitting under the big fig tree knitting. After a while she gets up and goes for a walk around the complex. Her walk leads her up to the gigantic Jacaranda-tree and behind the bushes with acacia. She disappears into the staff houses. She is very proud because I gave her some knitting yarn and she has produced a baby cardigan in beige and black. Now the needles are quickly rotating down into the light green colour. Already she is some 10 to 15 cm into the pattern, which looks rather complicated, but it is all up in her head. The knitting needles rotate with her swaying gait. Although she is thin, her bum still has a good shape and moves erotically. All men in Africa are fixated on the bum, and after all these years I have now also got that fixation. She makes the stitches like we do in Denmark when we are crocheting, because that is how she has been taught by the British. The African women always knit the same, as they have first learned, and never try a new knitting pattern. Many of them can knit and do crochet, even when they cannot read or write. That is why they stick to the patterns they know instead of learning new ones. But it makes it harder to sell the same thing over and over. Once the foreigners have acquired the tablecloth and the bedspread, they look for new products. Even when these women can read and write, they prefer to stick with what they know and do it by routine. Perhaps there is a lack of ambition and creativity. They prefer that life remains the same.

There is no more knitting yarn in Zimbabwe, and the women do love knitting and talking at the same time. When times were better, they would stand by the roadside, waiting for the combo-bus and chat together. The needles would move rapidly and the bodies would gently rock from side to side like in a dance, to calm the baby on the back.

Salome is now getting ready for a walk outside. She is dressed in her maid's uniform with matching pinafore, but the starched cotton cap she has replaced with a knitted one in Rastafari-colours – not because it is cold or building up to rain, but she wants to look smart. Had it already started raining, she would have put on a shower-cap. Oh, how the knitting was missed in the street life since I came back, and the fact that Salome can stand on a street corner with busy needles, is a matter of prestige for her.

It is with mixed feelings that I go shopping in the daytime. Normally, I start in Bon Marché to save time and petrol, but I also feel stressed out, now that Clyde needs three healthy meals a day. He comes home for lunch every day. Outside the supermarket I am already prepared for the big price increases since I last did my shopping, as the last eight days with power cut has meant that I had to discard most in the freezer – giving it away. The two garden boys, Rafael and Givemore, were very happy and exclaimed spontaneously, "It is like Christmas, Madam." Then they clapped their hands with palms and fingers together.

Salome was overwhelmed too. They all had some chicken, beef and ostrich, as did our Austrian friends, Tut and Edgar, and Leslie at Alo Alo, because they have a generator. Our generator from the factory never really worked properly; it cooled the meat down, but never froze it.

First I find mushrooms and oranges, and hot green peppers for curries. The staff in their green uniforms and white pinafores are just packing them into trays, but *very big trays*. I quickly ask if I could get a smaller portion, but the lady says, "No, Madam. You have to buy one big tray."

"But you only use one pepper for one stew," I argue. "At least make it into half a portion and put a new price on it."

"No, that we cannot do. That is not our policy," she explains unsympathetically and puts on the self-sticker with the price."

You cannot get blood out of a stone. I should know that. So I forget about it although thinking, how bloody stupid when so many customers could be made happy, if they sold smaller portions.

When I return home I receive a telephone call from Denmark. Gert and Lizzie are not coming as planned in October, as Gert has fallen ill. At the hospital in Denmark they diagnosed an aggressive cancer in his lungs. Since the diagnosis he has deteriorated rapidly and his family has taken steps to get him admitted to Arresødal Hospice.

Clyde is shocked to hear the news when he comes home. Although we both knew that Gert had problems with the healing of a wound on his foot, the fact that he is now a dying man is incomprehensible and a big shock to all of us. The two Catholic nuns, Nancy and Sweet Rit, call us and their voices are full of sorrow. "Let us pray for our friend," they say. We are all at a loss to understand this sudden turn of events and the fact that we shall never again see Gert at the end of the table with his fat Havana cigar and clink the crystal glasses high in the air with him.

Because Clyde fought the same disease, it is difficult for him to write off an old friend, although he is so much older. We therefore advise him to go to France, and send him an envelope with *Ngoka tea*, which he must drink three times a day. Many Africans have gotten rid of malignant cancers by drinking this tea, and Clyde has assured me that the tea is produced by a renowned witch-doctor in Tanzania.

CHAPTER 5

THE PARTY MUST GO ON!

O ur social life is very demanding at the moment. First there is June and Dan Bailey's art exhibition at their galleries here in Belgravia. The theme is "Shouldering the Burden" and it is an exhibition full of imagination in abstract forms. A young Belgian artist is exhibiting her work of art from the sea. She has produced some shell-looking sculptures, many of them inserted with pearls, and has produced a very beautiful glaze in an attractive wine colour. The idea is good, as many of them could actually replace live flowers in vases, especially useful if you are a busy career woman. But I am surprised when I meet the artist, who has neither snorkelled nor dived in the sea to get inspired. She seems restless and in too great a hurry, as is typical with people from Europe.

The guests are the old guard of Harare, a small circle of perennial figures preoccupied with self-preservation. They are Harare's yuppies, *the young, the rich and the beautiful* from Harare's nightlife. All are standing with a wine glass in the hand and look carefree. But on closer inspection you see that there are cracks in the façade; the good humour is only skin-deep. Because they are not so young anymore, daily life has become a struggle and some of the smiles are covered up to take the attention away from some molars now missing. I am witnessing the poverty in Zimbabwe, which has also reached Harare's yuppies.

"Bodie, did you get any wine?" Dan Bailey asks and pours more white wine into my glass. "You know that *a day without wine is a day without sunshine.* That's what they always said in South Africa."

At the cash bar I find Dusty Miller, who is a journalist. He is a food connoisseur and critic in the weekly independent newspaper. While he is consuming an intoxicating drink, he is gazing over the party.

Meanwhile, Clyde has made contact with the principal of the International School and is probably trying to get an order for school furniture.

We meet a physiotherapist called Didier with his girlfriend. He is still very attractive with an athletic figure and looks like a tennis pro, and he has got the strength to manipulate and massage the international clientele who can afford his treatments. A woman is standing close to him and looks stunning from face view, but from behind she has jelly bum and jodhpur thighs.

Clyde and I make an early departure from the galleries.

During the next few days we are invited to a number of national days with international embassies. These events have one advantage: you only have to stay a maximum of two hours. The ones that stay longer are almost demonstrating a craving for human contact and are usually the ones only being invited once a year. Those of us who are invited officially or on business generally leave early. National days are now celebrated in the middle of the day to emphasize the official and work-related reason for the celebration.

The countries are mainly represented by ambassadors or their deputies. In the old days, staff members of lower ranks were also invited and included attachés and administrative personnel who mixed freely with those of high rank. But the growth of bureaucracies (in part because foreign aid budgets have ballooned) has marred the pleasure in this regard. Diplomatic functions now accommodate only *high-ranking* officers. The hierarchical pecking order is more visible than ever before with ambassadors and emissaries strutting around like peacocks, or perhaps it is more like ladies and gentlemen of the court around the royal elite. It seems ironic really in these modern times that feudalism has returned. Should you be so lucky as to have the attention of an ambassador for a few minutes, you will notice that his glance wanders uneasily from one object to another. He cannot afford to lose out on an opportunity to meet ministers or other dignitaries. If His Excellency (let's be honest, there *are* only few womenfolk among them, although to punish Mugabe they are now in higher numbers) sets eyes on such a species, you'd better be prepared for a surprise amputation of your conversation with him, as he moves with unexpected speed towards the VIP, which in diplomatic terms stands for a *very important person,* not to confuse with the medical term: *vasoactive intestinal polypeptide.* It is important to be seen, important to show you are one of them and used to walking on the red carpet. Although I have been accused of being a butterfly, when I flutter off, it is only that I cannot be captivated for long by the flashy appearance and nectar-like allure from these peers and it is, after all, better to move on than to be discarded.

The Mugabe government is almost like some kind of dirty word now, and this is especially evident on national days. The German *lady* ambassador has consequently invited several nuns and religious representatives, resulting in a colourful fauna in the landscape. I recognize many of our Dominican nuns in their white/black habits. Other orders are dressed all in crème-coloured habits. The chorus, organized by the Anglican Church, are in shiny purple garments, looking very much like university graduation gowns. The German ambassador, who is strikingly beautiful with her gypsy looks, has on her long lean body hung some national costume from South Germany. Although the colours are dark and befitting a funeral, they match the red carpet she is standing on to bid everyone welcome. She recognizes neither Clyde nor myself, even though we sat at the same table at the Italian Sixtieth party. She is high-spirited from standing on the red carpet shaking the hands of the dignitaries, and has little memory or warmth. Or perhaps like me, she is afraid of being discarded, so she makes it short.

The celebration takes place in the official German residence surrounded by six acres of land in a distinct African landscape, where the Msasa trees are growing along the upward slope. These wild trees are first red and only become really green after the rain, when they have finished flowering. Huge tents have been set up to accommodate long serving-tables and under the shady trees are placed small round tables and chairs, where you can sit comfortably with a glass of wine and have a conversation. All German citizens are invited and many are enjoying themselves.

Exactly an hour after the official time of arrival the formal entertainment begins. The normal protocol is not followed today, as President Mugabe and his henchmen are *persona non-grata,* so they have not been invited and we miss their exchanges of speeches praising one another. In her speech, the ambassador emphasizes the importance of *unity* and compares it with the unity reached in East and West Germany, after the Berlin Wall fell.

The two national anthems are played after that. The Zimbabwean national song called *Ishe komborera Africa*, which replaced the old Rhodesian tune *Ode to Joy* from Beethoven's Fifth Symphony, has a strong effect on everybody. The song makes you feel happy, strong and part of the African struggle. They used the South African song *Tshotsholotsho*, meaning "to go forwards" and changed a few words. Every African knows the tune by heart and their beautiful voices are echoed between the Msasa trees. As more and more voices are joining in, the crescendo is like a rising tide. Then the anthem of Germany, *Das Lied der Deutschen* by Haydn, more commonly known perhaps as *Deutschland, Deutschland über alles,* is sung, and it brings to the party a peculiar mixed atmosphere of Oktober-fest and military parade.

Unexpectedly, I meet many old friends, both from my riding lessons with Claire Pierce (cut short though when I had a fall and fractured my neck), but also from the Belly Dance Club. My German dentist Gerhard Lung from Chinoyi is also there and next to him his wife Sonja. We greet each other warmly. After a while I find a chair next to the Catholic nuns, as they possess such vitality and worldly wisdom, which I don't find among the other guests.

As per tradition Clyde and I are also invited to South Korea's national day, which is held at the elegant Meikles Hotel in the middle of the city of Harare. Meikles Hotel is especially beautiful now, surrounded by the flowering Jacaranda-trees. These incredible perennials during the month of October (that we here call the *suicide month*) are completely bluish purple and have an array of colours like an artist's palette. On some of the avenues they are in such close proximity that their gnarled branches close in at the top, making it look like a big tunnel. Immediately after the first rains the clusters of flowers fall to the ground, and it is during that short period that the whole city looks completely blue as if covered with blue carpets. In the background there are Acacia trees with bright yellow flowers. Out in the streets the people are shielding themselves with colourful umbrellas against the unrelenting sun, because it is midday and it is the hottest month of the year. Like the flowers and the trees, the indigenous black people have been given colourful complexions and cheerfulness. The indigenous white people are more peach-coloured, living behind crème-coloured iron-barred windows, and are totally addicted to *pink*. This is very evident from their interior décor both inside and out and is carried through in their dress code. They have been living in this reminiscence of colonial times for decades, because Zimbabwe is isolated like an island and changes are few and far between.

Clyde parks his blue Mercedes outside the Harare Club, which in the old days was an exclusive club for the gentry. Women could not be members. As we walk along the street towards the hotel, we are accosted by homeless beggars and criminal "guards," who want to watch over our car. We normally pretend that we are deaf-and-dumb and avoid eye contact with them, unless Clyde is being *street smart* and behaves like a gangster.

The hotel lobby has still got that international upper-class look, but in the Stewart Room, where the party is held, you see a red carpet full of spots and the large patterned Axminster carpets from England have seen better days. They need a good chemical deep clean, but the chemicals are hard to get these days and a complete replacement of the carpets would have been the better option in good times. The wall tapestries are still more beautiful-than ever before, but then of course they only look better the older they get.

The Koreans obviously have a different policy from the Europeans, so we see numerous black government officials from the ministries and other high-ranking people. The protocol is followed to the dot and the Korean Ambassador makes a speech in honour of the Zimbabwean President. It becomes uproariously funny when His Excellency gets mixed up and toasts "Robert Gabriel Mugabe, President of the Republic of Korea." A few hysterical laughs are heard and the mix-up is especially popular with the Shona representatives. After sipping champagne, the microphone is handed over to his counterpart, who then repeats the same phrases and praises the co-operation between the two countries. We all stand up straight as the national anthems are played. *Ishe komborera Africa,* or *Tshotsholotsho* as I still call it, feels as close to heart as my own national anthem. Lastly, the host country plays the Korean anthem *Aegukga*, a patriotic song with choir and military instruments.

Just like another cattle show we greet, are seen and keep circulating, because everybody is so busy. We forget about the standing buffet, as the local officials have already taken over that part of the room and are busy stacking their plates full, and from experience we know that only crumbs will be left behind.

A couple of days after, there is yet another national day, and that is Austria's. Like the Germans they have invited many ordinary people as well, right down to grass-roots level, and there is a swirl around you with long German words. Totally different from the Danes who used to have two national celebrations: one for the Danes and one for the official representatives and other high-ranking people. Now there are no more Danish national celebrations, since the embassy closed down due to the political instability.

Whilst circulating I meet old girlfriends, both German and Austrian, and some of them I know from belly dance.

The Austrians have also chosen Meikles Hotel for their venue, but the atmosphere is totally informal and relaxed. They serve generously from the snack tray and constantly pour wine.

Young, beautiful bohemian Renate is stuffing herself and exclaims apologetically, "Sorry I'm talking with food in my mouth, but I am so hungry!"

Like many people these days there is very little to eat at home because of the crisis and many are unable to bake bread, as the flour is in Mozambique and has not been able to cross the border due to the lack of foreign currency. Although Renate has always been a skinny belly dancer, she is now looking almost ghostly as she is a mere skeleton. Her pale skin looks extra pale surrounded by her carrot-coloured Rastafari hairstyle. Yesterday, I was so lucky because the Baron's gofer, Watson, delivered a big packet of flour and it makes me think about what I can bake when I get home, if we have electricity. Forget buying bread in the shops. There is nothing!

Among the guests I get eye contact with Harvey Schwarz, who is Jewish and a lawyer. His wife, Arlene is a pianist, but she did not come. Harvey is alone. I know him well from the time, when I was a diplomat, as he acted as a lawyer for our embassy. Harvey has that old quality of decency and liberal education that enables him to keep cool and not hunt down every celebrity like a bird of prey. He is totally relaxed as he stands talking to Justice Gubbay, who was forced to leave his official duties, the only reason being his white skin and his willingness to take on cases from the white farmers. Harvey starts introducing me, but Gubbay says, "Oh, we know each other."

It has become typical for these get-togethers that you never discuss politics, and the diplomats avoid the issue like the plague. All seem to have strict instructions from home neither to express personal nor official opinions. Once it was all different, but today there is a greater demand for human resources who have the highest expertise in idle conversation.

CHAPTER 6

HELP THY NEIGHBOUR

Every day it gets more and more difficult to find groceries and prices are soaring. Clyde is now helping with shopping, as he no longer needs to be at the factory constantly. We try our old supermarket at The Chase, as I noticed yesterday that the women folks behind had a mini-market and were selling 30 eggs for 4 million Zimbabwe dollars. But then I did not have that much money.

"Today they cost 5 million, Madam," says the African stall holder.

"You must be crazy," says Clyde with serene contempt, "I can drive out to Cripps Road and get them for 2-1/2 million."

"Oh, Clyde, why can't we just pay the extra million?" I ask him earnestly, knowing well that Clyde is not updated on the food market and add, "We will just end up spending the same in petrol."

But Clyde is stubborn. He refuses to pay 5 million for a tray with 30 eggs.

"I am going out to the factory anyway to check on the scotch carts," he explains. I glance over to another stall, where they have carved soapstones, an art mastered by the Shona tribe. From a distance I hear rapid drumbeats. Must be they are drumming for rain again. The sound is coming from the mountains behind Domboshava.

Out on Cripps Road in the industrial area there is a petrol station and they used to have eggs according to Clyde. But now they are sold out. A few busses are parked further down along the road, filled with passengers. On top of the bus roof there are stacks of chequered plastic bags from TM Supermarket and they are stuffed to breaking point. These handy bags are used all over by the Africans because of their multi-functional use and capacity for load with the box-shape and double stitches. The strong zippers give them strength like a suitcase and even when you fly to London you will see these TM plastic bags on the conveyor belt among all the expensive suitcases, filled with goodies that you cannot get in Zimbabwe.

There are also boxes with cooking oil, sugar and salt on top of

the roof among the stacked plastic bags, next to carriers with other
necessities for daily life which the family in the *kamusha* needs from
relatives working in town.

There are heaps of litter among the dead elephant grass, as the
passengers throw out their garbage from the busses and cars and the
pedestrians drop theirs too. The town is looking more and more like
one big scrapheap. But that the Africans don't see. They do not see
how ugly it looks and they are not worried about pollution.

"The busses are only allowed to drive when the guard has checked
what they have paid for the petrol," explains Clyde. "If they have
been charged more than the government fixed price, they will not be
allowed to travel."

A short distance away from the busses there is an African woman
with a tray of eggs balancing on top of her head. She is wearing the
typical wrap-around skirt in colourful African patterns. On her feet is
a pair of black canvas shoes. I look at the tray hardly moving despite
her undulating walk, but it is only half full of eggs.

"150,000 per egg!" she shouts turning to look at Clyde from the
side.

"Take them!" says Clyde, by now waving goodbye to his boiled
egg for breakfast.

"Those two are cracked, I don't want scrambled egg," I tell the egg
lady, continuing, "and please include the tray, otherwise the others
will crack too." She was actually about to put my eggs in a thin plastic
bag and keep the tray. I then get the tray with 9 eggs; the 2 cracked
ones she keeps for herself.

The next morning I boil two eggs for exactly seven minutes, half
soft, half hard as Clyde likes it. But the eggs are almost black and
stone hard. The egg timer must have problems. "Clyde, we need a
new egg timer. It does not work any longer."

"Let me first examine it inside," says Clyde with a voice like some
gynaecologist. After the examination he claims it has been fixed. But
the clock is ticking wrongly and not the right time. Suddenly it seems
all so unfair, the whole situation, when we are talking about millions
of dollars on the black market and fortunes to pay for petrol and air-

conditioning for the Mercedes, and I can't even get a new egg timer. It is the fate of women, to fight for everything, especially their tools. In the end I may get a new egg timer from Johannesburg, but right now it is just so intolerable, the whole situation, my life is totally dependant of others and even the smallest items that I need cannot go unnoticed.

Then a day later, when Clyde again gets a black egg, it dawns on him, "I think she sold us *boiled* eggs!" We look at each other and break down laughing. It never occurred to me. But the egg timer is still not working.

Clyde's secretary is a Muslim and her name is Naila. She has invited us for dinner at her parents' house. It is to express their gratitude to Clyde, because he paid for the mother's hospital bill, so now she has invited us for a home-cooked Indian dinner. They live in an area where there are absolutely no road signs or numbers, not even home-made ones, but finally we arrive at No. 37, which Clyde seems to recognize. There is a light at the gate. Naila arrives and opens the tall gate with a key. There are no flowers in the garden, no shrubs or palm trees. Nor are there romantic storks on one leg or decorative toads like the Hindus have around their gardens. It really looks very neglected.

We enter the lounge, which is lit up by a neon tube casting its harsh light over the very heavy ship-wheel furniture loved by Africans, in solid wood with dirty upholstery. The TV is very domineering in the room, but they have switched it off. Naila is getting more and more overweight, but compared with her other three sisters, she appears almost small, as they are all extremely obese. They all greet us. The mother has henna-dyed hair and a surprisingly good figure, but after a little while I realize why – she is simply working for the whole family without any assistance. She has been in the kitchen the whole day to prepare this meal for us. Naila's father looks wild and has a long grey chin beard reaching down to his chest. He greets us warmly wearing his typical white doti from India and has a grey waistcoat on top of it. His complexion is sallow and sickly and he appears as if he is mostly indoors. Had I seen him in a dark alley, my heart would have pounded.

"Do you want Coke or water?" asks the father. Both Clyde and I choose water, because Coke is probably too expensive for them and neither of us like sweet pops. Clyde glances towards a pair of green flags over the entrance to the lounge.

"What are these flags?" he asks. The father explains proudly that the flags are in honour of Mohammed's birthday and points towards the Arabian inscriptions.

"Have you been to Mecca?" Clyde asks to get the conversation going. But he had not been there.

"Neither have I, but I was close by one time when I lived in Jeddah before the Gulf War," I say eagerly and carry on, "I could only travel on the *Non Muslim Road*."

After that the conversation eases, until the wife announces that food is on the table. We take our seats according to instructions and I sit between Clyde and Naila. The husband and the wife sit next to each other. The other daughters sit opposite us. There are plates with *samosas* and *chilli-bites* on the table for snacks and a huge stack of the Indian flatbread called *chapatis* as well as *pappadams*. There are several small bowls with pickles. As we reach for the *samosas*, rice and chicken curry are put on the table. The wife asks if we want a knife and fork, and Clyde says immediately, "I am happy to eat with my fingers." Like all Canadians he is used to eating with his fingers or using chopsticks at the Chinese places. I prefer cutlery and accept it.

The daughters dig down into all the dishes with all fingers rather ungraciously and wring the food around in the sauce without any embarrassment. The sophisticated movements from India of using the *chapati* as a tool to avoid getting greasy is unknown here. A toilet roll appears that you can wipe your hands on.

Despite the primitive surroundings the food is delicious. The tablecloth, which is in the same colour as the Mohammed flags, is full of spots. The conversation rises as the meal progresses, despite the fact that no alcohol is served.

It becomes evident that Naila is the only daughter who is working. The best-looking and slimmest of the daughters has a boyfriend, who arrives during dinner. The newly-arrived reaches over the table, shaking hands with everyone and presents himself as "Mr. Khan." The meal continues and Mr. Khan gets up, as he has no time to stay.

We ask if any of them have been to India, and it is confirmed that both parents have been there. But Naila refuses to go with them if they go again. She is deeply suspicious concerning her parents' intentions. It appears the mother grew up in the State of Gujarat with her parents in a very big house. She lived there until she was 18 years of age. At that time the father travelled to India to collect her and marry her.

"She was a postal bride," declares Naila full of disgust for such an arrangement. Which brings about the father's explanation, that he had in fact seen a photograph of his coming wife before the arranged wedding took place.

He tells the story with evident pride and says, "She was one sister of a pair of twins and I chose the one on the right. It cost me 10 American dollars."

As I have seen many excellent pre-arranged marriages in India and want to avoid any discord between us, I change the subject and tell them that India has a special place in my heart, as I lived there for four years during the period when Prime Minister Indira Gandhi was murdered. They all derive amusement from this, as if I played a role in the assassination attempt, and could I not repeat the same here in Zimbabwe to get rid of a certain tyrant?

"And I love the way you greet each other in India, with both palms against each other up in front of the face," I continue and make the movement.

"That is not Muslim. We don't greet like that. That is only the Hindus," says the father, "and the Muslims don't say *Namasté*, they say *Salaam Alaaikum*. Also it is only the Hindus who wear a *bindi* in the forehead." Hearing this, Clyde sends me a look that says, "*There, you really put your foot in it, Bodie!*"

I quickly move on to compliment the healthy home-cooking, which is so much better for all of us instead of all that *Westernized fast food*, but all the daughters, including Naila, love fast food, especially chips with lots of vinegar and salt on them. Obviously the mother never had any authority in the home to set the rules; perhaps she was brought up to be humble. She does not talk very much.

The dessert arrives at the table and it consists of a delicious *halva*, which is a kind of milk jelly, totally made stiff with saffron, almonds and exotic spices. One day I must get that recipe from Naila.

The whole evening has cheered me up, and as we take leave I remember to say *"Salaam Alaaikum,"* which pleases the father and he answers warmly, *"Alaaikum as-Salaam."*

The days go by like the minute-hand on a watch. Everything is routine, morning becomes evening, and tomorrow is another day. Like the tree in our little garden, which is called *Yesterday, Today and Tomorrow.* It is not a big tree, more like an overgrown bush. There were two of them on Montgomery Road, one was purple and the other one was pink. It is like life in Africa, you forget time and place, routines are all laid out and you forget even how old you are.

Routine is what brings harmony to the African. He likes routine and continuation. I used to make timetables for them, one for the house and one for the garden: Monday tasks, Tuesday tasks, etc. Their efficiency rose so much that they ended up having more time off.

My gate bell rings. Somebody is at the gate. *"Gogogoi!"*

"Who is calling?" I ask.

"It is me, Friday," replies a smiling voice.

I immediately open the automatic gate and Friday enters and walks briskly towards my house. He smiles and greets me politely in the local manner, clapping the palms and the fingers together, *"Mangwanani."*

"Mangwanani, Friday. *Makadii?"* I greet him first by shaking his hand, then I step back a little and clap my hands together, cupping one hand across the other as local women do.

"I am here, if Madam is here." As he makes this simple statement, I see that he is unhappy and in pain. He has lost weight.

And who would have thought it? That the job Clyde and I found for him to remain on Harry Pichanick Drive, taken on by the next tenant after us, was no good. She had given a good impression at first, saying that she was a widow and worked for the American embassy. But it was only OK for the first couple of months. If Clyde had not continued paying salary with inflation into Friday's bank account for six months, he could not have survived. Because of his many years of service on Montgomery Road, Clyde had made this special arrangement. When we decided to buy the townhouse, there was no servants' quarter, otherwise we would have taken Friday with us. The garden boy, Elias, got a job in the factory.

Friday now tells me that he has only received 450,000 Zimbabwe dollars every two weeks for the last 4 months.

"Now I go home to Ares," Friday says. He is talking about his wife, who now looks after four grandchildren, because their two daughters are dead, I expect from AIDS.

"My other daughter is also sick," Friday continues, "but it is different than the first daughter that died. Her stomach is very big, but rest of her very thin."

As I listen to him I get the impression that the daughter is undernourished. Friday asks if I have more of those herb pills that cured Ares. Then he starts talking about the new *Madam*. I knew she was coloured and came from South Africa.

"She pesters me all the time about things missing. Where is ma Vaseline? Where is ma spoon?" says Friday, who during so many years in our employ *never* stole. Friday is the finest African gentleman and so polite and such a good person. "New Madam has two teenage children and they get many visitors. Next day they can never find their things. New Madam does not say Friday is stealing, but she goes on and on asking me where is it, over and over."

Now Friday cannot take it any longer, he wants to go home to Ares, because he cannot live from the salary he is getting, and the New Madam does not give him any food.

Knowing that Ares and the children will starve if Friday does not have a job, I ask if he wants me to find a new and better job for him. I will ask the embassies and the nuns and Father Ryan and Brother Paul. I give Friday a stack of money, because I know that he will never ask for help. He brightens up like the sun, but although smiling his face is deeply furrowed with sorrow, and for a moment it looks as if his head is very far from the body, because he is so thin. But with Friday I know it is not AIDS – he loves Ares with all his heart, since that day in his early youth, when he met her on Tapson's Farm. That was in 1966, when he started his first job. But the farmer lost his first farm in Karoi and Friday at first did not join the farmer to the next farm in Marondera, but chose to live in his kamusha together with Ares for two years.

I first met Friday one fine day by the stone wall outside Rhodesville Supermarket. He had shown me his black book, as it was customary to have such a book with references, but in Friday's black book there was only one reference, because he had only had the one job. It was from farmer Tapson:

Friday resumed his occupation with me after 2 years of absence and has worked for me since that date. I found him honest, reliable and a good worker. He cooks reasonably well.
—*Marondellas, 12 August 1978*

I never regretted that decision by the stone wall when I employed Friday, despite the fact that he had not had other jobs and could not read or write. In itself his name made up for any lack of qualifications and as Clyde said, "I would have employed him on the spot too, especially with a name like that. If he is Friday, I am Robinson Crusoe, and either he can do the job or he can't do it."

And time would show that Friday was the best cook we ever had, despite being illiterate. When he cooked, the food had flavour and it didn't matter that he could not make starters and dessert, as I could do that myself, when we had visitors.

Originally Ares also worked at the Tapson Farm in Karoi, but then they started having children, and she went home to the kamusha. They had five children: Diana, Gangsai, Petty, Takwana and Tawenda. Takwana means in shona *we are enough*, and Tawenda means *we are too many*. Now of all the children, only two are left and Tawenda is sick. Friday comes from Chief Makope's kraal in Nyamupfukudza and was born around 1947. His whole life he struggled and never had enough to keep body and soul together.

Now Friday reminds me that since I gave Ares the herbal medicine and told her what to eat, her arthritis disappeared and never came back. Also she no longer had high blood pressure. Perhaps if I have more herbs, Tawenda can be cured too. He looks hopeful and returns to the subject of the new Madam.

"That one was fired from Amrican," explains Friday with his special pronunciation of America and it is his impression that she no longer cares to work. That is why she is now paying him a salary less than 10 per cent of what he had been promised. "That one is no good and doesn't know how to clean house. That one clean floor with *mutsairo* like people from the bush." Friday shakes his head in disbelief and explains to me, "Madam, it is not even a broom, it is made from grass and you have to bend all the way down to the ground, when using *mutsairo*. Eh, that one, no pay, no mealie meal."

As he talks I have made some notes about Tawenda's symptoms. I can then ask advice from Dr. Vick or Dr. Simone at the Convent. I promise to call Friday and we have agreed that if he is unable to get to the telephone, he must return in three days.

There is definitely something about syncronicity, for that same evening Brother Paul passes by. In fact he is looking for a housekeeper, but as I tell him about Friday, he says that he is afraid he is too old, and how is he able to take messages from the telephone and make notes, when he cannot read or write.

"He can write numbers up to ten," I explain, "and Friday *never* forgets who has called! He can make the best roast beef dinner with roast pumpkins and roast potatoes, real homemade farm cooking that has flavour, and he serves it with Yorkshire pudding! He polishes shoes and he irons shirts and he never even once made a burn mark on them. He doesn't even pinch sugar. He is in love with his wife Ares and never sleeps with other women. The only job he ever had was the one with Farmer Tapson from 1966, until he came to work for Clyde and me."

I notice that Brother Paul starts looking rather interested, but then he apologizes, because it is not a decision he can take on his own. He must first consult with Brother Benjamin.

THE NEXT DAY BROTHER PAUL calls to let me know that the two monks have decided to take on Friday for a trial week.

I then make a telephone call to Harry Pichanick Drive, and the son Dusty answers the phone. "Hello, Dusty, it is Bodie. Could you pass on a message to Friday that I have some medicine for his daughter, who is ill?"

Dusty promises to pass on the message, but several hours go by and I hear nothing from Friday. Either he was not given the message, or perhaps he has gone home to Ares. But then the gate bell is ringing.

"I got job for you, Friday, it is with Brother Paul, whom you know. And he lives together with another brother. They have just moved to Highlands and want to have you for one week on trial." Friday looks as if he is receiving the Revelations and we arrange that all he has to tell the new Madam is that Tawenda is sick, therefore he wants to go home to Ares to assist nursing her for one week. Then he must say that he will return to collect his furniture to bring them home. As the new Madam did not pay him a salary for six months, he must ask the son Dusty to find a bakkie and pay for the petrol. It is only two hours' drive to his kamusha.

Then I proceed to prepare Friday for his new job. "Just do exactly the same as you did for *Amai Tsitsi* (that is my African name) and forget everything about mutsairo. Brother Paul and Brother Benjamin are good people. Make that roast chicken with roast pumpkin and roast potatoes first. Then another day make that cottage pie and the other dishes we used to make. And just ask, 'Where are ma shoes for cleaning, and ma hangers for the ironing?' Then Master will know you have experience and know everything."

"Oh, Madam," whispers Friday and looks as if he just won the lottery. On the way to the gate I explain to him, "Brother Paul will come tomorrow Sunday to pick you up here. But don't worry, after one week he will *so* happy to have found Friday that soon a big salary will follow." Friday and I share a conspiratory laugh together and we are both in high spirits, as Friday has indeed struck it lucky.

Sunday morning Friday arrives an hour too early. He has a bundle under his arm, containing blanket, clothes and a few necessities for one week. I give him a bag of mealie meal and a little cash, so that he does not have to ask Brother Paul for anything.

Just three days later Brother Paul phones me. "Bodie, we are keeping Friday on a permanent basis. He is doing an excellent job!"

EVERY DAY THAT GOES BY, we get more and more desperate, as there is no money in the bank. Even the Baron cannot get any cash. I follow Clyde's advice and try various branches, but every time I get the same reply, the staff often yawning from sheer boredom. I have tried all my authority tricks, including *"Could you please give me that in writing,"* but when poverty comes in at the door, love flies out the window. *THERE IS NO MONEY.*

Outside the banks you see endless lines of people hoping to get cash, and more are lining up for sugar and cooking oil. All the shelves in the supermarkets are empty, apart from a few rotten cabbages and dry scones. Nearby a few vendors are selling marmalade and Mazoe orange juice. Some mothers have had to give their babies this sweet commercial drink, when their breast milk has dried up from their daily diet of starvation.

Waiting like that in indeterminate queues, one turns into a cosmonaut, losing all sense of time, becoming weightless and dizzy. Time might be measured in thousands of light years and has totally lost its meaning. Standing upright in the baking sun creates hallucinations of water and figures of distortions like the optical phenomena in the desert, because even with an umbrella and a sun hat it is unbearable. This is probably how one would disappear into space under torture. If you do not get a heat stroke, you end up in a raging frenzy and start arguing with others in the line-up. We are losing our nerve because they are lowering our dignity and grinding us down to base equality; the ultimate humiliation of mankind. We are shepherded with a stick, like sheep.

At the end of June, President Mugabe forced businessmen to slash prices of all goods and services, believing he could crush inflation. He claimed that the high prices were caused by the private sector trying to topple his government, and that there was a conspiracy against him from the governments of the Western world. His intervention only resulted in higher inflation and nourished the black market, as the country ran out of wheat. That was before Clyde and I returned, when desperate people had stormed the shops and stripped the shelves of merchandise, as the government had encouraged them to do. Later on, the stolen goods were sold outside the big supermarkets at black market rates. As the police were especially keen on observing the price fixing and used their uniform to legalise the robbing, you will see many policemen's wives behind the long wooden tables, where you can buy carbolic soap and cooking oil among other things.

A WHITE FARMER HAD A farm on the way to Mutare near Halfway House. He is passing by our house with his three children dressed in school uniforms. They go to school at the Convent, the same school President Mugabe's children attend. They are unsure about their future, as they have lost their home, but still they seem happy and content as only children can be in such a situation. Their father, on the other hand, is unhappy and about to give up.

"I am like the Jacaranda-tree in Africa; I am imported and don't belong. If you see a single Jacaranda-tree far out in the veldt, you can be sure that a white once lived here," says the white farmer, who is very tall and impeccably dressed. His eyes are sad as he looks down towards his brown crepe-soled shoes, but he continues: "Once I asked an African: *What does it mean to be indigenous?* He answered: *It means you are homemade.*"

"They don't understand all these words," I remark soothingly. "Our old housekeeper Nazarious thought that a white-collar worker was a person who works for TV. You see, it is not the ordinary people that are causing all this trouble. It comes from the top and it is caused by the politicians."

I disappear into the kitchen to make tea and return with four mugs. The white farmer is staring into space, as he quotes, "There are four questions in Africa that will show if you belong:

Is maShona and maNdebele equal?

Is the Jacaranda-tree an indigenous tree?

Is Nkomo of the same importance as Mugabe?

Are women in Africa equal to men?"

He looks at me and gives me the answer to his torment. "If you correctly answer all four questions with a NO, then you don't belong in Africa. You are just a visitor." Ironically, when he speaks, he uses *ma* in front of the nouns, just like the Shonas, as he was born here.

Because of the farmer's desperate situation, I give him two bricks of money before he leaves. These are the last two bricks in the mini-safe and they were meant for emergency. It's all or nothing. Hopefully Clyde will find a solution.

As the family has left, I pull the chair out by the diningroom table and I play for a long time with the words, but finally I put these words down:

I wanted to find you a present
but all the shelves were empty
or full of zhing-shong.
Then I saw that they had cards
for every occasion
and my eyes fell on these 2
autumn leaves of the Maple tree
when I thought: They are like us
2 leaves that have blossomed
only to be caught by the strong winds
and end up in such
beautiful autumn colours.
Happy birthday, my darling, and many more
beautiful Autumn leaves
      —Bodie

CHAPTER 7

REST IN PEACE

I n the middle of November our friend Gert dies. One of his loyal friends sent us this message:

Dear friends,
   This brief note is to inform you that Gert has left us.
   He died Thursday at 6 o'clock in the evening at Arresødal Hospice.
   His 3 girls were with him. I arrived at 6.30 and said goodbye to a friend who meant a lot in our lives. He looked very nice and calm.

The two nuns, Sister Nancy and Sweet Rit, call to tell us that they are coming over to have a drink with us in memory of our mutual friend. Avis and Zeb also phone us and for half an hour we turn over all the lovely events we have shared together with Gert and Lizzie. Zeb is angry because he had such difficulties to get the connection through to Denmark, and then when he finally succeeded the daughters said Gert was too weak to speak.

"But he didn't need to say anything. They could just have held the phone to his ear and I would have said to him, how much I appreciated all those years of friendship. I just wanted to say *thank you*." Zeb sounds grief-stricken and it was a sad blow to him that he was not given that last chance. Even when we are old and have had a long and good life, there are always parting words that we never had the opportunity to say, and we only need those last few minutes.

Tut and Edgar call us and it is decided that Edgar and Clyde will visit Gert's farm to make sure that the staff carry on regardless.

Around *sundowner time* (as we call the time in Zimbabwe when we get an intoxicating drink under the last rays of the sun), a big wine-coloured Holden Trooper arrives at our parking space. Even though I cannot see anybody through the dark mafia-windows from the sides, I know that the nuns have arrived, as I recognize their vehicle. An old German lady lives across the gate and she had pressed the button to open it, when she also recognized the big four-wheel drive. Sister Nancy always drives that vehicle, as it is suitable for the bad roads in the African bushland.

I run through the courtyard towards them and we embrace after they come down from the high steps of the vehicle. Clyde also comes into the courtyard and suddenly he has tears in his eyes. It is difficult for him to speak about death and have it so close, when you are yourself living on the brink of the precipice.

"Shall we sit outside on the veranda or inside?"

"Let us sit inside, it is more private," suggests Sister Nancy and sits down in one of the peach-coloured recliners, while Clyde takes the other one. Sweet Rit and I sit across in the velvet sofa. Clyde opens the cork in an Australian wine bottle, a brand unknown to us, but nevertheless precious, as I had hunted it down on my latest shopping safari.

"It is also better to be inside, because when it starts raining, all the flying ants are pouring into the house," I declare quickly and get up to close the veranda door and it closes with a slam from a gust of wind. I turn the key around and return to the velvet sofa.

"Here's to our friend Gert. We hope that where he is now, there is his favourite Havana cigar and a good glass of red wine," says Sister Nancy with a smile. We all lift our glasses and clink them in the air against each other. Sweet Rit is showing her grief on the outside – I know she is also distressed about her younger brother being sick in Germany.

After the bottle is empty the two nuns apologize that they have to leave early as there are so many problems at the moment, but they are very relieved that Clyde and Edgar will drive out to Gert's farm and make sure that everything runs smoothly. They have tried to call the staff, but the telephone lines are not working in that area. Before leaving they give me a plastic bag with German coffee and a homemade bread loaf that Sweet Rit has baked.

A FEW DAYS LATER CLYDE and Edgar inspect the farm in Ruwa,

which is about half an hour east of Harare. They want to make the staff tremble a bit, because there have been quite a rash of robberies lately. Edgar's wife Tut says she would dismiss the whole lot. Being Swiss, she would never have tolerated the way things were managed. She and Edgar are organized and have a place for everything and everything in its place. During Clyde's preparations to pass by and collect Edgar, I phone them up and suggest that I have a cup of coffee with Tut in the meantime.

"That is definitely not a good idea, because Monday is her washing day and then she puts clean sheets on the bed." Edgar is very stand-offish with me. When he talks about the wife, he says *she*.

When I tell Clyde, he laughs and says, "That's what all the Suisse are like. You can't just change their daily routines. And certainly not start drinking coffee on your washing day!"

"It reminds me about Mommy Sine, who really had a washing day, but that was because she only had the washing room once a month and on that day she had to wash, put the clothes through the wringer and then iron everything. But we have moved on, haven't we? With automatic washing machines and dryers?" I look at Clyde waiting for a response, but he does not answer.

That same evening there is a power cut on Duthie Road, where Tut and Edgar live. Poor Tut had her shoulder operated in Switzerland shortly before their departure to Zimbabwe and suddenly it is all too much; the daily life is just too full of obstacles.

"Invite them over here, we'll just eat what I am making anyway," I suggest to Clyde. Tut and Edgar arrive within a few minutes, and she is carrying a tray with her green salad and the egg salad as well as a cold potato salad. We combine everything with the spaghetti bolognaise that I had made, and Clyde opens a bottle of red Drostyhof from South Africa. The meal is more special than many of the arranged dinner parties, because it is so spontaneous. For two months nobody has seen any beef, so the simple meat sauce is like a gourmet dish. Clyde sets the table in a hurry and I notice through the hatch that he has put knife and fork on the wrong side. It seems to be a Canadian custom, as I have seen many of them using the knife with the left hand and eating with the fork in the right hand. I quickly correct the setting and return to the kitchen, whilst commanding through the opening, "The white dinner napkins and the crystal glasses, Darling." I am standing by the stove stirring the pot.

The evening is one for the memory bank as we feel giddy and laugh a lot, and even Tut is funny and remarks during the evening that *of course we could have taken a cup of coffee on her washing day!* We make eyes at each other knowing that sometimes our hubbies *misinterpret* us.

"How did you meet Gert?" I ask during that evening, and I end up getting the full story of these veterans in Africa:

Plus, who originally owned Gert's farm in Ruwa, was Swiss and had his domicile in Switzerland, but 4 to 5 times he would travel to Africa each year. He employed Edgar Schurz as a jack-of-all-trades and administrator. The first trip they went to Uganda, from Entebbe to Kampala, where Plus and Edgar had offices in the Applo Hotel. They were following up on an irrigation project, Garamotjomere close to the Sudanese border. Eventually, Plus became in charge of the project that had been negotiated with everything prepaid, but unfortunately the materials had not been included in the negotiations due to lack of funds. Plus and Edgar stayed in Uganda, until Idi Amin came to power.

They made many excursions to Murchison Falls and travelled to Enimiers over the Falls. Some excursions led them to Simriki Park on the Congolese border. It was here they saw thousands and thousands of antelopes and other wild animals. In those days you never went on a safari hunt in vain, because wildlife was plentiful. Not like today where you can drive in your jeep for hours without seeing any animals.

Plus had a license to hunt and hired a professional hunter and they were in luck. They hunted from the jeep, but Plus, whose fingers were all thumbs, never shot anything. In the end the professional hunter set his rifle aside to give Plus a chance, but Plus was not good at targeting and he shot a buck in its hind leg. The poor animal tried to flee on 3 legs and consequently they had to follow to relieve it of its pain. In the end the professional hunter shot the buck.

They also had license to shoot elephants, but that was not Plus's preference. They came up close to an elephant that day, but when Plus saw that it only had one tusk, he suggested that they called off the hunt.

When Edgar went to Uganda the first time with Plus, it was because he had opened a ball-point pen factory to export across the continent including South Africa and Zimbabwe. That was how he came to Zimbabwe, which in those days was called Rhodesia, but they made their money in Ghana. They followed up on various projects, first in the timber trade – that was before in-dependence – but then they started their first transport of timber to Takoradi Second Harbour. It was here that they met the Dane, Gert Hjorthede. Plus always had political contacts on a very high level, he knew the right people and he succeeded in establishing several industrial businesses. In 1956 Ghana became indepen-dent, but that did not stop Plus, as he still knew the right people in the right places and he began to build a factory that could convert cocoa beans into cocoa butter. He had common sense to minimize the volume and started a second factory, a cardboard packaging plant, in order to export tropical produce. He did not stop there – then he started a glass factory, but it was a white elephant, because it was not suitable to be taken over by blacks, who lacked the expertise which the whites had. Finally, they sold pipelines from the Akosombo Dam in Upper Volta to the city of Accrá in order to supply water.

Their Odyssey even led them to Sierra Leone, where the story goes that in the 15th century they believed that the thunder from the port came from the roaring lions in the mountains. Like many adventurers of his time, Plus was also involved in diamond ex-port and shipping and here again via the shipping, he kept meet-ing Gert. The businesses were booming and they sold helicopters, aeroplanes and trains. In between the time was spent to build a palm oil factory and they started exporting palm oil to England. In Freetown they electrified a whole street in co-operation with a Swedish company, Frans Electric, and installed 2 sulzeber en-gines to generate electricity for the BBC.

It was under the same agreement with Sweden that they went to Zimbabwe to produce electricity there. Some projects were established in Matabeleland, but the whole plan never succeeded due to lack of funds, even though 80% of the money came from international aid funds donated by the Swedish government.

In 1980 Plus received a lot of money in commission in Sierra Leone, and that became his downfall. He became reckless and lived beyond his means, as he wanted to live life to its fullest. He went overboard and started with the rental of a Lear Jet from a leasing company. Edgar was put in charge and asked to collect him in Accrá, then they flew back via the Algerian oasis Tamamrazat. They went to a lot of places and ended up in Marbella in Spain, where a luxury villa had been rented, but it was not good enough enough for Plus. A villa next to it belonged to Kindy Graff Schönenburg and was called "Quinta Maria Louisa." That place suited Plus. Edgar stayed in a club in flat No. 1 with Tut and the children.

The Lear Jet was used as a shuttle service between Santa Margarita and Zürich and between Zürich and Geneva. At least 2 to 3 times they brought business people to Geneva, and 3 limousines with drivers were hired to bring the guests down from Santa Margarita, where they stayed at the Imperial Hotel. Plus occupied all the top floor there, including The White Chapel. When the guests had to be entertained, he rented a big yacht with captain, cook and servant for daily cruises.

Plus was not his real name: he was born Adolph. He was fat and ugly and a homosexual. Behind the external appearance was a clever man with many talents and he knew how to seduce people with flattery. He would kneel right down to the feet of the high-ranking blacks and in a begging voice he would utter, "Oh, please, please, honourable Minister... I BEG you!" He knew the impact of a white man kneeling for a black and he knew their superstitions and swore by their ghosts and their forefathers.

At one point in his life he adopted Sidney Watjuku, who was the son of his cook. But despite the fact that everything was invested for his adopted son's future, such as school in Suoz in

Switzerland, Sidney became a loafer and a complete waster.
Everything he wasted on sports cars and girls. The first sports
car was a Volkswagen, the next an Alfa Romeo and the last one
was a Porsche. He would walk into all the shops and order goods
to be sent home, but he would omit to pay for it. He had no morals
and no honour.

Plus married a local black girl despite his sexual preference –
he was only attracted to men. And BLACK men only. Black boys.
He never touched a white boy. He always lived in a hotel. It was a
costly lifestyle and when he ran out of money, he would ask Edgar
to help out. Over the years Edgar had to pay for many of Sidney's
bills and he was never refunded.

Gert was in charge of Shipping Tacomrande. When Plus be-
came ill, he came back to Europe and asked Gert if their many
businesses could continue for 6 months. More and more bills re-
mained unpaid, some concerned Gert's company Scanship, but
many others were involved, among them some Norwegians who
exported palm oil in a 1973 venture. After the communist-leaning
government of Ghana nationalized all large foreign-owned com-
panies, and the oil crisis began, the country found itself without
transport fuel. Saudi Arabia said it had freight oil, if Gert would
come and collect it, so an oil tanker and 2 freighters were sold to
the country to import transport fuel and facilitate the export of
palm oil.

At one point Plus wrote a letter of guarantee to Gert that the
farm in Ruwa with all its contents was to belong to him if the debt
was not repaid. Shortly afterwards, Plus passed away, and that
was how Gert in the end of the eighties became the owner of that
beautiful country house with farmland, in a country where he had
never lived but where he was to get the best experiences in the
autumn of his life, and have the best friends.

All of us are full of ghosts of the past and the evening went by
so quickly because of the pleasant atmosphere. On the way out to
the parking area we exchange the traditional three kisses, which is a
Swiss custom and embrace each other warmly. It occurs to me that

it is strange how the Swiss have such a warm way of greeting, when they are so reserved.

As Clyde and I return to the lounge it is all full of flying ants, because we left the door open. That is what happens when you have the rainy season. They have big brown transparent wings and glide around the room like little glider pilots. They come out of the ant houses, where they were born, because their nests are now full of water. Then they fly around in a constant speed and they have to be careful that they do not lose any of the four wings, because if that happens, they drop down to the ground. Within 24 hours they must find a partner and get pregnant – otherwise they die. If they succeed in getting pregnant, they grow fat as a worm, because they are so full of eggs. In that way the next generation is secured. But then they are not needed anymore. Make no mistake, *the life of a termite is short.*

Nothing has changed as far as the bank is concerned. We still cannot get any money and I have to humiliate myself just to be allowed to write out a cheque, because in most places the swipe-machines are not working, or they spit out a note saying, "Refused," even though the amount asked for is only 41 million and Clyde has recently deposited 300 million to our bank account.

In Spar Supermarket I see a Greek yogurt in a big container, but the shop assistant says that I cannot buy that one, as it is "off," meaning it is too old. So I suggest that he sells it to me for a smaller sum, because I only need to use 1 tablespoon of it to make my own homemade yogurt. The normal price for this yogurt is 6.5 million Zimbabwe dollars.

I talk with my hands and explain to him how I used to make yogurt in India. "You take one cup of milk powder and five cups of milk. You whip it together and let it boil up. Now you cool it down until you can stick your little finger in it *without* burning it and then you take a little of this lukewarm milk and mix it with the yogurt-starter. Now you add the rest and put it all in a bowl. Now you isolate it for 12 hours and after that you have a big portion of yogurt." I look at him with a smile, but it is also an appeal.

In the end he swaps the price-sticker with the one from the liver paté, so I end up getting the old yogurt for 1.3 million.

As I later tell Clyde about it, he shakes his head. "They think you are nuts, Bodie. And the Africans are scared of loonies."

Clyde is very quiet these days, as there are problems acquiring raw materials for the production of scotch carts. The Baron has not delivered the wheel shafts, but has sold them to somebody else. Again there is no electricity in the factory.

CHAPTER 8

THE CHINOYI DENTIST

I t has been on my mind for a long time.
"It is time for our check-up at the dentist, Clyde!" I say it very firmly, more to convince myself. Because of Clyde's illness and all the journeys to get him fixed I am beginning to get worried after 18 months without dental hygiene. We get an appointment two days later and on the day in question we get up very early, as we have to be with the German dentist in Chinoyi at 8 o'clock in the morning. First we have to eat our breakfast with fresh fruit, homemade orange- and beetroot juice, oat porridge, boiled eggs and green tea, so I get up with the birds.

It is not raining heavily, just a drizzle, when we start and one of the garden boys stands with the hosepipe and is watering one of the flowerbeds. He carries out the task as if he is hypnotized and he probably doesn't even notice whether it is raining or not.

The trip is like an excursion and a reminder of many years in the past. Many times have we driven this stretch, both when we went on Clyde's houseboat *Timela* on Lake Kariba, but also when we used to visit our rondavel-style African lodge at Mazvikadei Lake. Shortly after the round-about by the West Gate Shopping Centre the familiar landscape with eucalyptus trees starts. Even when driving in Clyde's heavy Mercedes we constantly feel the bumps in the asphalt. We are already quite a way outside of town, but the Africans walk and walk, with bags or boxes balancing on their heads and babies on their backs sitting in the wrap-around towel. Meanwhile, we are passing Msasa trees, indigenous Bauhenia bushes and Umbrella trees. The trees are smaller now because of the land reform, which they have named *Sunrise II Reform.* Instead of all the trees that used to be here, there are now scattered primitive African huts that are almost falling apart. They have no electricity and no water, and live from day to day by chopping down trees and making a fire for preparing their food. In the beginning they sold firewood by the wayside, but now there are so few trees left that they hardly have enough for their own cooking. On the radio we hear a monotonous voice announcing: *Your land is your prosperity, your land is your prosperity...*

Some faded lonely signs are still placed along the road painted with the words *"Worms for sale,"* but no worm-dealers are there any longer, because it has become more and more rare that the white folks stop to buy worms on their way to Kariba, where they used to go fishing on a regular basis. Now if they *do* go, it is no longer considered safe to stop. *A hungry man is a dangerous man!* Here the white man used to live, surrounded by wild stretches of swaying savannah grasses. He was caught on the edge of life, isolated and abandoned.

Always when we cross over the Great Dyke, I get that special feeling and the same happens today. Like being lifted up from above and then you see it all from up there. The stripes in the asphalt are almost gone. Sitting along the roadside is a whole family of monkeys. There is a single Frangipani-tree and a Jacaranda further away out there on the veldt and I recall the white farmer with his three children, who said it was not an African tree, but it was put there because people like me had planted it; people who wanted to show their flag and their special colour to this endless fauna.

As we pass the old railway line, Clyde remarks that there are no longer any passing trains, as it is not used any more, but I still glance in both directions, just in case. The railway tracks in Africa have never had good visibility, because the road makes a sharp turn exactly where you have the level crossing.

Outside Banket, which is about 100 kilometres from Harare, I see the iconic huge corn silos that were built with Danish aid money, now empty and no longer used, yet another white elephant that is towering above in the outskirts of this village. Funny, how these development engineers always want to build such domineering monuments, almost like penis symbols. That thought enters my mind, but the next instant I am relieved to consider that Clyde's project with the Baron is so very different with its ox-driven carts and the ploughs. This appropriate technology would also have been better in the past, if you wanted to help the poor in Africa. Unfortunately most development aid was assisting the already rich commercial farmers.

Clyde has always been a man of few words, so it is good that I am a dreamer. There is not much of an interaction with him, not because he is driving; that is just the way he is. If it wasn't for his choice in music, it wouldn't be so bad, but it is streaming out of the loudspeakers rather loudly, after he put in the CD. He can play these monotonous beat rhythms from the 1960s indefinitely, and it is not the quiet romantic tunes he likes to listen to, it is the disco music.

There is yet another railway track. It is the track to Mangura Copper Mine. As Clyde sees me scanning the two sides, he explains, "It used to run once a week, now it is only like once a month."

On the bare fields that used to be covered with trees, you see men and women working hard with their hoe and badza in the heavy red soil to plant their mealies. There are the only two tools needed in Africa: the hoe and the badza.

There is still a road sign for Manyame River, but after the hospital I see no more signs. They must have disappeared in Chinoyi like Harare. Further ahead on the main road we pass two traffic lights, but none of them are working. Then we arrive at Dr. Lung's Clinic. We open the car door and greet the private guard, but the noise of the huge generator drowns all my words. Inside, in the reception, Dr. Lung's wife, Sonja, is sitting but she gets up immediately when she sees us and gives us a big hug. Sonja and Clyde have a very special relationship, as they have both survived cancer treatment. Today is a special day for her, because she has a record of five years' survival and she says in a tone of triumph, "We are survivors!"

Shortly afterwards, Dr. Lung arrives in his military jeep and due to the constant problems with power cuts, he has changed his look and let it be. With his designer-stubble he looks more like an artist than a dentist. Out here far away from civilization and white people he has for many years run a modern Western dental clinic with implants, jaw surgery and ceramic crowns. He is also an expert in removing silver amalgam fillings. He hunts around the area towards Karoi and Kariba and claims that he sleeps and drinks water with the elephants. When he arrived in the nineties, there were still many German farmers in the area and many had come after independence and bought farms, as Zimbabwe had earned the reputation of a stable country, although black. But after the year 2000 everything changed and most of them left the country, only a few had enough savings to buy a house in Harare. After this rural exodus many whites are now only investing in beautiful Hollywood-smiles, which they can pay for in Zimbabwe-dollars, a currency now regarded totally without value. I remember this safari-guide, who came in from the bush and sat in the dentist's chair for eight hours. In between he was given a couple of local anaesthesia and when night fell, he looked like a movie star with a perfect toothpaste smile that would last his whole life.

Everybody in reception gets in a good mood because of the dentist's wife, who supplies happy music from her little radio and chats with everyone. She used to be a radiographer and worked like that in the beginning, but when she was diagnosed with cancer, she stopped doing it and left that part to a local radiographer. Once I also had a torture treatment and shouted to Dr. Lung, "Gerhard, give me an extra high dose of the anaesthesis, or I shall surely scream!" but having read on my lips what I said, he answered: "You can scream and shout, I will not hear anything!" As a child, Dr. Lung had become deaf after a penicillin treatment, and now he is totally against using prescription medicine, even after jaw surgery. But I must say this, their hygiene at the clinic has a high standard and I have never heard about infections like you do in the West.

"It is completely perfect!" declares Dr. Lung, after cleaning with a combination of airflow and ultrasound. Then it is Clyde, and I send a little prayer that everything is OK, because he has been through so much. But as he comes out, together with the dentist, both Clyde and Gerhard look like two naughty school boys. The smile says it all.

We ask Dr. Lung if we can pay by cheque, because we cannot get any money in the bank, but he makes a deprecating gesture; he does not want anything. He is simply full of joy that we are still here, but for a brief moment his face is distorted and he holds one hand behind to the back. The many hours standing in awkward positions have left their mark, but he wants to avoid surgery.

"He did look a bit worried," I say looking at Clyde behind the steering wheel.

"Of course he is worried. He is under the same threat like the rest of us that they will take over his business. So he is working like hell to get the most out of it."

"But he is in a different situation. He is a dentist," I say, a little surprised.

"Makes no difference. The same will happen to him as with the farmers and the industries. Sooner or later they will invade the clinic and take over," Clyde has that finality in his voice.

"But he invested so much buying all the latest technology from Germany; the X-ray machine and the CEREC machine to make crowns and restoration. Besides he came many years after independence. It would be so unfair."

"Let me be clear on this. They do not care. They will take what they can get or smash it to pieces. Many of the German farmers in that area came after 1980 and invested there. That did not save them."

Clyde turns up the volume indicating we have talked enough and we are back after only 1 hour 15 minutes. He drops me by the gate and continues to the factory. As I walk down the path, I see Salome knitting under the big fig tree. As she sees me, she stops her work and asks, "We have power, Madam. Do you want me to finish the ironing?"

"Oh, that would be nice, Salome, but only if it suits you," I answer.

In my kitchen I prepare a cup of green tea for both of us and we sit at the round dinner table and enjoy it together with a couple of biscuits.

"Has Madam no children?" she asks, as she is putting extra sugar in the tea cup, because like all Africans, she has a sweet tooth.

"No, I never had children, because I met my husband too late in my life. You shouldn't have children when you are old. But it is not a problem, because my husband has two children and one is married with two small children."

"That is not the same," says Salome. "They are not your children and they will not look after you, when your husband dies."

"You are right, of course, that it is not the same. But my husband has recovered from his sickness, so I will not be alone."

"He is coughing a lot." Salome glances at me sideways and her quick glance speaks volumes. Then she gets up to bring the tea cups into the kitchen sink and adds, "You should have got children, even if it was too late!"

CHAPTER 9

CHARITY

I t is the middle of November and the bloom of the Jacaranda-trees has been taken over by the Flamboyant trees, which has given the city an orange shade. The big clusters of flowers look like elder flowers, but the colour is a deep orange like the Tibetan monk's habit.

The diplomatic wives in Harare, who officially are called *The Diplomatic Spouses* and unofficially *The Spice Girls,* have sent out formal printed invitation cards for the *Charity Gala Ball.* They have an association in Harare whose purpose it is to help the poor. We arrive at the Golden Palace, which was once called the Sheraton Hotel, but now they have changed the name to Rainbow Towers. The theme of the evening is "Tiri Tose," meaning *we stand together,* and the dress code is gala or traditional costume.

As we walk up the wide staircase with marble steps, we hold on to the railing as not to lose the balance on the arched steps. On the foyer of the first floor we present our invitation cards and receive instructions where to sit. Then we enter the big Jacaranda rooms with huge glittering chandeliers. The rooms have not changed, but the chairs have been redecorated and are now covered with all white fabric, tied with a bow at the back. The Japanese ambassadrice, Mrs. Yuki Yoshikawa, is dressed in an enormous costume, which changes her otherwise petite feminine figure to look almost monstrous like a bird strutting its feathers, while she is holding the microphone to welcome the assembly. She is confident as she reels off all the phrases that she has heard in her husband's many official speeches and her own speech is delivered in a monotonous pitch and very quickly. "Excellencies, ladies and gentlemen, captains of industries, distinguished guests... I welcome you all to this auspicious occasion...."

It reminds me of Sunday School as a child, when you learned things by rote, saying words you did not even understand the meaning of, and often with no intonation due to lack of understanding. The guests are dressed in elegant robes, very décolleté, showing a lot of cleavage. And there I thought that sequins had gone out of fashion, but oh, they are back again, everybody is bespangled, but in a new fashionable way. It is the Hollywood style in scanty dress that is in now, if you are married to one of these oligarchs, who go for younger and younger wives, looking like they have to compete with Naomi Campbell. As they glide to and fro with the photographers after them, I am, in my imagination, transported to the Oscar Award ceremonies: the thin straps on their shoulders and the small underpants with G-string, that you clearly see marked through the thin almost see-through garments, the ample bosoms that on some of them could compete with Anna Nicole Smith, who is now dead. The grey men have become more powerful and reserved, and their wives learn quickly to copy their fleeting and casual encounters, rushing along to meet the very important persons, the VIPs. The women from West Africa and the few Arabian countries that are participating are dressed differently, many of them in national costumes, and from Nigeria and Ghana they have added their festive headgear.

The servants of the diplomatic spouses have worked endlessly with assistance from the top chefs of some of Harare's leading restaurants and have created an orgy of exotic dishes from 25 different countries, from Brazil to Ethiopia, South Korea, Sweden, America and many more. They do all this to help the poor, many of whom live homeless and without a roof over their heads a stone's throw away from the elegant Rainbow Towers Hotel. I glance up high and look into the enormous square-shaped crystal chandelier right over our table, its many sections with mirrors and copper and crystal drops hanging on gilted wires, and I hope that the lamps have been checked recently, so that they do not suddenly drop down on us. The damask tablecloths and the napkins are shining in competition with the diplomatic spouses' diamonds.

Our table is Swedish, and besides the ambassador and his wife there is a Swedish professor, who is a surgeon. His wife is German, sitting next to the Swedish lady consul and a retired Lufthansa director. In the course of the evening I notice that there has developed a romantic feeling between the airline guy and the pretty blonde consul. I sit quietly and observe this and it makes me happy, because he had tragically lost his wife last year, when she expired after having swallowed a tiny piece of chicken bone. She did not die right away, but some two months after the incident, because she was that kind of person, tenacious of life and never complaining. She apparently thought that the uncomfortable feeling she had when she swallowed would eventually go away. When she finally went to the doctor, it was too late. All of her insides had become infected. Those two romantic birds are not so young anymore, but the woman has started to look younger and started to laugh again after the divorce that took her down a peg.

Clyde and I are representatives of *captains of industry*, which is the reason why my husband has brought along the company cheque-book to enable him to donate a few hundred millions. But he is smart: he donates them to buy his own school furniture and he knows that it is a good cause for the ladies' fight against poverty. Our wine bag contains a couple of good bottles: one is a deep red Cabernet Sauvignon from Robertson's Winery in South Africa and the other is a French Rosé. There are also two bottles of vintage wine on the table, donated from 14 wine-producing countries. Interesting that the Muslim Ethiopia donates wine. Even Congo has donated.

Around 8 o'clock the microphone is taken over by the master of ceremonies, Stan Higgins, who is very professional and used to instructing big groups of tourists. He explains how we can avoid unnecessary queuing and long waits if we follow his calls for the sumptuous culinary buffet. The big copper dishes are heated underneath with small containers of paraffin, which are no longer available for the poor. They have to make their firewood with an axe and cook their meal slowly, before they can eat.

There is no shortage here. It is obvious that the supplies to the embassies take place via other channels: the cooking from Ethiopia is *Injera and Doro Wotte*, fish fillets and vegetables are from Malawi, *Beef Pilau* from Tanzania, *Kalio Ayam, Oseng-Oseng Tahu and Jamur* from Indonesia, *Chicken Curry* from Pakistan, *Tourtière Meat Pie* from Canada and a Sudanese mealie meal porridge with *Waika & Tamia*. Sweden has produced a real *Jansson's Fristelse with ansjovies* and Japan is serving delicious *Chirashi sushi and Nimono tofu*.

The arrangement is amazing, a remarkable culinary experience, and it helps you to enjoy it if you are used to living in a diplomatic environment. The poor mother with the child strapped onto her back, while she is begging among the chauffeur-driven limousines and the SUVs, would never know how to appreciate these dishes and would not know how to observe the rules of etiquette. But then, of course, the poor would never be invited to such a function.

At the Japanese buffet stand I meet Yolanda Lee. We have not seen each other for several years, but we used to socialise, when I was a bachelor and diplomat. She still looks stunning. We immediately recognize each other and in two small sentences I explain that Clyde and I now live with one leg in Harare and one leg in Canada. She and her husband Donald and their Chinese family once introduced me to the casino life, and we stayed at the Mont Clair Hotel in Nyanga. Already at that time, before the inflation started, the Chinese would fill their shopping bags with money to prepare for gambling in the casino. They would bring along their nanny to look after the little ones, while they were gambling.

The dance floor is opened by two professional dancers, the female in flowing crème-coloured chiffon garments, matching her partner's crème-coloured jacket. After this opening of the ball many couples join in and soon the dance floor is full. At our table No. 6, the men also get up and start to ask the ladies for a dance. First I dance with the Swedish professor and later with the Lufthansa director. Suddenly I am in the arms of the Brazilian ambassador. Clyde is always slow to ask me to dance, but he finally holds me very close to his chest. It feels so good, far better than when he used to wildly dance the jitterbug, as he did the first years, and where I always felt I was dancing alone. Now, unfortunately, I am always guarding him, to make sure that he is OK, that he has not gone pale or vacuumed his drink, all because I am not quite sure if there is some terrible danger lurking in one small cell.

As he looks OK, I relax and start mixing with other people that I recognize at the other tables. There is Solveig, the Norwegian ambassadrice. I like her because she is down-to-earth and does not show off. At the next table there are two African ladies of ample proportions;

for that reason it is very difficult to tell their age, because the chubby faces are hiding all the wrinkles. I know both of them; we met before at Elisabeth and Peter Haruna's residence, the Nigerian Army general who has now gone back to Nigeria.

"Are you still teaching belly dance?" asks Jaminah and bends down towards me with her full Nigerian headgear, as the music is very loud.

"No," I explain, "I had to give up the dance when my husband was diagnosed with lung cancer. We travelled to so many places for treatment, even went to New York University for a screening, but we won the struggle!" Behind my lively voice is hidden pain and a feeling of powerlessness, but I continue politely, "How are the general and his wife?"

Jaminah looks both surprised and sad. "So you didn't hear the tragedy, no? One year ago the general was killed as the plane crashed. There were seven generals on board, apart from the crew. They were all killed. It was sabotage."

I look totally shocked and call Clyde, who reacts the same way. Later he says, "I heard about that accident, but it never occurred to me that Peter was one of the casualties." General Haruna had been very close to the late President Obasanjo before his death.

We have reached a point where it is time to break up, and the host and hostess have left. Outside the hotel the air is cool, but with the wine and the atmosphere in the blood we hardly notice the chill. In the porte-cochère of the hotel we meet Vicky and Rick from the Food & Wine Society. They have been dining up at the Penthouse Restaurant and Vicky is so happy to see me that she gives me a bouquet of red roses.

She asks if we heard what happened to Ray. No, we don't know what happened.

"He was terribly burnt," she tells us. "It happened when he poured petrol from a plastic bottle into the carburator. Probably, he was in an intoxicated state, because he asked the garden boy to turn on the ignition key, so the car could get started. But the carburator fired back, which made him jump and then the petrol splashed all over him. In one second he became a burning torch. Fortunately, his wife Winnie heard his screams and quickly grabbed a blanket. She rolled him on the ground and shouted to the gardenboy that he should spray him with the hosepipe."

I remember on another occasion at a very lavish party at Haven on Earth, where the men consumed a lot of alcohol in the bar and Ray later went for his car to go home. He had steered towards the swimming pool instead of the asphalted driveway and one wheel was hanging over the pool edge, but fortunately at the low end where there were steps.

CHAPTER 10

THE PIANO TEACHER

I am on my way to my piano teacher, Miss Moss, and driving on Churchill Road. As I come to Borrowdale Road I turn left. The lights are not working and it is amazing how many cars are on the road considering that you can only buy petrol on the black market. A street vendor is standing waving a packet of toilet paper, and another stretches a bouquet of flame lillies towards me, as I am passing by. The flame lilly is Zimbabwe's national flower and is protected – illegal to sell because of its protected species status. Strikingly beautiful with delicate red-yellow petals, all parts of this plant are extremely poisonous – its reputed use in murders and suicides, and to poison dogs, eerily comes to mind.

It is difficult to get over the crossing, because nobody respects the rule of yielding to traffic from the right. I turn into the road past St. John's School, where many people have been attacked. That is the reason that I always keep my handbag and my music books in the trunk. The local radio station is playing Rap music between the news. If you do not know better, you could be fooled. It all sounds so normal, as the broadcaster reports about the storms and floods that have ravaged the country. He makes it sound like the tsunami in Thailand, giving the impression that our government is struggling heroically to normalize the conditions. All the power cuts, says the broadcaster, are directly related to the climatic changes and are caused by the West.

As I arrive at my destination I notice that the rules have been changed. The guard on duty, although having known me for the past six years, will not let me in until he has entered my name in a black protocol. He is enjoying the superior role and using it as a power game.

"Please hurry up, I am late!" I say.

In one second I see him turning his role into an abuse of power, as he lectures me. "You must come on time." Then he slows down with the entry in the protocol.

This is Africa in a nutshell: to delay as much as possible; to put a spoke in somebody's wheel; to show power towards a white person. I ignore him and use one of Clyde's tactics, to start driving slowly towards the gate, which he then opens ever so fast. On the parking lot I open the trunk to take out my bags. I always enjoy walking the last part of the road to see what is flowering between the row-houses. There is the blue Petrea cascading over a white wooden fence and some bees are swarming around it. It is an imported tree, just like that big Flamboyant-tree in the background with the coral flowers. But the Flamboyant-trees like it here, even though it was a maritime tree from Madagascar.

Miss Moss is a delicate older woman of English origin, but she was born here in the old Rhodesia and lived part of her life in Cape Town. For many years she owned a little bungalow on Montgomery Road, but six years ago she moved to this protected complex. Her figure looks almost miniature and her hair, which is snow white, has always got a shine to it. She has a very friendly smile despite the fact that she is reserved in her manners. Her teaching is full of authority and can even make me nervous, especially if I have not yet grasped the theory and make mistakes in compound time or play *adagietto*, when it should be *animato*. It is now more than 10 years ago that I started my piano lessons with Miss Moss and she permits me to call her Joyce. She often asks if I want a cup of tea, but I normally refuse, knowing that she has so little means to live on. As all older people in Zimbabwe, they have no pension and only God knows how they survive. "By the help of God," says Miss Moss, while she pushes her paper handkerchief into the sleeve of her cardigan.

Today she is looking quite elegant and she is wearing high-heeled sandals. Like a rainbow at sunset I see the afterglow of her youth. She is mysterious and full of secrets. Once she was very beautiful and had been a concert pianist. I can easily imagine that: how she once sat in a long gown with a side slit, and it must have had that same blue colour as the petrea outside, and she would show a hint of bosom, because even now it is still curved despite her thin figure. The high-heeled sandals that she is wearing today show off her slim anklebones. She must have seemed unattainable, beyond the reach of most men, like a Snow Queen, in those days. Now she is less reserved than she used to be, although she smiles less because as times get harder, she can no longer afford the dentist. Every time she is about to smile, when I say something silly or funny, her hands automatically reach up to cover her mouth.

"*Tatefe*, you remember this one, but if it is tied, *Taéfe*, then the melody is *taéfe ta ta*, but here you can see, it is *sat ta*." We are far into the duet that Miss Moss is trying to teach me, but in one moment her concentration is interrupted by a garden boy standing in the door.

"Yes, Martin, are you finished?" asks Miss Moss with the same authority as she is using as a teacher. The garden boy Martin gives her a big African smile and answers, "Yes."

Miss Moss continues, "Can you come back next Tuesday?"

Again the garden boy smiles, "Yes, Madam."

"At 2 or 3 o'clock?" asks Miss Moss with her command voice.

"Yes," says Martin.

"But which time?" asks Miss Moss with desperation.

"Same time," says Martin and I can see that he has no watch and doesn't know what time he came.

"OK, goodbye, Martin, and remember, next time you start with a cup of tea," says Miss Moss thereby ending the audience with the garden boy and returning to the duet. "Where were we? *Sateate....*"

She has a baby grand piano, and it fills up the greater part of the whole lounge. Every time we change seats at the piano, I get a bruise from the bookshelf. There is just too much furniture, because Miss Moss brought all her furniture from Montgomery Road, where she also had a sun lounge. At that time you could walk around the piano, which had the centre stage in a separate lounge with a reddish wooden floor, always shining from many layers of wax. Next to the piano she had two Persian rugs, and a big framed picture of political Beethoven was hanging on the wall. When Pauline used to come to practice the movements in an opera, she would normally stand on the red Persian, while Miss Moss sat at the piano directing her and correcting her. Often Pauline sang in German.

Now all Miss Moss's furniture has been stacked like a shop with second-hand furniture, because she can't let go of any of it; she loves every shelf and every chair. There is dust everywhere, her eyesight has deteriorated and besides, you don't expect an artist on her level to go around and dust. It has become too expensive for most to have a servant. The garden boy Martin is not employed by the occupants but belongs to the complex like the guard.

My lesson passes quickly and I stuff my notebooks and music books into the Bourdeaux-red snakeskin bag from India.

"How is Clyde?" asks Miss Moss.

"Fine, fine, but he is working too hard with the production of the ox-driven carts," I explain. She is fond of Clyde, because once he collected her bridge-table, took it to the factory and returned it totally fixed and polished.

"Thank you for the eggs," Miss Moss sounds a little apologetic. "Do you mind if I share some of them with the other residents here in the complex?"

"Of course not, Joyce, I know how hard it is at the moment and we all have to help one another," I say to her with a wave of my hand. She waves back standing there in solitude in the stable door.

Clyde brings home a section of the pink *Zimbabwe Gazette*. Sister Nancy has taken a sample out to the factory to show him an article about himself. The article describes a stinking rich dude and industrial tycoon that I don't seem to recognize:

As the nation starves, the ruling Zanu PF party is pumping out billions to local Engineering companies for their production of scotch carts to be distributed in rural areas in a move aimed at gaining more votes in the presidential and parliamentarian elections to take place in March 2008.

Close sources have indicated that a Harare engineering company, Edisan has been selected to manufacture 10,000 ox-driven carts as well as an unknown number to the Engineering firm McDermaid among other companies. The source says that the boss, Clyde Simeon, who is a filthy rich dude with his own private jet, has already been paid an undisclosed huge amount to produce the order and is presently importing material to be used from neighbouring South Africa. The manufacturing of the carts has since been made the major project by the company.

Zanu PF engaged in the project a few months back and Zimbabwe Gazette understands the party has already started distributing some of the carts. The scotch carts are also being manufactured in Gweru and Bulawayo.

Currently, Zimbabwe is experiencing a severe shortage of food, especially basic commodities such as mealie-meal, bread, milk and cooking oil. Many locals have gone for up to 5 months now without even tasting bread which is only available on the black market at an exorbitant cost of $500,000 a loaf.

"We are still in Phase I of the production, which will see us manufacture 3,000 scotch carts. However, it is difficult to meet the end of year deadline and target as well. Last week, two haulage trucks arrived at the company from South Africa. One offloaded brand-new tyres whilst another one offloaded tins of paint to be used in making the scotch carts," said a source who preferred anonymity. "The company has also recently hired new staff so as to cope with the work. There are rumours that we might not be breaking for the festive season holiday because Zanu PF wants all the carts before the beginning of next year," added the source.

Furthermore, the company supplied chairs for the Harare International Conference Centre (HICC) and the President's office. Musician, Prince Tendai frequently visited the company collecting Zanu PF metal badges. Zanu PF has a tendency of using maize seed and fertilizers to buy voters in the rural areas. The party has always used some blackmail in addition to using military force to have people cast a vote for it. Village heads in form of Chiefs are used to coerce villagers to vote for the party candidates or have no maize or mealie-meal given to that person, family or village.

The source says soon after the company ventured into this project, employees noticed some magnificent changes. Suddenly, they were now given transport allowances in cash and on a weekly basis.

"Clyde, it must be those pictures on the wall in your office. The ones of the Boeing aeroplanes," I say to Clyde after having read the article. "That is why they think you have a private jet!"

Clyde shakes his head. "They are crazy all of them. And the irony is that all those years, when I represented Boeing, I never earned a cent. I had to pay for the prestige it gave and never sold a single aeroplane." He stops talking, as he is seized with a fit of coughing.

"You are coughing a lot more," I remark. "What did Dr. Cunning say?"

"He says it is the phlegm that is coming up because of the radiation damage. It is like the mine workers that he used to have as patients. Tomorrow, I am going to see a physiotherapist that he has referred me to and she will slap me, so all the phlegm comes up." Something about the whole thing makes me feel very uncomfortable, as Clyde never recovered completely after the last flu.

But we all carry on, and I continue my normal life and my piano lessons. The last couple of times I have noticed that Miss Moss takes very long to open the door. I think she is always on the loo. Also I see pain in her mild face.

"Is everything all right?" I ask.

"Oh, I do have a small problem," admits Miss Moss and explains, "It is my colon. I am going to have an examination inside. It is on Thursday. But I am sure it is nothing serious."

But, it is serious. After her colonoscopy Miss Moss says, "I am going to have surgery. There is a huge tumour and it is malignant."

I try to make her talk more about it, but she dismisses me with a brusque reply. "No! Let us talk about something else." Then her voice gets kinder, as she continues, "We must practice as much as we can, so that you don't fall behind. That is my duty. That is what I am here for and what I am good at. I was born for that. I do reckon that you know a lot of these health issues, because I have seen how you look after Clyde. But not today. I have complete trust in the doctor who is going to do the operation."

Then we practise the pedal and try a Christmas song. On the way out of the stable door, Miss Moss hesitates a little before remarking, "I wonder what I have done wrong?" She shakes her little face with the short grey hair, but it is more to herself than to me that she addresses the question. As I walk along the path towards my car, it dawns on me that she really believes God is punishing her for something she has done wrong.

When I get home I make a phone call to Brother Paul and tell him about Miss Moss. He remembers her very well from the Shangri-La Restaurant, where Clyde and I had invited him and the nuns for a lunch with Miss Moss. Miss Moss had enjoyed so much sitting next to Brother Paul.

"I shall immediately drive over to the hospital to see her, before she has the operation," Brother Paul assures me. "At which hospital is it?"

"Saint Anne's," I say and everybody knows that it is a hospital for cancer and that it used to be administered by nuns.

After his hospital visit, Brother Paul comes by our townhouse as I run out to his rusty old car to greet him. The evening has already taken on the afterglow and soon it will be completely dark. He blends in with the darkness, as he is dressed in his formal dark brown monk habit. It is a long cape with cowl and his blue jeans are completely covered. But his braided rope belt that he has wrapped around his waist lights up, as it is white. On special occasions he wears this traditional costume from the Franciscan order. Because it has started raining, he has pulled the cowl over his head. He looks just like a hangman from the Middle Ages.

Inside the lounge he pulls down the cowl and crosses the legs, as he takes a seat in one of the peach recliners, revealing more of his blue jeans. He assures me that Miss Moss is quite at ease with the situation and, as she is a strong believer and belongs to a prayer group, they are paying for the surgery.

"When I left she was quite cheerful and even blew me a kiss," says Brother Paul with a naughty look in his blue Irish eyes. He tries to brush away a strand of hair, but as it is crew-cut there is nothing dishevelled.

"I am very grateful that you went already today," I say, and add, "Miss Moss admires you a lot. She often talked about you after the lunch and the conversation you had at the table."

Friday after the surgery I drive over to St. Anne's Hospital. The buildings are now run down and have not been maintained since the nuns gave up the administration. But still all the signs of their presence are everywhere. I approach the reception desk to inquire where to find Miss Moss. The receptionist is African and looks at me with one eye. The other is totally without life, as it is a glass eye. Perhaps she has had retinoblastoma, I think, pitying her. During the last year all the literature I have read has been about cancer and nothing else.

"She is in the Intensive Care Unit," informs the receptionist and adds, "Go straight and take the elevator over there." She is surrounded by flower arrangements, which are for sale. But as it is typical for Zimbabwe, they have all been made disproportionately to be viewed from one side only, like a spray on the coffin. I don't buy any of them, and besides it is probably not allowed to bring flowers to the Intensive Care Unit.

As I get there, I ask if visitors are allowed.

"No problem," says one of the nurses. Her uniform looks very much like an army uniform. A male nurse in a blue cotton suit is checking the numbers over the cardio-surveillance equipment over Miss Moss's bed. But she already has visitors and I hear two voices chanting words over her head like they are embalming her. "She loves Jesus. God loves her. Jesus is receiving her." The words come from two middle-aged women, probably from the prayer group that Brother Paul talked about, who were paying for the surgery. On the night table I see Miss Moss's Bible with the cross-stitch embroidery to protect it. A lot of patience was demanded in sewing this cross; it is made in very fine stitches. The two holy ladies depart and I sit down on the chair. The monitoring machine is making noises and the male nurse tries to stop it.

"You are too short; you can't reach," says Miss Moss with her friendly voice and continues, "What did Dr. Flesher say after the surgery this morning?"

"He said that the surgery went well. There were no metastasis, but they made a colostomy," replies the short male nurse.

I look at her face that is taking in the information, and suddenly she looks very old and tired. Only now do I notice that they have put a bucket under the bed with a hose attached to the bucket from her internal organs.

"It can be changed later. Mrs. Lang had that done," I assure her, as I hold her delicate hand with many blue veins in mine. She then glides into sleep.

CHAPTER 11

DOUBLE RAINBOW

Clyde comes home in between inspections at the factory and I always stand ready like a dutiful wife with sandwiches and fruit. As soon as he sits down, he presses the button on the TV remote control and follows the sports programmes intensely, and after that he watches poker tournaments and teenage soaps. If I do not protest, we would never watch the news, but right now he is taking advantage of me cooking supper.

Before darkness falls, we decide to go for a walk around our area in Belgravia. Each time we take the walk it is obvious to us that this suburb, that used to be very elegant, is so quickly deteriorating that it will eventually end up looking like a slum area. The Africans throw things everywhere and you often forget to look up into the beautiful trees, when you have to watch every step you are taking in order not to fall into the deep holes and break an ankle. It makes me angry and sad. Last time we walked, I saw a hole over 1 metre in diameter and with the rain it looked like total erosion. That was the day I picked up the fallen leaves from the local Kaffir boom tree. They were so amazing with their coral flowers that from a distance they looked like tulips. That is why many of us call it the *tulip tree*, instead of using the derogatory term Kaffir tree. The first whites called the blacks *kaffirs*, meaning infidel, and that name has stuck like bad names do. Ironic, how the children of the same people today study at universities and deny creationism, when they still talk about kaffirs. The minute the flowers fall to the ground, they no longer look like tulips. They are actually bell-shaped with a yellowish colour around the edges.

In the evening we see two good movies: *Faith of Potatoes* and *Step Up*. The first movie is made in South Africa and describes vividly the combination of extreme religion and irresponsibility. Already in the first part of the movie you notice this, when the preacher, who is also a farmer, drives the tractor together with his work boys and two of his own children and the sister's son. They sing wildly and happily, when the accident occurs. White and black, this is something I have noticed many a time here in Africa: they are just so irresponsible, both with regard to nature, the children and big dogs. Always you see a bunch of kids on the back of the bakkie. "Typical pommy," says Clyde and I add, "Just like Britney Spears when she drives her luxury Mercedes with a baby on her lap!"

The other movie *Step Up* is my kind of movie and as Clyde also likes to dance, we enjoy watching it together.

Zimbabwe is a country where you, over the years, are confronted with many individual racial and cultural differences. During the Second World War, when the British used the country for training troops, all nationalities started coming, and when the war ended the immigration numbers rose. First, it is the pronunciation. You know straight away who is Italian or Greek, and the local Africans pronounce the English language in their own way. As for myself I suppose I am a mixed cocktail from all the countries I have lived in, but here in the southern part of Africa, they always guess that I must be German or Dutch, because that is all they know from the Afrikaans language in South Africa – even though I would not dream of saying *workmanship* with a single V.

Then there are the physical characteristics, and here I am not thinking in the terms of black versus white. The British have very small dainty feet, even the men, and the women have a short torso therefore showing a lot of cleavage. The first time I saw Clyde, I knew immediately he could not be British, because he had such big feet, just like Danish men. The British are often seen with overbite and it does look cute when the children are small, but later on they get problems with their teeth. Their fine delicate facial skin is the envy of many, but unfortunately it wrinkles more than an oily skin. They all seem so *petite* here, the English, and it makes me feel very big and clumsy. I used to like being tall, but not anymore. When I put on my high heels, my head reaches above Clyde's. Eventually I started buying shoes with lower heels. On my arms and legs I am full of long white hairs, but the African beauty salons are very efficient in removing them with hot wax, to such an extent that I always have to remind them only to do half of the leg; otherwise, they put the hot wax right up into my private parts. The Africans themselves have such a smooth skin on their arms and legs without any hair, and interestingly enough they do not seem to get wrinkles until they are very old. They also constantly apply Vaseline or Shell motor oil. Or perhaps it is the *Sadza,* the porridge that they make from mealie-meal and the *relish* with kale which they serve with it, that keeps them so young-looking. With their incredibly long arms, they can reach almost to the ground with their hoe and badza. They do not seem to have a hip bone and if the African men sit on a bench or an ottoman and lean forward, then it is like seeing a *cleavage* between the buttocks. The hair is kinky and cannot grow longer than 12 cm, and even that length normally requires a perm first to straighten it out. The many *dreadlocks*, which you see around a lot is a painful fashion, because first they have to twist their own hair into tiny plaits, and after that they glue on hair pieces. Such an adventure is very costly, but then it also lasts more than a month.

The Africans and the Rhodesians do not seem to notice changes in temperatures, perhaps because they are used to unheated houses with no insulation. Their traditional round houses, which are called *ron-davels,* are probably warmer with the thatched roof. The Rhodies can stand in their thin garments with no sleeves on the coolest nights and make this statement, "It never gets cold in Africa!" The Africans will one minute wear a thick winter coat, the next a thin shirt in Cuban colours; it does not matter to them how the temperature is. They are both used to wearing open sandals all year round and their children play around barefoot. Often the Africans will put on a knitted cap, not because the weather is cold, rather because it makes them feel fashionable. It is the same with their babies in the towel on their backs; they always wear a hat. I can imagine how it was indoctrinated into their heads by the British: "You must wear a hat in the sun!"

Clyde and I look at things differently. He grew up in Windsor near Toronto, and early in life he was introduced to the American lifestyle, as Detroit was so close. He almost drove a car while he was still wearing nappies! Money and big industry means a lot to him and his main interests in life are entirely devoted to sport, cars and sailing. Over the years I have made an effort to turn him into a greener and more artistic person, and although he *has* been tainted, it is not very predominant I am afraid.

Outside I hear some voices. It is Clyde, who has invited a younger couple for *sundowner,* as we call that hour of the day when we enjoy a drink in the sunset.

"White or red?" asks Clyde to make the choice easier, as he is not much for mixing cocktails. It is wine or beer. The lady guest and I choose white, the men prefer red wine.

"A day without wine is a day without sunshine," says Gavin, before tasting his wine. He is a young man, working for *National Geographic*, but he was born in Zimbabwe. His girlfriend, Birgit, works for an international aid organization. After the first bottle of South African red wine, Clyde starts opening bottle No. 2. We ladies continue sipping; there is still a lot left of the white wine bottle. The conversation is lively and pleasant, while we do idle girl-talk.

"I never liked my bottom," Birgit confides in me and she gets up from the chair so I can see for myself what she regards close to a deformity. She turns her head around and glances down on her behind. "See how it sticks out too far, and it is too big. I am very conscious about it."

"I can't even see anything abnormal in the size," I declare honestly. "In any case, it is much nicer than a flat one. We must have a little shape. Just look at the Africans, they are proud of their behinds and the men see it as something very feminine and beautiful." As she does not look convinced, I continue, "My sense of beauty and this idolizing of one specific race has changed as far as I am concerned, since I came to Africa. Every type has its own beauty. But in your case, what is your problem? I would not consider it big, even if I had never been to Africa."

We are having a nice time, until we start discussing politics and farm invasions. At that moment the good atmosphere fades away like morning dew and all the niceties have gone. Birgit is totally biased and on the side of the indigenous people only. She elevates them to a higher level with regard to race and traditions, as if they are far superior to the white race. She defends the violent farm invasions as if it was their *right.* As if somebody has the right to ravage and plunder and destroy your home and the work of a lifetime, because of past injustices.

"I do believe, it is more a question of class difference than race," I suggest diplomatically.

Now Clyde is voicing his opinion: "It is exactly the same with the Indians in Canada. They think they can continue using the same excuse all through life, even though it did not happen in their lifetime."

Gavin supports him 100 per cent.

"But, we should not forget that the blacks are also their own worst enemy. They oppress their own people and have always had a feudal system," I suggest, but the warm atmosphere has cooled. Birgit is unable to regard the discussion from a neutral angle; she is totally fixed on the racial connotation. She does not even seem to listen to other arguments.

The minute I have said it, I regret it, but it just comes out, as a result of the looting and the farm invasions I know about, including a religious white family fostering 17 children. Quickly they became a very large family, as they found children abandoned in public places, after their desperate parents had lost everything and fled the country. The first little boy and girl had been sitting in the old Harare International Airport for hours when they found them, because the parents had said that they should just wait while they went to buy tickets. During all those hours the flight had already been in the air for a long time and was in another air space. The children did not know the destination. One month later they found two other little children outside Spar Supermarket. The couple lives in a big farmhouse with a few acres of land in Marlborough. As the farm invasions grew, their family grew. The smallest child was only 18 months when they found the baby. Over the years they have worked in co-operation with Interpol, as it is their hope that the children will one day be reunited with their biological parents.

Gavin's girlfriend looks at me with a hypnotic stare and says, "Give me all the information. Hearing this story, I am convinced they are being abused!"

I look at her totally astonished and remark sharply, "You have got it totally wrong! It is a fantastic family and I can assure you they are not taking advantage of the situation and abusing the children, sexually or otherwise."

"You are too narrow in your definition of abuse. There are many ways of abusing. It could, for example, be that the children don't get the education they deserve and if in general they are in the wrong environment," Birgit lectures.

My eyes become two narrow slits and I assure her again that the children are being taken good care of, and besides I have heard that they have now found most of the parents. I add this just in case, although it is not true, but I have to get her off that dangerous track, or she might do some investigation on her own and try and take the children away to have them institutionalized. How wrong I was to think I could persuade her to see things my way.

Instead I try to move on and tell her about the Danish farmer Wolle Kirk and his wife Birthe, who were attacked on their farm called Bhara Bhara. First they tied up the wife and then they sat on top of Wolle and stabbed him 17 times. He sustained serious injuries and one arm was shattered, but the worst was that the attacker hit him right in the eye, and they later had to remove that eye. This story, so close to me, makes no impression on Birgit; she is not even interested in hearing about the suffering of the whites. She interrupts and states that it only the suffering of the blacks that counts.

What a relief it is when Gavin changes the subject and moves away from this tense political subject. He starts talking about the Victoria Falls.

"In full moon you can see a double rainbow," he explains and I remark, "I have never seen that, even though I have been up there so many times with foreign diplomats, friends and family."

"It was the same for me," explains Gavin with a beautiful voice that sounds like a science narrator on TV. He stretches out his legs and crosses them over and I look at his light complexion that looks very Nordic, as he continues, "I grew up here in Zimbabwe, but it was only much later that my attention was drawn to this phenomenon with the rainbows. It happened when I saw an amazing shot in *National Geographic*. I noticed there were two rainbows. Later, I saw this wonder myself and never have I seen rainbows so bright, so vivid. It happens because you have this combination of the light from the moon and the clouds rising from haze and mist and light. That is why you see two big arches in the sky. They say that the colours of this double rainbow are reversed: the upper one being blue, yellow and red. The lower arch is red, yellow and blue. As the sun declined, the rainbows ascended until they reached the clouds of spray above the horizon. It spans the whole river for nearly a mile."

"Your story is so fascinating," I exclaim and clink my wine glass with him. "I simply must see this. Double rainbow at full moon. It sounds like a terrific sight. Like a complete circle."

So in a way the evening has a better ending than I first expected because of Gavin's story.

THE VERY NEXT DAY I ask the nuns about this rainbow phenomenon. Sweet Rit, who has seen them in sunset, describes the strong colours in the rainbow. She says that the second rainbow is a reflection of the first one. They call it *Lunar Rainbow* or Moon Rainbow. When Clyde comes home, we also talk about the rainbows. We agree it is very much like a *fata morgana* in the desert, this optical phenomenon that creates illusions because of distortion of light by alternate layers of hot and cool air. In the same way it disappears very quickly. Both of us recall how we, as children, have tried to run to the rainbow, but all the time it seems only further away. Before we sold *Haven on Earth* in Highlands, we had in one of the guest rooms a collection of Thomas Baines, who was famous for his paintings of Victoria Falls. Even though we did not have the originals, the prints were also very beautiful and spoke volumes. Baines was a member of the Livingstone Zambezi expedition, recruited for his valuable observations as a painter. Many amateur photographers have tried to capture such phenomena like rainbows and snow-clad mountains, but it is here that the brush of the artist can catch details far beyond the capabilities of a camera.

CHAPTER 12

LIVING IN FEAR

A s we are approaching Christmas the days are full of frustrations, because of the shortage of food and cash from the bank. Sister Nancy calls to remind us that the Governor of the Reserve Bank, Dr. Gideon Gono, will make a speech that same evening regarding new bank notes being printed in Germany. Despite the power cuts we can still see TV with the extra installations Clyde has made. The President, Robert Mugabe, has just been to Lisbon and got scolded by Angela Merkel, the Chancellor of the German Federation. It made him very angry and he has nicknamed Denmark, Sweden, Holland and Germany *The Gang of Four*.

SWEET RIT IS FRUSTRATED OVER the dirty lounge suites and chair upholstery in their house at Strathaven. They love living there, because it is a real house and not a nunnery. They have called it *Shalom*. Avis said to her that she must ask me to come over with my steam cleaner, so I drive over there with all the parts, including the pistol that literally shoots away the dirt. Very efficiently all the dust mites are removed, and the rings in the bathtub. In between, Sweet Rit shows me around the whole house. It is very cosy with a courtyard with red stones, pretty verandas on both sides and two lovely Labrador dogs, one of them a little mixed. Sweet Rit has brought them each a bone and they sit nicely on their bums as if saying *please*. It brings back both sweet and sad memories, as we had to put our dogs to sleep when Clyde became ill.

Daisy was a Bearded Collie and Lucky was of many a mixed race, smaller in size than Daisy and with quite a lot of Alsatian in her. She was almost black and had a construction like the back of a lopsided bakkie which had been hit a number of times. Clyde and I had collected Lucky at Philippa's Kennel, where there were many orphan dogs. She had begged us to choose her, rattled the gate to attract us and not look at the other dogs and she was the favourite of the old African keeper, who said to us, "This one here is a very fine dog and only two years old!" Later on we discovered that Lucky was much older, but as is typical in Africa, they say what you want to hear. In her past life Lucky had been a street dog, which was the reason for her looks. When we first introduced her to Daisy, her slim little tail was lowered between her legs. She was afraid. But Daisy gave a jump towards her and kissed her and from that moment on they were friends. Because Daisy had never experienced anything bad in life and was never nervous, she was a lover. She learnt quickly to give a kiss on the cheek and often chose the lips instead, as she copied Clyde and me. Every day she would wait for Clyde on the lawn for hours and when she heard the noise from his car, she would bark happily knowing that the minute he got out, he would throw the blue rubber ring – how she loved that game – to fetch it and bring it back, over and over again. What she had not expected was that Lucky was a competitive and smart dog who soon enough learned all the dog tricks. Lucky even became so cunning that she would hide behind one of the flower pots to be ahead of Daisy.

The day their life ended was carefully planned, but it was a painful experience. They both had a pill to relax them, before I went to the Indian vet in Avondale, bringing along a big box with cash payment. As the owner of the veterinary clinic did not have any petrol, I collected his African vet and his assistant. The two dogs never knew what was happening. Daisy never made the slightest noise, she quickly became heavy and limp, and our faithful gardener Elias carried her out to the back garden to avoid Lucky seeing her dead body. Then it was Lucky's turn and she was given the same little prick. She whimpered slightly, as the needle went through the thin skin on her foreleg, but she quickly expired. Already, when Elias lifted her into his strong arms, she was deadweight. We did try to find them another home before this, but it was difficult because of the political situation. Besides, Daisy had a bladder problem since she had been spayed, and Lucky was from the beginning an old dodderer. Eleven years with Daisy, out of which she spent seven with Lucky. Sometimes dogs have so much personality that they fill more in your life than people.

Elias had prepared everything and dug a grave in the back yard, so *Master* would be spared the sad event. Using his hands like a tool he poured the red African soil over the fur of the dogs that had been so loved, Daisy with her blue rubber ring between her front paws. He finished the job by raking the soil evenly and used his bent fingers like a rake over the grave. When he was satisfied with the result, he took two different sizes of wood and nailed them together like a cross, which he then pressed into the soft ground.

My thoughts return to the present time in the house of the nuns. Sweet Rit takes me to the lovely big kitchen and the combined lounge and dining room. They have good quality teak furniture and orange lamps. All over you see the suffering Jesus hanging on a wooden cross, in the lounge, in all the bedrooms and in the chapel. I am pleased to see a big painting hanging over the sofa. It is a motive of a fisherman, painted by the local artist Peter Birch. We gave that painting to Sister Nancy, when we sold Montgomery Road, because many a time had she remarked on how much it reminded her of her own father in Ireland. It really has its place here in *Shalom*, takes away a bit of all the sadness from so many religious icons.

Sweet Rit apologizes that the home is all looking so neglected, but I assure her, "It is not *that* bad, Sweet Rit, and when we finish with the steam cleaning, the lounge will look like new. It is probably because you are such a perfectionist that it looks so terrible!"

"I think you are right there," admits Sweet Rit, "but unfortunately, that is my personality. When you have finished, I want to show you a book about personalities."

After my job has ended, we sit in the lounge drinking German coffee with homemade biscuits the nuns have baked.

"Look here, Bodie, we divide it into nine groups. That should cover all our different personality types and characters," says Sweet Rit and shows me the cover. "I am No. 3," she continues, "that is why it was so difficult for me to finish the project with the new Convent in Gossops Green. I wanted everything perfect."

"Although there were still a few things left to do when Clyde and I saw it, the main project was done and it is all so beautiful and the architecture is harmonious," I say.

"Correct," admits Sweet Rit, "but you see my health suffered. Now I have high blood pressure and problems with the neck. Dr. Auchterlonie wants to operate, but in Germany they say I should instead try to train the muscles. And although Dr. Auchterlonie is an expert in his field, he doesn't get any younger, and one wouldn't like to be under the knife that day his hands are shaking."

"Agreed, avoid surgery. Instead train your body and get strong," I support Sweet Rit and I am thinking of many tragic circumstances, where they had opted for surgery on the spine and never got a good life after. One of my girl friends, Irene, who had taken me to the airport in Copenhagen when I left for Zimbabwe in September 1986, ended up committing suicide a few months later after years of suffering after a botched operation. But I must admit that I never heard about mishaps in Zimbabwe and I have known two who had been operated by Dr. Auchterlonie. They were both fine after. But Sweet Rit is not so young anymore.

"Would you like to borrow the book, so you can find out what personality type you are?" asks Sweet Rit.

"Thank you, I would love to read it." I place the book in my handbag and, having this rare intimacy, I take the opportunity to ask a little more about the German nun's life. "Are you born to be a Catholic, Sweet Rit?"

"No, you don't have to be born into it. Like you, I and my family are of the Lutheran faith, but when I was a young girl and stepped into this beautiful Catholic church with all the lights and smiling faces, then I knew that I belonged there. This decision I have never regretted, but it was very hard for my family."

"I can imagine, because you are so close and they must have felt like they lost you." I suddenly see Sweet Rit in a much younger version, because her sincerity peels away all the layers.

On my way home I drive by Strathaven Shopping Centre and see the African women sitting under the Acacia trees selling veggies and cooking oil. The sun is still high in the sky, but you feel so much humidity in the air that you expect the rain will soon fall. As I get close to our townhouse, I see three children sitting behind a cardboard box. The box is used as a table and it has two bananas and three tomatoes on it. They pretend to be vendors, but their real purpose is to keep an eye on all the houses to find out about our routines. The automatic gate does not open when I press the remote control, so apparently there is another power cut. Gardener Rafael is standing nearby watering the flowers with the hosepipe, totally unaware of the first drops of rain already falling, but as he sees me, he sends me his big African smile and comes over to open the gate from the inside.

"It is soon going to rain heavily," I say.

"Yes, Madam, it has already started," says the gardener.

"Here is a little rice for you and Givemore for the Christmas holidays. I wanted to give you a Christmas bonus, but there was no money in the bank," I explain as I am getting the rice out of the trunk.

"I know it, Madam, no money, no food. It will be a sad Christmas."

"What did you used to do for Christmas?"

"Oh, Madam, I used to love Christmas. When I was a child, I lived in Murehwa and we woke up very early and went together with all the other boys in the village down to the river. There, we would scrub our cracked feet and wash our bodies. Then we would smear our bodies with Shell oil. After that we would put on the new canvas shoes and new clothes that our father had bought in town. It was a good life, Madam. We all had bread, rice and chicken and some of us even had a new shiny watch that could wind itself up. Those without anything to show would smear their mouth with margarine to show off. No one starved because everyone was willing to share."

"Hopefully, the new year will bring us luck, so that you can give your children more than you had yourself," I say to Rafael as I am closing the car window because it is now beginning to rain heavily. In the rear view mirror I see the gardener resume his work with the watering, oblivious to the wasted effort when it is raining.

As I park the green Mercedes in the carport, I wave to Salome, who is sweeping the grass with an inside broom and piling up the leaves.

Inside the townhouse I sit down in the peach recliner and open the book about the nine personality types. After I have studied the book and all the character traits, I ascertain that I actually belong to three types: No. 2, No. 4 and No. 5. No. 2 because I grew up with manners

of a finishing school; No. 4 because I very early figured out that I was
something special; and finally No. 5 when I admit that I sometimes
lose my temper and bound up like a rocket.

A COUPLE OF NIGHTS LATER we discuss the book of personality
types at Brother Paul's house. We are invited to his place together
with Sister Nancy and Sister Sweet Rit. Sweet Rit says that No. 4
sounds a lot like me and you are really supposed to belong to one
type only, she explains. But Sister Nancy also finds that she cannot
fit into one type, she feels she has much in common with several of
the personalities and then she tells us that Jesus belonged to all nine
types, so perhaps it is a good thing that I belong to three types. She
says it with devilish eyes.

Brother Paul has himself prepared the evening meal, because
our old housekeeper Friday has gone home for Christmas holidays.
Another brother, who lives in the house together with Brother Paul,
has only been in Zimbabwe one year, but before that he lived for
many years in West Africa. Talking about West Africa, our thoughts
are with our dear departed old friend Gert. Once he sent the nuns
tickets to come and visit him in Denmark. He had also invited Mother
Superior, who was German. He wanted them all to come and see for
themselves the country life north of Copenhagen. No doubt Gert realized that things were beginning to deteriorate in Africa, but he chose
to turn a blind eye to that and enjoy the last years of his life there.

"May he rest in peace," says Sister Nancy and gives a Hail Mary,
"hopefully he is now in a place with his favourite Havana-cigar and
enjoying a decent glass of wine." Looking around she raises her glass
and we all clink ours with her.

"Oh, how we miss him," I add, "but typical for him that he was active till the end and died on the battlefield. You just could not imagine
Gert ending his last years in an old people's home."

Brother Paul demonstrates a new talent, as none of us knew he was
such a good cook. But before we start, he asks Sister Nancy to say a
prayer. We all hold each other's hands during the prayer. She thanks
the Lord for bringing us together for this meal. The starter is a tuna

lasagna and the main course is oven-roasted pork chops. Dessert is a surprise with a delicious bread pudding served with homemade ice cream – a splendid piece of work considering the difficulties we are having just surviving every day.

The atmosphere is delightfully informal and has an uproarious hilarity from the Irish way of life. Even with so many nationalities among the nuns and monks, I have often noticed that they are always very cheerful. But then I look at the carved wooden cross of Jesus nailed to the wall and am reminded that we are in a holy house and that there are limits to our boldness. If it was not for the jolly atmosphere with food and wine, the house would seem cold as a prison, because the monks do not have the talent of making a house cozy like the nuns. Even the grand piano in the foyer is standing like a lonely soldier and looks more like a torture instrument than an instrument for music.

Brother Paul had a nasty incident with the police. They came in through the automatic gate as they followed a truck delivering petrol. Then they started an interrogation and the three policemen searched the whole house and found exactly what they were after: *foreign currency in pound sterling*. They immediately wanted to arrest Brother Paul, but on the way out they said that it seemed a very embarrassing matter for a man in his position. Seeing another way out, Brother Paul asked if they would impose a fine on him instead. The three guys had nodded with careful consideration and said that the fine in that case should be 80 per cent of the foreign moneys discovered and that a 20 per cent administration fee was added. Besides this settlement they also seized all the petrol coupons found during their search of the house and these coupons had in fact a higher value than the "fine."

We all live in fear. On one hand we cannot exist and live our daily lives without breaking their myriad of laws and regulations, and on the other side President Mugabe and his cronies are not inclined to change as long as they become stinking rich by looting the country of its resources, and manipulating the currency and the black market.

FOR CLYDE AND I, THE impact really started eight years ago when we were in Cape Town, where we lived part of the year. Over the radio we heard that there was no petrol in Zimbabwe. At first we just laughed and treated it all like a joke, because everybody thought that this was just a temporary inconvenience, but when we returned, the destabilization of the country started and violent farm invasions of white-owned farms intensified. The petrol crisis never ended; it became a permanent state of affairs and we began to wait in kilometre-long petrol queues, until Clyde found another way.

In 2001 they also started threatening the large-scale industry and many captains of industry were kidnapped and tortured, to force them to pay large sums of money to the "war veterans." During the months of May they also invaded Clyde's factories, and before that actually took place, they had infiltrated the whole organization and destabilized the spirit of the workers, who put forward claims and grievances.

On May 7, 2001, Clyde sent off the following letter to Southerton Police Station:

RP Officer in Charge
Southerton Police Station
Southerton
Harare

Dear Sir,
On Friday 04 May 2001 at 1230 hrs I was visited by a group of alleged War Veterans, demanding a meeting and threatening that I would be removed to the Zanu PF headquarters. Even though I mentioned that I had another appointment, they would not allow me to leave and was forced by them and some ex-employees to hold the meeting in the boardroom.

The meeting concluded that more information should be obtained and a further meeting to be held at 1430 on the Tuesday 08 May 2001. I wish to lodge a formal complaint about this harassment and request a police officer's presence in an emergency.

In addition to this we had telephone threats by an ex-employee, by the name of Herbert Phiri. He phoned my secretaries and told them not to come to work, as there will be big trouble. Mr. Phiri is currently being investigated by the police on alleged fraud charges. He is using this opportunity to instill fear into some of the employees. He continually phones me with threats, demanding money. This can be evidenced by the phone bills. I believe this harassment must be contained. Please advise me what I must do.

Thanking you in advance for your help.

Clyde Simeon

Clyde also sent a letter to the Ministry of Public Service, Labour & Social Welfare:

Dear Sirs,

After a visit by a delegation of alleged veterans bringing grievances of former employees, it was agreed at an emergency Board Meeting on Friday 4th May, only to find that the allegations by these workers and their grievances were unfounded. The Group has and will always abide by the laws of this country – laws which were passed in Parliament by the government and are specifically set out for handling all labour disputes. We refer to Statutory instrument 118 of 2001, Section 24, page 595, in conjunction with second schedule page 612. Every rule of law has been applied in every case. If there has been a discrepancy, we would be quite prepared to correct it, but to date we have not found any discrepancies. However, it seems that there will always be grievances from an employee when he does not understand the laws or rules.

We have no option, but to abide by the existing laws of this country. This company does not align itself with any political or religious organization and we will always be responsible to the government of the day.

Yours faithfully,

Clyde Simeon

CLYDE THOUGHT THAT THE AGITATION had subsided, as nobody turned up on the 8th of May, when the second visit of the war veterans should have taken place and policemen from Southerton Police Station were there to handle the matter.

But exactly three days later they arrived unannounced. In a crowd they stormed up to Clyde's office on the first floor. They attacked him viciously and pulled him down the stairs. The handling was so brutal that his leather belt was torn apart. As they heaved him into the waiting white combi-bus, he saw a large number of his workers stand in a line hooting and dancing, as if they were celebrating his final departure.

One hour later did I receive a phone call from Clyde's office informing me that my husband had been kidnapped. He was abducted by the war veterans, they said. Feelings of anger and desperation overwhelmed me at first. Then my feelings turned into dead faint and fear, because maybe I would never see him again, or he would be left somewhere in the wilderness, beaten to a pulp, with broken limbs and severe injuries on body and soul that would never heal. He would not survive. It would have been better if they had thrown him in jail. I sat completely still in the breakfast nook and thought, what could be done. The Management Secretary had told me that she already had called both the Canadian and the Danish Embassy. But what could they do? Write a demarche? Or a note verbale and express their condemnation, while all along the time to save Clyde was running out?

Suddenly I knew what to do. I remembered my African Shona girl-friend, Anne Knuth, who worked as a kind of protocol chief for the President and travelled with him on all his journeys. She is a widow after her husband, a Danish Count, had been killed by a Puma, which is the name of the Zimbabwean military vehicle that hit him on a road on the outskirts of Harare. The husband, Christian Knuth, had never been involved in politics and there had been no plans to eliminate him. What happened was a tragic accident. It occurred years before the farm invasions. I always kept in contact with Anne and it was a special relationship originating from the time I left Denmark. When I made plans to sell my apartment in Copenhagen, I gave her daughter, Marianne, some of the Danish furniture. Since then we had always been close friends. Surely Anne would help me.

I called the number to the President's Office, but was told that she was not available. Full of adrenaline I began shouting and that is something you would never do in the Shona culture.

"Calm down!" said the secretary in her very soft voice. But it had the opposite effect on me and I became almost hysterical.

"How can you say that to me, when my husband has been kidnapped and I don't know what to do!" I began crying like a wounded animal.

The voice on the other side remained friendly and she said, "I am going to find your friend Anne and I will do it now now. Just stay by the telephone and *don't worry!*"

That pop-song came back to me, ringing in my ears. *Don't Worry, Be Happy!* It was repeated over and over again at Lake Kariba's Seaview Hotel many years back – a popular tune that brought smiles to all the faces. When I first came to Zimbabwe, all of us were hopeful and believed in a free Zimbabwe without racial discrimination, and freedom and equal rights for everybody.

I was erect like a statue and sat motionless in the dim light in the breakfast nook. I hardly moved. Just waiting for the telephone to ring. A few minutes passed and I literally heard them pass from the noisy ticking of the grandfather clock. Then the silence was broken by the loud ringing. My hands were shaking as I grabbed the phone. It was Anne.

"What has happened, my friend?"

I told her very fast in a few sentences what had happened.

Anne was very calm and said, "It must be a misunderstanding. You must not worry yourself, we shall get him out quickly. That I promise you. And thinking about it, in this case it is not a good idea to use Comrade Chinotimba. Instead we will use Comrade Longchase. I will contact him and you just wait till you hear from him."

I was no longer passive and I immediately changed clothes. I had better wear a business suit in case I had to knock on doors to high-ranking people in the party's headquarters. Then again I sat down and waited, until the intercom sounded. On the small TV-camera I could see that it was the wife of the Danish Ambassador. We knew one another from being posted in India at the same time. I pressed the button to open for the automatic gate to let her in, but I was unable to speak.

The fear had returned. Inside myself I was praying and begging, *Dear God. Do not let this happen to us!*

Again a loud ringing came from the telephone. "I am Captain Longchase." He had a deep soft Shona voice. "I am a friend of Anne Knuth and accompanied her and the President to Malaysia. I am willing to help you. Do not worry. The only problem I have is that I have no petrol."

I laughed, almost hysterically. "I can drive. We'll take my car, I have lots of petrol."

To which the Captain inquired, "Where is the factory?"

"He is not at the factory, I think they took him to Zanu PF's headquarters," I explained.

"Oh. Then I don't need any transport. That is just on the other side of the street," explained Captain Longchase. "I will walk over there now now, don't you worry any longer." It felt good that he said *now now*, because in Africa if you only say *now* once, it does not mean right away, it can mean much later.

As the darkness of Africa fell, the dogs started barking, and then the heavy automatic iron gate opened. Clyde's car drove in with the dogs galloping behind playing in the rear lights.

In the bar Clyde poured a double strong whiskey and vacuumed it down. His eyes filled with tears, but they did not run down his cheeks, they just stayed there. His glance was hazy and there was an air of unreality about the scene, but he was in one piece.

"Pack immediately!" he said. "We are driving down to Cape Town." The servants were informed and I showed them where I kept extra dog food.

That night Clyde drove without stopping even once, and he only started to relax when we had crossed the South African border. Only the next morning did he let me drive and he lay down on the back seat, resting his head on a pillow and pulling a duvet over his body. He fell asleep and slept for hours.

Only twice did we make a stopover for meals and we avoided entering the town of Bloemfontein, but continued through the Karoo desert after darkness fell. That was why we never saw the beautiful scenery between the high mountains and the bare cliffs, or the sheep and the turkeys that are seen during daytime. Clyde flew like a madman and I feared that if he did not stop at some point, we would surely end up in the Kalahari Desert towards the west. In total we drove 2,500 kilometres and the rain was pouring down when we came out of the big tunnel at Paarl. It was like the Devil was after us and only when we arrived at our townhouse in Hout Bay at the foot of Chapman's Peak, had Clyde used up all his adrenaline.

During the following days I was told in fragments and disconnected sentences about his kidnapping. Immediately in the combibus they had started to brutalize him and it continued as they drove through the entrance gate to ZANU PF's headquarters, passing the rooster with its magnificent tail, which is their official symbol. Clyde had been put on a chair in the middle of one of the offices and the war veterans stood in a circle around him. To begin with they asked questions and when Clyde tried to explain or deny the accusations, he was slapped hard in the face. He soon learnt that it made no difference what he said.

It did not take him long to discover that his previous partner in the plastic company, Arthur Willoby, was already in the office and that was a surprise. He is a few years younger than Clyde and looks like the son of a British plutocrat. He was well-dressed with pressed trousers and shiny shoes. It was his coquettish laughter and shiny eyes as well as his white skin that separated him from the bystanders. In one instant Clyde realized that he was not there to help him. In fact he had been behind the arrest, as he in his crudeness believed that he could take over the whole group of companies.

Willoby was no longer partner in the plastic factory. What happened was that he misused the partnership and registered a private company in his own name. He would then transfer all incomes to this company, whereas all the expenses were debited the company they owned jointly. During the last 10 years the plastic company had never become self-sustaining, but always suffered losses, so the group company had to make good for the deficit and paid towards expensive machinery. Clyde only discovered this by chance, when Willoby travelled to England on holidays with his wife for more than a month. It was then that several discrepancies concerning the delivery of a nylon protective coupling came to light. As Clyde knew the owner of the company that had ordered the coupling, he phoned him up and inquired about the payment, but to his surprise the invoice was in another company name than the one he was partner in with Willoby. Clyde quickly arranged to have the mistake corrected and received payment, but he never mentioned any of this to Willoby. When the latter returned from overseas, the tables had been turned and Willoby was no longer in control of the production of the plastic company alone, hence it became impossible for him to run the profit into his private shelf company, which he had done for the last 10 years. Clyde is a very quiet man and never talked about the matter.

Arthur Willoby became constantly more frustrated over the arrangement and in the end he declared, "If you no longer need me, then I am leaving!" Clyde had answered that he could accept that. But then Willoby threatened to sue Clyde and take the case to the courts.

"You are very welcome to do that," Clyde had said, well knowing that if the case went to court, Willoby would be exposed as a criminal and put in jail. In actual fact, it was not only the plastic company that he had ruthlessly exploited. The main group company had also been used to finance Mr. and Mrs. Willoby's lifestyle, and the renovation of their private residence and the building of a hunting lodge near Mazvikadei Lake. Willoby had a habit of pretending towards the workers that he was also part of the main concern, and that was how he got away with ordering people around.

Now Clyde looked around in the room of the Zanu PF headquarters and he noticed three or four true war veterans. He looked at them and said, "I see in this room a few *real* war veterans. May I with all due respect present you to Mr. Arthur Willoby, who was a warrior in the Rhodesian Army for over eight years and killed many of your friends and family." This created an immediate shift in the atmosphere, and they began muttering threats among each other. Willoby then hastily left the premises foaming with rage.

At the same time the door opened for Captain Longchase, who in height measured the double of Clyde. He was immaculately dressed in a wine-coloured jacket and looked like a maître d'hotel.

"Mr. Simeon. Anybody here by that name?" he had asked with a very loud voice.

"Yes, that is me," Clyde had answered.

"Are you all right?" asked the Captain.

"Yes, I am all right!"

Then the tall man consulted with the people in the room in their native tongue and Clyde was free to go.

Later when we returned from Cape Town we renewed the connection with Comrade Longchase and thanked him for his assistance. Clyde even trained him to become a commodity broker, a job which he became very good at. He later established his own commodity broking company and used it among other things to assist white farmers in selling some of their machinery, after their farms had been taken. The Captain kept 25% in commission for himself and quickly became a rich man.

CHAPTER 13

A SEASON WITHOUT MONEY

As most of the shops are empty and totally derelict without the usual decorations, Christmas 2007 is over us without any warning. In a way it is a relief in our situation, but it is the first time in my life that I have not celebrated Christmas Eve and gone to bed that early. But Clyde is very tired and Christmas Day he is sleeping most of the time. Boxing Day we are invited for lunch at Zeb and Avis's. The two nuns, Sister Nancy and Sweet Rit, are also invited and so is the lawyer Harvey Schwarz and his wife Arlene. Both Arlene and myself order a tablespoon of whisky in a big glass of water before the wet lunch, as we both get a headache from too much mixing.

"Now I can play *Minuet in G*," I tell her proudly, referring to a music book with 18 selected pieces of Bach that she has given me.

"How is Miss Moss?" asks Arlene with a smile.

"Don't you know that she is in St. Anne's Hospital?" I enquire.

"No, I did not know anything about that," she says, full of sympathy, and listens to the whole story.

Arlene is born into a family where they were all professional pianists. Her mother was educated at the Conservatory of Milan. The family lived on Rhodes Island until Arlene was 11 years old, but during the Second World War the Germans came and terrorized them because they were Jewish. The mother had two pianos, both Bernstein and one of them was upright. But it was the other one, the grand piano, that the soldiers wanted to remove. Her mother begged the young soldier to leave her with at least one of the pianos. He asked her then, if so which one should he take?

"Take the upright one!" she said firmly. Which he did, but he got a look of surprise on his face, when she asked him for a receipt. After the soldiers had removed the upright piano, the family sawed off the legs of the grand piano and put a mattress over it and slept there till the war was over. When the British came after the war had ended,

Arlene's mother went to one of their warehouses, where people could get back their belongings and asked to get her upright piano back.

"Do you have a receipt?" asked the attendant at the warehouse.

"Yes, certainly, it is here!" said Arlene's mother and passed them the receipt from the soldier, which was folded neatly. They said she was the only person who had a receipt! She got her piano back. Every time I see Arlene, I think of that story of her life. In the beginning I never knew, she looked so carefree with her trendy short black hair and seemed to have an easy mind, like she was trifling away her time, with her soft frisky manners at the parties. She gave the impression of a rather protected woman in the upper class of society, who had never known any hardships.

"Have you been able to get money in the bank?" asks the hostess while passing around a serving tray with delicious snacks and decorated with edible flowers from the garden. She is very pretty and has natural blonde hair and blue eyes. She was born in Britain, but moved to Africa in her childhood with her family. Her little chubby shape and face makes her look years younger, and like Arlene she has a very stylish short hairstyle. Despite all the hardship Avis is able to maintain the elegant lifestyle. She is a true gourmet and has trained the maid Mavis since she was a little girl. Mavis can cook all the dishes, but now she works more backstage, because at an advanced age she gave birth to a son, having for many years believed that she could not bear children. The child was named Zeb after Avis's husband. Before Mavis disappears, she comes out on the veranda to greet all of us.

"How are you, Auntie Bodie?" she asks warmly and greets me with a sincere handshake first and then claps her own hands, one hand across the other as women do in Zimbabwe. In Africa it is polite to address you as "Auntie," and it makes you feel like you are family.

None of us have been able to get cash for weeks now. We all agree it is the big sharks that are out for ruthless exploitation. We sit on the shady covered veranda and there is a drizzle of water coming down from the skies. It is so relaxing because most of the time it is pouring down in buckets, and in the town of Masvingo they had so much flooding that people, goats and other animals were carried away by the strong current. The vegetables are beginning to disappear from the street markets, as the rain spoils all the new cuttings.

Zeb offers wine to everybody and Clyde helps him at the other end of the table. Like Schwarz, Zeb is also Jewish and carries the same upper-class manners. He is at least 20 years older than Avis and is beginning to show his age.

"Thank goodness we had power today," praises Avis. "Without power everything stops, and without water it is just impossible. We had to put buckets with water for each toilet and the shower was ice cold. Of course right now you can do without a warm shower, because it is so hot, but I thank the Lord every day when I get a warm shower."

"Yes, and the freezer can't be without power for many days, before the chickens go bad," Sweet Rit joins in.

"The worst thing I find is when the computer is not working," says Sister Nancy, while she is checking on her cell phone and pushes some buttons.

"And then all the desperate people that come to your gate and ring the bell all times of the day," continues Avis. "All of them have a story to tell about their hardships because they can't find work and they don't have money for food or clothes, indeed it is very sad. The worst thing was yesterday when a white European woman came to the gate and said over the intercom that she was 61 years old, she couldn't find work and she was hungry and needed help. It just bothers me, because I did not have bread in the house for ourselves, nor money, and besides you also have to be careful – it could be a trick."

"You never know," I agree and add, "During the last power cut we had to wash the bed linen and the clothes in the bath tub."

We all condemn the Zimbabwean government for giving us all these daily frustrations and then it is time for us to leave. Although we do not intend to break up the party, the sisters are also ready to leave.

Being only a stone's throw away, we are soon back in our little townhouse. There is still power and Clyde turns on the TV. Through the hatch I watch the news. All channels send the same news, whether it is CNN, Sky or BBC and they are all praising Benazir Bhuto as a heroic figure and presenting her as a champion of democracy. "You don't know whether to laugh or to cry," comments Clyde.

ALL THE CHRISTMAS HOLIDAYS IT is pouring down with rain. The rain is drumming noisily on the green metal roof. It makes Clyde restless, but the rest he gets from this weather does him good. We lie on the big king size bed and have left the window half open behind the mosquito net. The window seal has lost its varnish due to the constant splashing. As I lie there I enjoy listening to the sounds of the rain at intervals, first light, then heavy, beating like drumbeats and especially at night it has a calming effect. We are safe and dry, but the thoughts inevitably go to the poor and the homeless and the small-scale farmers, whose crops have all crumbled up when the rain drowned their harvest. Sister Nancy told me the other day that three family members had been killed in Mangura. Despite all the rain, the water in the well had been quite low and when the girl leaned forward to fill her bucket with water, she dropped it. Her brother reacted quickly and jumped into the well to retrieve it, but he never ascended. The other brother then jumped into the well, but the same happened, he also stayed under the water. The water was dead still and did not look dangerous. Finally, their cousin jumped in because he was a good swimmer, and if he acted quickly he could save the two brothers. But his swimming skills did not help him in this situation and he knew nothing about what was in wait for him in the deep waters. Clyde explained to Sister Nancy that it is the formation of methane gas coming from the mines that had poisoned the well. You feel nothing, but you immediately lose consciousness. The girl, who had lost the bucket into the well, went back to the kamusha screaming and now everybody in the village thought that the well was bewitched.

Clyde is watching a game of golf on the TV screen. He misses playing with his group who call themselves the Nomads. The group has members also in South Africa, Botswana and even New Zealand and Australia. After golf and showering, prizes are given out. They are eating together and drinking a lot of alcohol – all in fun. The dress is black trousers and a black-monogramed jacket with white shirts and a Nomads striped tie. Very colonial and very formal.

Since his sickness and long recuperation they had given him a medical handicap but he used to be a 6. A few times he has tried to play 18 holes, but he could no longer manage it; he became short of breath. Three times he has been attacked by the flu and his immune system is low. We discussed whether a flu vaccination might help, but Dr. Cunning had said, "Yes, that would be a good idea, but the government will not procure them." Like all other things, the shortage of goods has hit the health sector. Once upon a time we could get everything, even vitamins and supplements. Still I have supplies with me from Canada, but when they run out, it will be a problem. Fortunately, I brought a lot as I emptied all the bottles and put all the pills in zipper-bags and in this way there was ample space in the suitcase.

Although it is good for Clyde to get some form of exercise, too much will do more harm than good and it is so obvious that the rain is protecting him. It forces him to be more quiet and less energetic.

WE HAVE TAKEN A BIG bite of the New Year, and still cannot get any money from the bank, but Clyde believes it is only a question of a few days before the new bearer cheques are on the market.

In a way we are like the Israelis who worked themselves out of slavery in Egypt. If only we can produce thousands of scotch carts for the Reserve Bank and some of the ploughs that they have asked for as well, then we will be out of our slavery. Clyde says that the next production of scotch carts must cost 1.5 billion Zimbabwe dollars each and he has had horse-sense with regards to inflation, knowing full well that around the New Year and thereafter it will be even more difficult to get raw materials for the next 2,000 scotch carts. Now the tires are a problem. Perhaps we have to get them from China. The Baron was smart in getting approval for the big price increase, but he overlooked the problem of getting the raw materials and he does not produce the rims as fast as he should, so he is behind with his part of the production. Despite the fact that his part is such a small job, he cannot keep the pace with Clyde's production of the whole cart. He works in a different way and is never personally on the grounds. His African mentality also makes it difficult for him to speed it up.

In the government-controlled newspaper and the three half-controlled magazines, they write that the new government budget runs up in quadrillions. That means there are 15 zeroes after the figure! More exact, Finance Minister Samuel Mumbengegwi has estimated a budget of 7.8 quadrillions to the Parliament. As the pink financial gazette writes, it does not seem very high if you use the black market rate: 1.5 million Zimbabwe dollars to 1 US dollar. However, if you use the government's official rate of Z$30,000 to 1 US$, the budget runs up to 261 billion dollars, but as the pink paper says, nobody uses that rate – except when important people need foreign currency to make money. The paper also explains that in the United States six zeroes are equal to one million, nine zeroes one billion, twelve zeroes a trillion and fifteen zeroes a quadrillion. If you continue to a quintillion, you need to put 18 zeroes after and there are 21 zeroes to a sextillion. A googol goes up to 100 zeroes. Zimbabwe is the only country in the world that has quadrillions and we are also leading on the world scale when it comes to the highest rate of inflation, at the moment 14,000 per cent!

Most of Zimbabwe's budget goes to the army, the police and the intelligence service. They need to print an awful lot of money and to borrow yet more. However, 25 million US dollars has been put aside for mechanization of the agricultural sector and I hope it is out of that sum that Clyde will get paid for the scotch carts and the ploughs.

The Director of the Reserve Bank has pointed fingers at the black market barons, who are hoarding their cash instead of putting the money in the bank. He knows they are keeping it to buy foreign exchange, because 58 trillion did not go through the bank. Simultaneously, he makes a new rule to the effect that you can only put a maximum of 50 million of cash in the bank for private account holders and only a maximum of 200 million if it is a company account. If you need your own money, you are only allowed to draw 5 million as an individual and a maximum of 20 million for corporations. It does indeed sound as if the Reserve Bank Director is living on another planet than the rest of us and never goes shopping, nor does he operate any production.

EVERY DAY CLYDE AND I try our luck in the bank, but both of us return home empty-handed. The few items I can get in the supermarket on my plastic card cannot cover our daily needs for a normal housekeeping for two people. I am worried that I can no longer keep Clyde healthy every day. Constantly I am speculating about what to cook, perhaps a few dry beans boiled with a few veggies and brown rice.

I am interrupted by the intercom bell and hear Sister Esseldrida's voice. She is completely desperate, as she is looking after the old people. She asks me if I can change 400 Euros, but I explain that it is impossible to get any cash. Should the situation improve, I explain to her that the rate in that case would be 1,400,000 for 1 US dollar and if I multiply with 1.35 then we have Euro and the rate would then be 1,890,000. She does not look surprised – it is my experience that all the sisters are well versed in the economics of Zimbabwe.

We sit at the round dinner table that Clyde made out at the factory, drinking German coffee and gossiping like the wives in Jutland where I grew up. The nun spreads out her legs for comfort like the men do when they ride in a bus, but that is because she is fat. She is dressed in a rather old-fashioned habit from the Dominican Order in a light crème colour, because that is cooler during the hot season. I confide in her that in actual fact I would have no difficulties living with the shortages, if only we could get vegetables. Avoiding meat and processed food is, after all, better for all of us and better for the planet, I say, then ask her directly, "Don't you also find that this bulimia in fiscal policies is about to strangle all of us?"

Before answering, Sister Esseldrida wipes her forehead and then looks straight at me. "But Clyde is constantly expanding his production of scotch carts!" Although her voice is mild, it is also firm with her German accent. Then she looks into the ceiling and continues, "If only we could get rid of Mug—" She stops short and puts her hand over her mouth, as the maid Salome enters the room to remove spider webs.

"*Masikati,*" greets Salome with the greeting that is used in the afternoon and putting the duster aside, she claps her hands.

"*Masikati, Makadii?*" replies the German sister in fluent Shona.

When Salome leaves the room and walks into the bedroom I whisper, "She is a fan of his!" We decide to be very careful also on the telephone.

"At least now we don't have to carry all those heavy bricks," I say cheerfully, to see the bright side of things in relation to the shortage of money.

"I don't see any benefit in that," says Sister Esseldrida, "and when you said we could just use pillow cases for carrying the money, I arranged to have pillow cases sent from Germany, because they are much bigger. But now we have no money!"

CLYDE RETURNS HOME, BUT AGAIN he is empty-handed and the trunk is empty too. Still there is no money in the bank. The rate of exchange has gone down slightly from 1.4 to 1.2 million to 1 US dollar. That happens automatically when the market has a shortage of cash. The big sharks are now taking all that is available. They are becoming desperate, because they don't know if the ship will be lost with all hands like the *Titanic*. In their feverish efforts they become like vultures and greed is their predominant feature, as they empty banks and supermarkets or whatever store that they find with goods.

But daily life continues regardless. Although I have no piano lessons anymore, I still practice melody pieces using the pedal and I struggle with *Ballade pour Adelaide*. I try to do the shopping trip in a hurry and praise the green Mercedes that always starts, no matter what petrol is in the tank. I start at Bon Marché in Avondale, although I had sworn that I would not set foot in there again. But there is no place for pride any longer. Also my milestones have been moved, as desperation grows. When I do find a packet of washing powder for the automatic machine that is environmentally friendly at a price of 8 million (and mark you, it does not even need any extra softener) as well as two packages of longlife milk at a price of 4 million each, I feel so lucky. And there is a bottle of locally produced dishwasher liquid for 679,000 Z$ and fresh mushrooms for 880,000. This is the only place where you find mushrooms. As the queue for bread is not too long, I join it. But as I get close to the front, I am told by the other customers that there is no more bread. An assistant with glued-on hairpieces in Rasta style declares, "No more bread!"

But I notice that many people come out from a side door with bread in their hand. I go forward again and greet the assistant very politely, first with *Mangwanani* and then I clap my hands across one another before asking very softly, "Have you got bread for me?"

"No, Madam, bread is finished!" she says and turns around swinging her pigtails – a beauty for which she has suffered many hours.

My talents as an actress have always been useful and I manage to get a look of surprise in my face. "They must have started the next lot of baking, because I now see customers coming out from the storage room with bread in their hands." My smile feels big and African and not stiff at all.

"I also see it," says a Shona man next to me.

"Oh," says the Bon Marché girl with the Rasta style and passes us three people at the front each a loaf of bread.

As I walk through the supermarket I feel my spirits lifted because of the incident, and the fact that I have learnt to keep my voice soft as a Shona and managed not to explode like some New Year's rocket. But you cannot do it all the time; sometimes it is just impossible to be that humble. Besides, you can hardly hear what they are saying.

When I come to the till to pay, my total is 31 million Zimbabwe dollars. I do not understand it. "That is impossible!" I go through the receipt and notice they have charged 5,679,000 for that locally produced dishwasher with only 500 ml in it. A white lady and a tall gentleman support me and say, "No, that is far too much. Even the concentrated one is cheaper. Ask to have your money refunded!"

The lady at the till double-checks the price and regrets that the high price is the correct one, but she does not mind refunding me the difference. All the customers behind me stand very patiently waiting. Now I get cash money back, because I had paid with my plastic card. Hurray! It is like winning in the lottery. Now I can buy paw paws from the street vendor. A tall man in front of me and around my own age stands with his Cabs plastic card and he is only buying a packet of Colcom sausages. He is typically dressed in shorts with long socks and desert shoes, a kind of uniform among white men. But he is unable to pay with his Cabs card. I see his situation and say goodbye to my newly acquired cash money as I try to help him: "Take it from my cash which they just gave me for the dishwasher liquid."

"No, I can't do that. I know how impossible it is to get cash," he says.

"But it is all right," I say. "I know that you cannot get it in the bank, my husband has been to four branches without any luck."

On the way out of the supermarket, he says to me, "I feel so guilty about this, and it is not that I don't have the money."

"I know. We are all in the same boat," I say cheerfully. "Next time it will be me needing a Samaritan." We wave goodbye to one another and I do not even glance at the paw paws.

IN TM SUPERMARKET I LOOK around quickly to see obvious advantages. The Australian red wine Preston Vale has gone up from 2 million to over 25 million a bottle. Then there are 3 bottles of 2006 Gourdini Gold Medal wines from South Africa for 5,856,000. There is a Pinotage and one Shiraz. I put all 5 bottles into my trolley. This present political situation does need a certain intoxicating lift from time to time. Clyde does not need to be consulted first. He would just say, "Are you sure they don't have more?" He has just deposited 200 million in my shopping account and it is worth using my Barclay Prestige Card as much as I can, when we cannot get any cash.

I suspect the banks are now keeping the cash for their top people and have instructions to withhold them from the whites, to deliberately force us out or drive us to bankruptcy. It is just another way to create *black empowerment* and to take over white-owned factories, restaurants and other businesses. But Clyde knew this was going to happen; that is why he is working like crazy on the scotch cart production, hence the profit goes to us and the Baron gets the Empire. It is ironic, of course, that the Baron does not pay with money from his own enterprises, but with profit of our own company.

Hopefully, the Baron will soon get cash. He usually brings what we need, in big brown cardboard boxes that stink from the local bleach called JIK and carbolic soap. They will be stuffed with bricks of 200,000 and 100,000 bearer cheques. A small box will have notes of 10,000 and 50,000 to make it easy to change into US dollars, Euro or British Pounds. Sister Esseldrida is the most desperate; we must help her out first or the old people will suffer. Many of these nuns have long passed middle age, but they continue regardless and often risk their own lives to help children, old people and the poor in general. Sister Nancy is even more desperate, because during the *Murambatsvina* action, the government razed many houses to the ground and among them an orphanage which she had built for small children. Officially, the government had said that they would only demolish buildings without a building permit as a clean-up exercise, but in reality they came in with big bulldozers and ruined the livelihoods of so many with no apparent reason, whether they had a building permit or not. The intelligence service had warned that the people were preparing for a rebellion and the government reacted spontaneously and destabilized the people in the townships, because it was among the poorest they feared it would come. The little homeless children had in that icy winter been thrown into the streets and had to sleep outdoors with only blankets to shield them. That happened before Clyde became ill and Sister Nancy had said to him, "Clyde, I need delivery from you of lots of plastic tubing and wooden poles, so that we can make temporary shelters for the children against the rain and the cold." The very same evening we watched on TV the same middle-aged nun look straight into BBC's camera and ask with serene contempt, "How can anyone behave like that?"

A few days later the nun got a bright idea and asked Clyde to buy an old organ from her, "Clyde, I need more money for my children and, you know, Bodie can always play on it."

It was an old organ made in 1853 in Boston and it came from Father Gilbert of the Mount Darwin Mission. When the mission had been attacked by guerilla soldiers during the war between white and black people, the organ was the only thing they managed to save, before the missionary house was set on fire. Later Father Gilbert managed to get the organ transported to the Convent in Salisbury, which was later to be named Harare. This happed during 1966–67.

After the fire the Mission closed down and Father Gilbert left the country. His old Mercedes remained for many years on a Rhodesian farm and was used as a truck, after they had cut off most of the body-work. Coincidentally and by the irony of fate, Clyde bought in the nineties the leftovers of that vehicle, but at that time he never knew who it had belonged to. He planned to restore the car to its original glory and had intentions of buying a new body for it. He had contact with a real expert in Stellenbosch in Cape Town, and had seen it demonstrated how it ought to look, and the expert had advised him to obtain a body from Namibia. Father Gilbert never returned to Zimbabwe but fate would have it that Clyde and I came to possess both his old Mercedes and the organ from his time as a priest at Mount Darwin. Years later all this came to light.

Sister Nancy had been warned when she became a celebrity on CNN and BBC for saying her opinion, but she refused to leave. Now she is busy building a new orphanage and as the Africans do not have the best long-term memory, unless it is a matter of revenge, perhaps she is safe enough because they forgive easily.

DECEMBER WAS EVER SO IDLE, because there has been no money to count and exchange. But it is impossible to live without money and we have all made plans towards transporting these huge sums when they arrive. Myself, I use an airport carrier on wheels to protect my back. When I have to empty Clyde's car trunk, I use a lightweight wheelbarrow, which Clyde has produced at the factory. It is collapsible and folds like a baby pram. The banks are now threatening big surprises and say they will catch the Cash Barons in the act. The last thing Clyde heard was that the new bearer cheques are in print and we will get notes of 250,000 and 500,000 and even a big note of 750,000. However, we know that big notes are only a relief for a short time. It does not take long until inflation catches up again and the convenience of carrying small bundles will only be a short pleasure. The printing alone is already causing inflation. The street vendors are already preparing themselves and enter the supermarkets when they open and grab all the items that are in short supply, then they place themselves at a wooden table on a loose stand behind the supermarket and sell these items for three to four times the price. It causes a lot of chaos and new shortages for daily necessities. The street vendors no longer negotiate about the price; they would rather let the goods go rotten.

CHAPTER 14

THE END OF AN ERA

During my next visit to St. Anne's Hospital there is another receptionist and she is not as friendly as the one with one eye.

"She is in Room 218, but you are too early!" she says warningly. I look up to the clock in the hall and sit down for five minutes before I take the steps up to the second floor. It is better to exercise and not risk being caught up in the elevator if there is a power cut. These days you can't be too careful. The walls remind me of a chapel with several decorations of the suffering Jesus on the cross and pictures of Madonna. The usual smells in the halls are absent. You smell neither soap nor medicine.

In Room 218 two nurses in starched uniforms and badges on the shoulders are in attendance. The uniforms look like the ones from the Salvation Army. They wave me through and I look at that tiny face in the bed with hollow cheeks. One of the nurses remains in the room. She shakes Miss Moss and says, "Wake up, Mrs. Moss, you have a visitor!" Out of respect she says *Mrs.* Moss instead of Miss Moss. Miss Moss would have corrected her and said, "I am MISS MOSS."

"Do not wake her up. I can sit here on the chair and wait." I say it in a low tone as not to disturb the patient and I am shocked to see the state she is in. She looks as if she is dying, but perhaps she can hear me. I say hello from Arlene Schwartz and tell her that she has given me the most lovely music book with easy music pieces by Anna Magdalena Bach.

"So you'd better get better. I need to learn how to play them."

She does not move, but I continue talking, pretending she can hear me. "Keiko has left for a while, but I saw Jim at Bon Marché, and Brother Paul sends his love."

When I mention Brother Paul, she opens her eyes and looks at me. I continue, "Clyde is so much better and is stronger by the day."

The door opens and I am happy to see a familiar face from the music club. She sits down on the other side of the bed and like me she talks to Miss Moss, as if she can hear her.

"Joyce, I was in Fishhoek, your favourite place." She is referring to the town on Cape Town's east side, by the Indian Ocean with the much milder current than the Atlantic side.

Miss Moss opens her eyes once more and looks at both of us and she grabs my hand on the sheet. She tries to talk, but none of us can understand what she wants to communicate. She tries several times and she wants to sit up. After a while we leave her bedside and leave the room together.

I can see that her health has totally deteriorated.

During the next visit there are other visitors and I am told that the surgeon left for Christmas holidays and that there was a shift in nursing attendance, so Miss Moss became dehydrated and had to have a blood transfusion. Now she can no longer talk and she vomits all the time; that is why she is now a mere skeleton. Her head swings weakly as if she is without a spine and it cannot stay on the pillow.

"Up, hold me up," she tries to say. We manage to hold her up together with the nurse, but then she starts vomiting again. Another nurse arrives to give her an injection for nausea.

"She must first give her permission," says the nurse.

"Yes," says Miss Moss in a whisper from dry lips.

That night I pray to God that He will have mercy on her and let it end quickly. Why did they operate on her under such conditions, when she is 84 years old? One of my friends has told me that the surgeon that operated on her is called *the Butcher*.

During the later years I learnt more about Miss Moss and her life, but never from herself. She had once been a nun, but had for many years suffered from a clinical depression. Her childhood had been unhappy and the parents became divorced when she was a little girl and in those days it was a stigma and she felt very disgraced over it. She left for England to study music and she was such a talent that she became a concert pianist.

As a young girl she fell in love with a violin teacher and they knew each other for seven years. Nobody in the music club knew what impact it had on her and to which extent it affected her later choices in life and whether it caused her to become totally devoted to religion and her faith. They also did not know if he was the reason for her depression. She was accepted as a nun with an Anglican Nunnery, but left the Order after some years before her final ordains. She had her last depression about 11 years ago, at the time when I approached her and asked if she was willing to teach me classical piano. I was totally unaware about her clinical depression over the years and I only got to know about it during her final days. Once, it had been so serious that she just sat and stared blindly into the air for months. Perhaps it was another irony of fate that I did not grasp the situation at the time and just accepted when she said to me, "I am terribly busy at the moment, but come back in a couple of months!" After exactly two months I tried again and asked if her time schedule looked any better.

"What is your music background?" she had asked in a voice like an examiner.

"I have no background, but I learn very quickly when I like the subject," I admitted shamefully.

"Do you mean to tell me that you don't know the change from minor to major?" she asked skeptically.

When I confirmed this she walked over to her small mahogany desk and found a calendar, commenting in a businesslike manner, "At least you have not learnt anything wrong, so I will give you a time beginning next month."

Our friendship was always a bit formal. I respected her so much as an artist and teacher and I never tried to be familiar with her. Besides I felt I was a cultural ignoramus and was humbled and grateful that she had accepted me as a student. She introduced me into a new world of beauty and kindness and I began having a new feeling of self-confidence and lost the feeling of not belonging. Once I said to her, "Before I started playing, I always thought there was something wrong with me. I always felt like an outsider when they were all talking about sport. I went for riding classes and tennis classes, but it did not help me. Now I know that I have to find friends with different interests."

After four years of weekly training she introduced me to the Music Club. She said it was a very special club, as all the members were rec-

ommended and they were all good and humble persons. At that time
I was still on a very low grade, but I was received with open arms
by music lovers of all ages and from many different countries besides Zimbabwe. The club had both amateurs and professionals, who
played for each other. They came from far-away places like England,
Switzerland, Belgium, South Africa and Japan and they all mastered
various instruments. There were also two opera singers among them.
Once a month we would meet in different homes – with frayed nerves
if we had to perform. The toughest performance took place once a
year in the autumn, and everyone would be nervous for that occasion
when old members, who had made a career out of their music, joined
and performed alongside the rest of us.

In an ironic twist of fate I share the same experience as Miss Moss,
with an unhappy childhood as a result of a divorce, but as we were
both so formal, we never shared our common destiny and regarded
such revelation for both frivolous and improper.

Miss Moss died at the beginning of the New Year. Brother Paul
had continued his visits to the hospital and he also arranged that a nun
from the Franciscan Order came every day to see her.

Her funeral was different from what I would have expected. The
church was built in a modern art deco style and the minister was a
young black African. The parishioners consisted of an unusually
noisy big crowd, the women dressed in richly coloured dresses as is
custom in Zimbabwe. Some of them had, that same morning, already
participated in another funeral, namely that of Wessels Rautenbach,
who was suspected of being an international arms dealer. Officially
he is known for having the franchise for Hyundai and Volvo trucks.
Clyde has told me that his son, Billy, is suspected of having killed the
son of the Hyundai boss in 1996 in South Africa and for that reason
he cannot travel to South Africa, where he is wanted by the police
in connection with the murder and for having committed fraud. The
father, Wessels Rautenbach was killed on the way home from Lake
Kariba, when his front tire hit a big pothole in the asphalt. As they
were driving at very high speed, the three passengers in the car also
died.

As I stood at the entrance to the church none of the faces seemed familiar and all the laughter and the happy atmosphere made me sad. How could they be so noisy and cheerful when they were celebrating the passing away of such a quiet and humble person? It offended me deeply. The young minister, who was dressed in a white clerical gown, smiled broadly at the parishioners and said, "She is now in Heaven, we can smile!" He spoke from Psalms 14 and 34. It did not surprise me that Miss Moss had chosen a black minister, as she had once commented when I had remarked on the increasing number of Chinese in the country, "If they are yellow or if they are black, it does not matter! As long as they are good people."

They sang the following 3 hymns:

Praise My Soul the King of Heaven
Oh, I was made for this and
To God be the Glory, great things He has done

Several of the people made speeches in the church, more notably the former Director of the College of Music, Neil Chapman, who highlighted Miss Moss's tremendous tolerance in life. Due to her status as a pianist and the special role she had among musicians, she was given more attention at her funeral than she had been given her whole life! The opera singer, Pauline, who like me had come to practice with Miss Moss for many years, had been chosen to end the funeral with Mendelsohn's *Oh Rest in the Lord*. Her powerful voice filled the modern church and made up for the superficial behaviour in the beginning.

I never saw a coffin in that art deco church, nor did I know if Miss Moss was buried or cremated. But it was the end of an era.

Her funeral happened to take place at the same time the local police broke into several of the Anglican churches in Harare. Three ministers and a large number of parishioners were arrested, as there had been protests against the bishop that the government had appointed. They were dragged out of the church, and as the incident took place at the end of the service during the Holy Communion, the communion cups were pushed violently over, splattering the white altar cloth with wine, and the communion breads were tossed in the air. In the govern-

ment-controlled newspaper, it was stated that the churches had performed their services without proper authorization from the police.

Meanwhile the opposition MDC (Movement for Democratic
Change) party swore that they would repeat the same violence that
had taken place in Kenya if Mugabe attempted to rig the joint presidential and legislative polls due in March, 2008.

"You saw and heard what happened in Kenya. It is nothing compared to what we will have here, if Mugabe rigs the elections again.
You can't have a thief rob you twice and let him keep his hands!"
said MDC's Secretary for Information, Nelson Chamisa, as he was
addressing hundreds of party supporters at the launch of their election
programme in a suburb of Harare.

I LOST ANOTHER FRIEND OVER the holidays. Miss Denmark calls
me from Denmark to tell the sad news: painter Hanne Passer passed
away on December 28th. Presumably because she did not wish to live
any longer, explained Miss Denmark. It made me sad to think that her
life had lost its meaning, that there was nothing left to live for. Hanne
had lived in her own world of mystery, with birds, eggs and shells,
wearing flowing robes in the shadows of the nearby woodlands. *"I
must always live in the forest,"* she once told me.

Once she had visited us in Africa and brought with her beautiful Christmas decorations from Denmark, and she had given me new
strength in a world with such a different mentality. *"Don't change, be
yourself!"* she had whispered. She had been on a safari-trip viewing
all the animals from the jeep, scanning the horizon of wild stretches
of swaying savannah grasses and she had slept under the stars on our
houseboat *Timela* at Lake Kariba. In the daytime Clyde had taken
her fishing and in the night he taught her how to see the size of the
crocodiles. He would show her how their eyes would light up like two
torches in the black African night and the bigger the distance between
the eyes, the bigger the reptile. She loved to go fishing in the daytime
with herds of elephants and buffaloes on the shore and one day she
said laughingly to Clyde, "I will tell you this, Clyde. In my next life

I want to be a hippo. Imagine, then I can just stay in the bathtub all day long!"

When I told her that if you hear the cry of the fish-eagle, it means that you will return to Africa, she said after a couple of days with tears in her eyes, "I heard it. I heard the cry of the fish-eagle!" Although Hanne never returned to Africa physically, I am sure that her soul did.

CHAPTER 15

HARDSHIP AND INJUSTICE

Because Gert has died we drive out to see the conditions on his farm at Ruwa. We get up very early and hear several roosters crow in the early morning, almost as if to remind us which party is in power. First, we follow the Arcturus Road to avoid all the potholes near Ruwa Supermarket. Along the road there are big rocks and you notice them more now, as so many trees have been cut down. Then there are wild stretches of swaying savannah grasses. A local cowboy is directing a herd of cows with a stick so they can cross the road. He is barefoot and only a child. The cows are only skin and bones; in fact they are so thin that the skin has caved in between the ribs. They have built a lot of new huts in Ruwa, but there is no electricity and no running water. All the people in the fields bow their neck to the yoke, their long arms reaching down to the soil to prepare for the maize planting. The tobacco building is half gone, as the 600,000 acres of land are no longer used for tobacco since the whites were driven off their land. Sorghum is also not planted, although it is actually more healthy than maize. This is because of their attitude: *we have never done it.* The African looks back, not forward. His life philosophy is based on forefathers and the elder. The respect for the elder and the Chiefs is so great that whatever they do, it is accepted, they are above everybody else. I was told as a matter of fact, to become a Chief, you must have killed somebody. In the West we are often told by the Africans, "You used to do it," and true enough, but a long, long time ago, and the African does not have a past and a present tense in their language. They even did not have a written language before independence in 1980.

They have stolen cables for one of the boreholes at the Ruwa farm. The swimming-pool motor has also been stolen. As soon as they were told about the passing away of their master, the robberies started. Gert used to come three times a year to Ruwa and he had cut the staff down to only eight, but he also employed two temporary workers. "It costs me only peanuts," he used to say. From his time in Nigeria he called his employees *stewards*. When I first heard it, it sounded very elegant to me. Certainly much nicer than calling them *houseboys* as they do here.

When we return to Belgravia, we are still without electricity. This has now lasted for two days. It drives me crazy, when I see these long red streaks of red blood on the freezer shelves and I think about how I can save the meat. Perhaps I can store some in Avis's freezer. Oh, how I dread it, when I have to clean up all this mess. Outside I can see Salome sweeping the grass with the inside broom. It is all the same to her – whether it is a tiled floor, an outside patio or just grass – she has no concept of tools being only used in one setting. She smiles broadly, as she waves at me.

"Shall we eat dinner at Mama Mia's tonight?" asks Clyde.

"That would be nice," I answer with relief, "but what if we invite Avis and Zeb? It is our turn and I really cannot cook at home with the constant black-outs."

"No problem, Bodie. Actually, Nick owes me money for the repair of the chairs at the restaurant, so we don't need to bring any money."

This is what is happening now, we are surviving on barter, since we no longer can get money in the bank, and every time we eat at Mama Mia's, Clyde writes off the debt for repair of chairs. Nick is Greek and works day and night in the restaurant, which is a family business. We sit nibbling at a nice mix of all the Greek starters. Nick's son, George, who has given Clyde his smart Michael Schumacher jacket, opens the bottle of South African red wine which we brought along because it is still cheaper to bring your own wine. Although he looks like a boy, he opens the bottle with hidden strength. A topic of current interest is Zuma in South Africa. Is he going to become the next president?

"It's an exciting situation," says George, while pouring wine into the glasses like an expert. "He is not very fond of Mugabe."

"But he will do exactly the same. The man is a communist!" says Clyde with loathing.

George shrugs his shoulders and, like all youth, he is light-hearted and unconcerned. "Certainly nothing to worry about. Until 2010 they are too busy worrying about the *World Cup*. There is a lot of prestige in that."

Avis tells us about all her problems with a gall bladder surgery in South Africa. "Can you imagine that I had 16 stones in there? I could have died right there and then. You know the first diagnosis at the Trauma Centre was totally wrong." Despite the fact that she had her gall bladder completely removed, she still looks young and chic. She is trying to explain the ordeal, but Clyde is absent-minded and finds it hard to concentrate. The more he stops listening, the more Avis dissects with the precision of the fine surgeon the juicy details of his procedure. Clyde starts looking uncomfortable and begins to greet people at the other tables. It is a bad habit he has, to behave as if he is circulating in a cocktail party. In between we raise all four glasses and clink them together remembering all the good times in Cape Town, but now sadly, things are on the down there and it will end just like Zimbabwe, Avis and Zeb confide in us. Nobody down there can see it coming. Just like Zimbabwe they think it will never happen to them. Just driving down, every time you can see with your own eyes how things are fast deteriorating. Zeb drives that long way every time because he believes his health is no longer strong enough for the flight and he rather enjoys being at the wheel going first to Bulawayo, then driving through Botswana to avoid entering South Africa via Beitbridge and the Limpopo River.

"I probably have to give up flying as well," says Clyde to Zeb and tells him about his last ordeal to Joburg. On behalf of her husband Avis replies, "It is not a problem. You just find a cargo vessel from Cape Town to Hamburg. Then you can visit Bodie's friends and family in Denmark and then you find a ship bound for North America. When you have enough time, it is not a problem."

The evening draws to a close and, as always when you are in convivial company with good friends, time is passing and before you know it we are standing out on the parking area saying goodbye. We break up hastily as beggars are approaching us and others who want to sell flowers. Most of them are children. Clyde has a body language that does not look inviting and can spirit away most of them: "Get lost!" he says. But the watchman is treated with kindness and respect and Clyde hands him a big stack of notes for looking after the car. Gratefully the watchman claps his hands, *"Ndatenda, Boss. Fambai zvakanaka."*

"Sarai zvakanaka," replies Clyde fluently in the local Shona dialect.

WE ARE SOON TO LEARN about the growing unrest in Kenya. The sound of the drum travels as fast as the international media. President Mwai Kibaki refuses to accept that he has lost the election to Raila Odinga, the leader of the opposition. It reminds us of the year 2002 when President Mugabe refused to hand over power to Morgan Tsvangirai, but what is very different in Kenya is the fact that the people crowd the streets and they demonstrate wildly. The international news media report that the problem in Kenya is due to the many tribes and therefore an entirely ethnic problem, but if you examine the problem more closely, you will realize that it is the poor and downtrodden, the slum-dwellers and the marginal groups that are taking up the fight against the growing corruption, the uneven distribution of the wealth in the country, where only 10 per cent are benefitting from the wealth of the nation and more than half are existing below the poverty line.

One wonders why nobody is reporting the conditions in Zimbabwe because here we have more than 80 per cent unemployment. Businesses and production are dying, a great part of the population have emigrated, and we live with constant black-outs in the capital of Harare and also other cities like Chinoyi. All our food we have to pay for in black market rates and many homes have been without water for months. When Clyde last played poker with Nick the Greek, he heard that for a whole month they had no water coming out of the taps and his golf mate Andy has been without water for three months.

"They buy water from a road tanker that is called a *bowser.* It is pulled by one of the old army vehicles," explains Clyde and continues, "But it is expensive; you pay the same as for petrol and at black market rate."

NOW, WHEN YOU DRIVE AROUND Harare at night, you drive in total darkness. There are no lights in the streets, but you always see people walking. Especially after midnight you will find people waiting on a street corner hoping to get a lift to the workplace. The busses are almost non-existent or they are too expensive to use when compared with the salary that the workers earn. At the crack of dawn when the cock crows, people start queuing outside the shops or the banks hoping to be lucky today. The street vendors and the police have plenty of time to follow up on rumours concerning delivery of bread, sugar, maize-meal, salt and cooking oil. Especially the police have a clear advantage wearing uniforms, so they end up with more than they need for their own families, and benefit from resale. Their wives and other relatives are blatently running shops behind the police station.

Many admitted to hospital are now dying from starvation. Patients are just left there, wounded after attacks or accidents. Many others are left there with serious diseases. They stumble around in the dark searching for water and toilets and, as no one is there to help, their conditions are worsening. The doctors are on strike and the nurses work on shifts in three different hospitals, three hours at each place to avoid paying taxes.

There are 65 prisons in Zimbabwe and the inmates are suffering from malnutrition and pellagra beside all the other diseases arising from lack of hygiene and toilet facilities. Or more to the point, they are living in filth and it is disgusting! Pellagra is a disease from lack of proteins and vitamins, especially vitamin B3. There are no medical supplies, clothing, bed linen or supply of toiletries. The women are bleeding on the floor when they have their periods. It is dreadful to even imagine how they all smell when they are brought to court. But at the moment both the city court judges and the high court judges are on strike. No legal proceedings are taking place and whether you are guilty or innocent, you can rot away in jail.

The children of the street vendors are sleeping on the islands between the two lanes, oblivious to the cars rushing by; they are five or six years old. Mothers with small babies on their backs are begging in between the cars, wherever motorists are forced to stop. Many of them have become destitute since *Murambatsvina*. Before that government action they had a home, though it had been in the poorer neighborhoods in the outskirts of Harare. All their houses and shops were destroyed when the rulers feared that they would rise up. The military and the governing party's thugs were well trained by the North Koreans in destabilizing.

Looking back to the independence days, it was at the same time as Mugabe was being knighted and given honorary degrees by universities in the West that he gave orders to the Fifth Brigade. Their actions resulted in the genocide of over 20,000 unarmed civilians in Matabeleland, many of them women and children. The gruesome events happened in Lupane, Tsholotsho and Matopo and the districts are littered with the mass graves of people murdered by this North Korean-trained Fifth Brigade. These disturbances, which happened in the beginning of the 1980s, are referred to as the *Gukurahundi* era.

The people have always been ruled with an iron fist and since the violent farm invasions, Mugabe has always been prepared to "go back to the trenches" to secure his power whenever it is threatened. Although he kept referring to *Murambatsvina* as a precautionary measure to prevent accidents targeting illegal constructions and buildings, his real aim was to make sure of a general dispersal of the population. He used the land reform to force them back to the rural districts so that they would be unable to unite and make a revolt against him and his government. Armed police came in bulldozers and their huts and buildings were razed to the ground in a matter of hours, even those that had been built with pride and were surrounded with pretty gardens. During this very same campaign Sister Nancy's orphanage was destroyed, although it was built with proper building plans during 1975–76. Captain Longchase did not escape either. He had thought that with a record as a war veteran, he did not need a building permit for his warehouse, but fate threw him together with the poor lot and the warehouse with all its contents was crushed under the heavy plow of the bulldozer.

After this blitz more than one million people were homeless, and it happened during one of the coldest winters that Zimbabwe had experienced within the memory of man. Whole families lived in the streets in sofas and lounge chairs with children crying, because none of them could understand what had happened to them. Eventually, they reverted to occupations from time immemorial – becoming prostitutes and beggars – to feed their children.

To compensate for the tragedy, the government promised during operation *Garikai* to help the ill fated, but it became others than the Murambatsvina victims who ended up benefitting from this campaign.

Last autumn ex-prime minister Ian Smith died in Cape Town, 88 years old. The world has always praised the Zimbabwe government for allowing the previous leader of the country to continue living as a farmer in Zimbabwe. In real life this was not true, because the last five years of his life he had moved to the Cape when they drove him off his farm. I once met him, but I made no effort to get to know him more closely. For me he would always stand as a symbol of racism, someone who looked more back than forward, so much like the Africans, and caused hatred between the indigenous blacks and the white population. It just jars on the ear hearing the expression *black* versus *white* in every sentence and funny enough, when I think back, I never heard this expression until I came to Africa. They did not have such a distinction in South America, nor did they have it in India. But in Ian Smith's Rhodesia they had that constant need to inject this perspective in every context. Not just that, denigrating expressions like *kaffir*, which means infidel, and *Afs*, which is a condescending short term of African, were used constantly. In 1986 when I first came to Zimbabwe, you would hear Rhodies talking around you using the same words over and over again. They were like a swarm of bees buzzing around living most of their lives on high bar chairs at typical British style pubs. One expression I remember clearly is this one: "He is so *thick*!" and that was said about the victim right in front of him as he was serving in the bar where the whites drank heavily. For hours they would talk about the war, which they called UDI (Unilateral Declaration of Independence) taking place from 1965 to 1979. Prime Minister Ian Smith broke all contacts with Britain and the rest of the world and declared, *"No black shall ever govern this country, not in a thousand years."* You could therefore say that Mugabe got it all wrong when he turned all his anger towards Britain and accused that country of everything that went wrong and refers to "independence from Britain in 1980." Historically, it is more correct to say that as from 1965, Rhodesia became an independent country during protest from Britain, Western countries and United Nations who applied economic sanctions against the Ian Smith regime in solidarity with the black population.

The scars from the war went deep on both sides and they suffered the same losses, losing sons and daughters and other relatives. Now they were in a situation where their own brothers in the West condemned them. It has been said that in Rhodesia the government did not make the same mistake as in South Africa by legislating apartheid. Although there is some truth in the fact that they did not make *written* laws to separate the population, the fact remains that their *unwritten* laws hindered secular humanism. Both South Africa and Rhodesia continued an antiquated colonial behaviour against non-whites, as they became very insular – their respective governments caused an isolation policy, resulting in total resistance towards the modern development that took place elsewhere in Europe and North America. They also maintained a distinct class system which they did not want to let go of. It was the old established society, the old boys club, the elites system of the Old Europe where they came from. Many inferior whites of poor background also suffered from their *petit bourgeois* prejudices, as is so vividly described by the British author Doris Lessing. Ironically, most historians have chosen to ignore this reality and stubbornly maintained that it was a war about *race,* perhaps out of fear of opening a Pandora's box with far more complex problems, or perhaps they were forced to write with the political correctness of their era.

Only much later, when the atrocities in Matabeleland came to light in 1997 with the report compiled by the Catholic Mission for Justice and Peace were these problems debated, but unfortunately the world conveniently seized on *tribalism* as a reason for the massacre. True enough, Mugabe's opponent Joshua Nkomo was Ndbele and when Mugabe slaughtered his people, he thought he could eliminate this threat, as they would all vote for Nkomo. Being rather a small tribe compared with the Shonas, wiping out 20,000 of them was very

significant. In truth Zimbabwe never had the tribal problems that existed in South Africa. The problem was merely Mugabe's insatiable
greed for power, and he was prepared to eliminate any obstacle in his
way. He follows Pluto, the god of the dead and the ruler of the under-
world, and on the path where he has walked is a significant number
of mates who have died under mysterious circumstances including
Josiah Tongogara who was killed in a car crash shortly before independence in 1980. Tongogara was popular with the working class
and with veterans on both sides of the civil war. Much later, when
Morgan Tsvangirai became the leader of the opposition before the
violent farm invasions from year 2000, the problem was not tribal,
because he was also a Shona. The problem was that Tsvangirai was
a threat to Mugabe's universal power, as he came from the workers
and represented the poor and downtrodden as a union leader. Even
worse, he had no war credentials and leaned towards the philosophy
of non-violence. He was looked down upon for this reason, and the
army generals refused to accept him as a future leader.

During the time that Ian Smith ruled, Mugabe was imprisoned
for 11 years. It happened in 1964 when he was convicted of terror-
ism. The same happened to Nelson Mandela in South Africa, but he
remained in jail for 27 years. When the West later accepted them as
world leaders, their crimes were forgotten. It has been told that while
Mugabe was inside the prison walls, he apparently had surgery to his
testicles due to cancer and indigenous people were of the opinion that
he could no longer father children. The only child he fathered was
with his first wife Sally from Ghana and tragically that child died
as an infant during the armed struggle. When he later had children
with wife No. 2, Grace, after Sally's death, many had doubts, because
they did not think he could be the father. On the other hand, it is
possible that he sought help abroad and benefitted from new medical advances. Zimbabwe has always been full of rumours and there
are many stories about the fateful surgery. Some whites have told
me that the white surgeon, who performed the procedure, did it to
save his life. He later had to flee the country when Mugabe became
President for fear of retribution. Perhaps at that time the doctors were
an arrogant lot and I wonder if they were any better in communicat-

ing with the patients than they are today. Considering he was dealing with an inmate, one wonders if Mugabe's consent to surgery was ever obtained, or whether jailors were handling all matters autocratically. I mean, if they literally cut off his balls, or even one of them without his consent, one can understand the hatred that rose in Mugabe. As a comparison, if I were to wake up from anesthesia without prior consultation with only one breast and a black had operated on me, I could also turn racist.

Other things I do not understand. Why did Mugabe hate his own people? Why did he torture the villagers in such bestial ways, like cutting off their ears and tongues? How could he use such cruelties to win the election in 1980? They said it was to create fear, so everybody would vote for him.

Despite the fact that Ian Smith had a good economy during sanctions and seemed able to remain self-sufficient, Smith realized that he could not continue his policy of isolation indefinitely and decided to submit to the Lancaster House Agreement. Mugabe and his competitor Nkomo from Matabeleland met and agreed to a cease-fire in order to have a peaceful election. Mugabe's party in Mashonaland became the winner and a few mandates went to Nkomo's party headquarters in Bulawayo. Ian Smith won many mandates, but not enough to win the election.

For many years Mugabe kept his hatred hidden. When I met him at official functions and once with Minister Amina Hugh, I got the impression of a cold and arrogant person who never looked you in the eye. When he was praised to the skies by the international top diplomats, I was silent. During those years, when he played the same tune as the West, he was described as an intelligent and intellectual man. None of them could see that he was a cunning fox. They failed to judge his strategies and manipulations, even though his lust for power was so obvious in retrospect, first as Prime Minister then as president and when he made himself *Executive President,* it was already too late. By then he was the sole commander. In those years the West did not attach importance to emotional intelligence, where leaders were concerned. They had, in a way, rather a lot in common with the Zimbabwean army generals, who respected Mugabe more than Tsvangirai.

Once I met a Danish farmer, whose wife was a whole-hearted Rhodesian. She told me that after independence her own farm workers and servants had come to her and said, "We are now comrades!"

She had answered, "I can assure you that I will never be your comrade!" In this way some blacks were discarded, even though they were willing to forgive, forget the war and be one big family – because they did not even know what a communist was.

This farmer's wife shared other thoughts with me about a political system that had been suggested instead of majority vote. It was based on a point system, to enable you to grow as a voter and become more informed and qualified. It is called *meritocracy* and the farmer's wife said it was far better than democracy. So for education you would get so many points; for paying taxes, you would get some more points; and if you had savings in your bank account or owned your own house, you would get yet more points. Even self-made people would get points for their achievements. I do not know if it is possible to work out a point system which would be fair to all, but on the face of it one would think that the wealthy and the golden youth are endowed unfairly in their cradles with too many points under this meritocracy system.

WE NO LONGER HAVE ANY convivial gatherings and only get together on a very informal basis. It has become too difficult with the food shortages. One night I say to Clyde, "I have a pork filet and I can make potato curry with beans and eggplant. Why don't you ask Tut and Edgar if they want to come for supper?"

Clyde phones them on the mobile right away and as he sees how much food we have, he suggests that we also invite Romano and Zsa Zsa. Tut and Edgar arrive first, as they live closer and it is not yet dark. There is a strange misty haze with a temptation of the last ray of the sun trying to go through that heavy cloud blanket. We are all laughing as we exchange the obligatory three kisses as is custom in

Switzerland, first on the one cheek, then on the other cheek and then back to the first cheek.

"Tut, I must ask you. Have you ever seen a double rainbow at full moon at the Victoria Falls?"

Tut straightens up her slim long body and looks up into the sky, her long dark pony tail reaching far down to her waist, as she says, "No, but I can see it here now!"

All of us stare and it is quite amazing, because we actually see two huge arches across the sky. Clyde runs in to collect his camera and quickly shoots the picture, but only one arch appears. The next moment Zsa Zsa and Romano arrive. Like Clyde he shortens his name, so we always call him Mano. Quickly we tell about the phenomenon with the double rainbow, but now it has disappeared. It was only there for an instant and we cannot even see the one rainbow that appeared on Clyde's camera. All we see is a heavy cloud.

Tut and Edgar have brought a bottle of Beyerskloff and Mano has another bottle of red wine from Italy. Besides the wine, he has also brought a big blue box with *panettone*.

"I know that cake from Tuscany and it is to die for," exclaims Tut.

"We are going to have it with coffee afterwards," I say.

There is a very special atmosphere around the round table, it is perfect when you are six and it has the right size for all to clink glasses in the air. Zsa Zsa and Mano sit closely together and they have a twinkle in the eye and send each other amorous glances like two young lovers. Mano is dandified and looks very charming. Zsa Zsa is wearing a more formal outfit, but like most Italians they both look elegant and have good manners. As always, Zsa Zsa's hair does not stray with even one hair, her hair remains in the exact pose it is combed and she does not use hairspray or other aids. She is born with that thick wavy mane and many believe she is wearing a wig or a hat. Once, when she went to her eye doctor in France, he said to her, "Please take your hat off!"

Once more during supper we discuss the double rainbows that some of us saw on arrival.

"It must be a good sign," says Mano with his soft Italian accent, smiling while he looks out as if the sight is still there. But all he is seeing are the darkened clouds with a slight rosy tint on the edge.

Clyde agrees and cites, "Red sky in the morning, sailors take warning. Red sky at night, sailors delight!"

"Come si dice, Mano?" asks Zsa Zsa in Italian.

Mano pushes the gold-rimmed glasses higher up on the bridge of his nose and continues in Italian:

"Roso disera, bell tempo si spera."

He says it soft like a caress, but like Zsa Zsa I also need to have it translated. He translates, "Red in the morning, good weather, you expect," which exactly contradicts Clyde's weather statement.

Clyde gets a grin on his face and says, "I like this one better: 'At the end of the rainbow there is a pot of gold'."

Suddenly I notice that Zsa Zsa has the red and white dog bag at her feet and I exclaim, "Really, Zsa Zsa, you must let out Muffin. He has been so quiet that I did not even notice he was with you!"

As soon as the zipper is pulled back, Muffin shoots up like a rocket.

Muffin is a tiny Yorkshire Terrier who was brought up from South Africa by folk singer Matthew Beyer. Clyde arranged the purchase, after the previous Muffin died during the long flight to Zimbabwe when the Italians first arrived. The dog was old and the heart was not strong enough for the long journey. Zsa Zsa was completely heart-broken and could not imagine her stay without a Muffin.

Matthew had travelled from Johannesburg and crossed the border at Beitbridge holding the tiny Muffin under his leather vest without anybody even noticing the creature. Although all documents were in order it was far more expedient not to declare the puppy. He was also so small that he should have been called Crumb. Matthew's German girlfriend, who had been a judge in many a dog competition for Irish Wolfhounds and Rhodesian Ridgebacks, had thoroughly examined Muffin and found that he had all the characteristics of a noble Yorkshire Terrier, and she predicted that the silverfish look in the face would spread all over. Ironically, Muffin lost even the few silver strands on the face and the new hair that grew out was totally black and that chevelure became his markings all over – apart from a few brown splotches on his feet. Overall Muffin represented a very noble and good-looking version of a South African-bred Yorkshire Terrier, but Zsa Zsa and Mano were later to spend an absolute fortune in veterinary bills, as they found out that Muffin had a very difficult set of teeth with an uneven bite. Besides this problem it was discovered during their last visit to Europe that Muffin had a gluten allergy and could not eat pasta, which was some sort of a tragedy, considering he was expected to grow up as an Italian dog. But despite the initial difficulties, Muffin has become their *bambino* and plays a superior role in their life. He understands everything in Italian, French and English and has an extraordinary intelligence. Unfortunately, besides his allergenic problems, he was also born with an acute intolerance to black people and he barks viciously at customs officials and the guards on duty.

MUCH LATER THAT NIGHT, CLOSE to the hour before dawn when you typically have nightmares, I wake up and think about the double rainbows and Victoria Falls. They are named after Queen Victoria when Dr. David Livingstone discovered them in 1855. The indigenous Africans called them *Mosi oa Tunya*, meaning *The Smoke That Thunders*. The power of the Falls is like love, the deep cascade of pounding waters plunging in a full crescendo until it is cut off and spread in many directions. Like love's pain across the chest it is so extended and rises high and mighty, its ending almost as powerful as the fall itself. The extreme height is the acropolis versus the bottomless abyss. The culmination of the peak is the connection between love and pain, the greatest happiness and the deepest sorrow, these foaming white furry masses that rise up so high that they look like snow and then plunge down to a deep pond that appears illuminated with the shade of sea-green water, reflected in an orgy of colours from the surrounding cliffs, water and the skies. The token of love is inside this mortal combat. One moment I am the bird Phoenix rising renewed from my own ashes; the next moment I am deep down in that bottomless pit. We are healthy, we are sick, we are strong, we are weak, everything is echoed in the opposite extreme, as reflected in that gorgeous double rainbow, but it was just an illusion in a fauna of strong colours. I can only watch, not touch.

THE NEXT DAY CLYDE COMES home for lunch and says, "They have stolen 4,000 peanut butter jars."

"Oh, no, how could they do that?" I ask, appalled.

"I am not sure, first I must study the security camera to find out," says Clyde with eyes downcast. Meanwhile, as I mix together brown rice with a little mayonnaise, put it on top of a lettuce leaf in between two slices of bread which have been buttered with peanut butter, Clyde continues, "Each scotch cart is now 4 billion, we make 300 each times 46, that gives us 1.2 trillion every week."

Then Clyde becomes completely quiet. He only speaks a few words at a time and his sentences are short. He is a man of few words. As I look at him, I see his once so magnificent hair having turned very grey and the bald spot on top of his head has grown bigger. He constantly wipes his mouth with the cotton napkin. Even though he is a simple man, he refuses to use paper napkins. He has a coughing attack and continues chewing after. He is only drinking water with the sandwich. Inside his head there is an invisible goal. Nobody can stop him from reaching that goal. He drives the factory day and night.

CHAPTER 16

EXPLOITED

M iss Moss often spoke about the little chapel close to our original residence on Montgomery Road.

"Clyde, do you remember Rhodesville Chapel on the little side road off Montgomery?"

"Yes, of course, it is on Wavell Road, just past Rhett Butler's house, The Faulty Towers," Clyde recalls.

"Miss Moss often spoke about that little chapel and at her funeral it was mentioned by one of the speakers. He said that over the door frame of the hand-carved door a number has been carved into the wood. Year 1915, he said. He also said that the chapel had withstood two world wars, tsunamis, the armed struggle and many other events. I would love to see it inside," my voice is trembling slightly.

"We could go over there now," says Clyde and suggests that we drive in my car. I hand him my car keys.

Clyde takes some odd routes these days to avoid some of the biggest potholes, some of them having turned into huge craters. He crosses over into Old Alexander Park, where Tut and Edgar live and continues up to Sandringham Road along Botanical Garden. He managed to get by the worst scarring of Churchill Road and turns right into Gunhill. It is confusing now with the new road and round-about behind the prestigious Orange Grove, but the low veldt landscape is beautiful because there are still trees. Some primitive police barracks are situated very close to the road. The clotheslines are full of washing although it looks like rain. It occurs to me that the value of the prestigious estate houses must have gone down a lot when this roadwork started. Once I wanted to live on this street, which they nicknamed Hollywood. Now Clyde takes an almost straight direction through the new round-about and suddenly we are back on the familiar street called Glenara Avenue. I easily recognize Glen Shee although the road sign has been stolen.

"Wait till you see how beautiful they have built the house on Glen

Shee, on the land that they bought from us," I rhapsodize to Clyde, as he is indicating with his turn signal and turns into Glen Carron Avenue.

"The wall is almost the price of the house," Clyde observes as he looks at the high concrete wall that has been painted in brown and crème to match the house. In the background I can catch glimpses of the original house that we renovated years ago and then subdivided the property, as there was enough land for two houses.

"Oh Clyde, I am so happy we got rid of all this," I sound like a chatterbox, as I continue, "How do you feel, do you regret that we disposed of all of it?"

"No," says Clyde with a conviction in his voice. "Not the house boat, not the lodge at Mazvikadei nor Haven on Earth."

"Good, because we did the right thing. Imagine if we had to start selling out now. It would be an impossible task." I turn my head and glance along the white durawall concrete fence, seeing our old residence on Montgomery Road, where we got married. The ceremony had taken place in the combined bar with Jacuzzi, because it was the only room that had a pastoral atmosphere to it with the high beamed ceilings and the glitterstones on the floor. The piano had also been placed there to distract from the otherwise Rhodesian looking bar, turning it more into a piano-bar. Apparently, the new people care for the place, because new flowers have been planted outside the wall, but the Golden Shower rose is still there, cascading over the ugly double twisted barbed-wire fence.

We turn into the narrow Wavell Road and pass Rhett Butler's house and enter a yet more narrow road that looks almost like a farm track. The elephant grass grows high on both sides until we come to the back of the Indonesian embassy. On the left is a painted sign that reads *Rhodesville Chapel*. Clyde explains that the place used to be open to the public, but now it has a gate and the gate is locked with a padlock. The place looks uninviting and secret like a grave. It is so well hidden behind bushes and tall elephant grass, it could easily go unnoticed.

"We can't enter today. Perhaps another day. I will talk to Rhett, then we can enter from his property," says Clyde.

At home we are able to follow the American caucauses in New Hampshire, as our TV is still working with Clyde's inverter. The way it is represented by the international media makes it sound like a horse race: will Obama win, or will Hillary Clinton win?

"Funny, how some of them say *caucauses*," I remark humourously, "sounds like carcasses!" In my mind I see all the skulls lying in the safari park. I continue, laughing, "I must remember that one when one day I go on stage in Montreal for the Comic Talent Show."

"That is not even funny, Bodie. I really hope you give up that crazy idea. The Canadians will not think you are funny," Clyde shakes his head and looks a little embarrassed just thinking about it. As a precaution he adds, "Don't give up your day job!"

His cell phone is ringing. The two nuns, Sister Nancy and Sweet Rit are coming over for a glass of red wine. They warn us that they are touring friends' houses and can't stay long – are just about to leave Avis and Zeb with whom they have spent a holiday in the beautiful Nyanga highlands. I suppose they can't say they are pub-crawling! A few minutes later I spot two tall figures in the courtyard. As all people growing older, the nuns have started to look more heavy, but they carry with them the spirit of the young and the pose of athletes.

"When did you return from Nyanga?" I ask.

"Two days ago. We spent three days up there and Zeb drove us around to all the familiar places," explains Nancy.

"Yes, we have really been around," adds Sweet Rit, "because we also went to Masvingo to see Dr. Vick and Dolores at Saint Theresa Mission." Dr. Vick is an American doctor, who for many years worked as a missionary doctor, since he was young. Whenever he gets time off and goes to Harare with his wife Dolores, he enjoys a game of golf with Clyde and later the four of us meet in the evening to have dinner at some restaurant. This is the high life for them – to come to Harare and see how we are living the Life of Riley, well, to them we are. In the mission village where they are living, quite far from Masvingo, they have nothing, no restaurants and no shops and apart from the church no cultural life.

The nuns have many stories to tell and one is about the terrible flooding in the Masvingo district and the danger of driving. There was this blue gum tree totally blocking the road and the driver had to speed up to avoid getting stuck in the river of water. Dr. Vick did not have the same fortune. His car got stuck, but by the grace of God a black man appeared out of the blue on a tractor and he was able to pull him out. But that favour costs Dr. Vick a whole container of precious petrol. There was no other way, the driver of the tractor had to be compensated. Dolores is taking a break; she is going back to America for two months.

The prices are sky-rocketing to an extent where I can hardly remember them anymore. Butter now costs 45 million Zimbabwe dollars, this is ludicrous, and the oranges over 4 million for only 1 kg. Although they have now printed new bearer cheques, it is still very difficult to get cash.

Out at the factory eight metres of angle iron has been stolen and in the process the thieves have broken down the durawall trying to haul it over. That iron is really heavy; they must have had a truck waiting outside.

"They are not allowed to leave angle iron outside," says Clyde, obviously very upset.

He is now studying the security camera together with Hilton to find the culprits, both as far as the peanut butter jars are concerned and the added problem with the angle iron. On the camera you can clearly see them loading 14,000 peanut butter jars onto the truck in dispatch. They should only have loaded 10,000. The police promise that they will make the workers confess.

After a couple of days in police custody the four workers continuously deny that they have loaded more than 10,000 jars and when they are shown the evidence on the camera, they say in turn, "*We only loaded 10,000!*" As this goes on, the police say to Clyde that they must find other evidence, as the camera is not accepted as evidence in Court.

"But these cameras are used internationally against terrorists," I say crossly. "In London and Madrid and many other places, these cameras are accepted as evidence."

"Yes, I know," says Clyde in a low voice and his face looking all drawn, "but this is Zimbabwe and they make their own laws from day to day. Even if we can prove that the cameras cannot be tampered with, they will still say that we did not supply sufficient evidence."

NEXT DAY CLYDE COMES HOME and shows me the new notes that the Baron got in the bank. There are 10 million dollar notes in a reddish-brown colour, a 5 million dollar note in a bluish shade and a 1 million dollar note, which I have yet to see, because the Baron wanted to secure the big notes first. Like the old notes they are issued as bearer cheques and look exactly like the money in a Monopoly game. I am impressed about how little space they take up and cry out, "Does that really mean that we no longer have to carry money in transit bags, pillow cases and wheel barrows?"

"As long as it lasts," says Clyde in a gloomy tone of voice. "The inflation continues regardless and in a short time the money will have lost its value, so enjoy it while you can, because it won't be for long."

As he walks down the hallway, he mutters under his breath, "We have problems with the Reserve Bank. They are now unwilling to pay 5.5 billion for each scotch cart, as they have agreed to."

I run after him. "But Clyde! That is crazy. They know how much we paid for the imported products, all the angle iron and the tires. We are now getting less than what they paid for the first lot. Why can't they just accept that you quote in US dollars, then the price remains the same."

"They will not do that," says Clyde and he starts getting agitated and angry. "How many times do I have to tell you?"

"But the Baron has to do something, we cannot deliver with such losses," I say very firmly and decide that I must secretly discuss the new situation with the Baron.

It is still raining day and night, and all over the roads are deteriorating. Some places the potholes are turning into massive craters. You are risking life and limb if you drive into a deep hole filled with water. The power supply has become extremely erratic and often we only have electricity for a few hours in the night. I cook our food on the small gas stove and we sit in the candlelight hoping for the power to return. When the power cuts are lasting for too many hours, Clyde cannot even watch TV, as his battery and inverter needs recharging on a regular basis. I am now washing clothes in the bathtub and I find myself getting more and more irritated.

Clyde tells me that the rate is now 4.5 million. That is for 1 American dollar, and RTGS is 7 million when transfers are made directly to your offshore account. The minimum wage at the factory is at the moment 150 million Zimbabwe dollars per month. How do they survive? It is even worse for domestic staff, gardeners, housekeepers and maids in the households, earning only about 40 million a month. Do they live on rats? In actual fact we have just entered the Year of the Rat, 2008, according to the Chinese and we hear this mentioned a lot because the Chinese colony has grown tremendously since Mugabe started his *"Look-East"* policy. The Chinese are becoming very influential in the whole system with all its ramifications and like the Africans they avoid paying taxes. When Clyde deals with them, he always has to pay in cash, because they avoid the banking system.

The supermarkets have hardly any products left on the shelves and the little meat you see around looks as if it has been defrosted several times. The vegetables are slimy and wet. Also our water has turned funny. When you cook potatoes, brussels sprouts and cauliflower, you get this horrible aftertaste of dirty water despite having rinsed everything. Everywhere you see huge lazy flies with blue wings enjoying the sparse food on the shelves, and the fruit is covered with tiny fruit flies.

In Silver Glory at Kensington Shopping Center I study the shelves and the prices. Even locally made products cost a fortune; there is no longer any comparison with prices in South Africa or in England. Shopkeepers just charge whatever they think they can get or you can pay, there is no budgeting frame relating to transport costs and normal profit, there is no logic behind it and there are no rules. Because of short supply and big demand there is absolutely no shame.

A young chap with dreadlocks stares at the box of Jungle Oats. It costs 52 million Zimbabwe dollars. He shows his disgust and an old white lady supports him, her voice full of determination despite her frail looks, "We ought to boycott it all, it has gone too far!"

A broad-faced Chinese girl joins in, "But this is not right. It is 4 to 5 times more than what we pay in South Africa. And even products made in Zimbabwe have sky-rocketed the same. Look at this flour – the price is 45 million. Where are we going?"

I join in the chorus as well. "And this JIK here, made in Zimbabwe, is now costing millions."

The Chinese girl continues, "Toilet paper at 91 million for 9 rolls!"

"It is cheaper to use the new notes from the bank than using a roll of toilet paper," says the young guy with the dreadlocks.

"Yes, but they are too dirty," says China girl, laughing widely with her small mouse teeth. It makes us all feel good to laugh out loud, we have broken the ice after having been in confinement with all our feelings pent-up inside for so long, and it is such a relief to submit to this orgy of laughter. The relief is so rewarding, and the feeling of unity in this crazy situation is like new hope.

CLYDE COMES HOME FOR LUNCH. The Reserve Bank has still not paid him what is owed, but the Baron is having a meeting with the Minister of Agriculture to make sure that we are paid just enough not to go bust. We should have been paid 7 billion Zimbabwe dollars for each scotch cart, otherwise our losses with all the imported raw materials are not covered. Unfortunately, the engineers at Reserve Bank try to underpay us as they do not care if the whole country goes down. It is this attitude that is so hard to understand: that there is no ambition nor sense of guilt, nor responsibility. Whether they work in the bank, or in the supermarket or in our factory, they do not seem to worry or care. If the roads, buildings or sewage collapse, it does not matter to them. But they like to be smartly dressed, have a cell phone in the hand and have the hair glued with extensions to make dread-locks. They do not really mind waiting for hours for bread, for money in the bank or for the bus. They are a patient lot, I must say.

Everything in Zimbabwe is about waiting and wasting time. When you go to a restaurant, Clyde says the waiter actually believes that his job is to wait. "*I am a waiter. My job is to wait and serve.*" Worst of all is the bureaucracy, it is like a jungle so thick, you need a machete to cut your way through. Clyde is wasting days of his life in this chaos

trying to follow all their regulations and laws, the latest being the declaration of a luxury vehicle, a SUV Mercedes 320. Not that it is any of
his usual business, but Clyde always tries to assist when it concerns
Canadians and Danes. This vehicle belonged to a Dane and it was his
intention that Gert should enjoy his last years in Africa being chauffeur-driven in an exclusive and safe car, instead of the combi-bus he
had driven for many years, which looks like the cheapest public transport. Now, that Gert has passed away, all the difficulties in declaring
it through Customs and the expenses in this connection have become
a big hurdle. Typical for Gert, he never checked the present rules and
probably thought a few bribes would solve all matters along the way,
like they used to do in West Africa. The heir of the Ruwa Farm had
given him the car because it had the steering wheel in the wrong side
and when the car was originally bought, it was for his young wife
who was being treated for a malignant disease in England.

On the third day with Customs, Clyde returns and says to me,
"You have to pay 130 per cent of the car value plus the freight costs
in customs duty. I was only able to get the price down to 41,000 US
dollars, as they have to follow approved documents from the Internet
on secondhand cars." My husband looks tired and worn out – the last
bout of flu has drained him and left him with phlegm and fluid on the
lungs. Since we returned, he has had three attacks of flu.

"Did you tell them in compassionate terms about the background?"
I enquire through the hatch to the kitchen.

"They don't care!" Clyde's voice sounds irritated, containing the
frustrations he is feeling these days.

"Why don't you take me with you?" I ask cheerfully expecting
him to decline.

I am surprised, when Clyde says, "I would like that."

Now I am stuck with it. I had secretly hoped he would say no.

THE VERY NEXT MORNING WE take off towards the industrial area
passing through a landscape full of containers, most of them from the
Danish Maersk Line. Clyde warns me that the agent is a real bitch and
all of them out there are the same. Even worse, they are all women!

The one he has mainly dealt with used to work for the Tax Office, and you cannot reason with her.

"Good morning," I say in a merry voice and look around the office that is only an on-site hut, built out of a container. "Oh, it is you, Nomsa, who has had all this work with our vehicle, and I heard that you have quite a career behind you coming from the Tax Office." I can hear myself elevating her position and making it sound as if she is a Deputy Minister.

She looks very proud. I continue explaining to her my own lack of experience as far as the computer is concerned as I left my career as a diplomat some years ago, but I manage to make our undertakings in government circles sound very similar. Nomsa starts showing me how they look up the country where the car comes from, then they base the value on the original price there and then they calculate year and mileage.

"Oh, Nomsa. Now I understand why it is so high. Denmark is far higher than any other country as far as cars are concerned and that is because we do not produce any cars there. Everything is imported. So despite the fact that the car was owned by a Dane and sent from there, it was never declared and used there. They only sent it via Denmark for transit. It came from Britain."

Nomsa asks me if I want to sit down and I can feel we are in harmony. Politely, I say to her, "No, thank you! I don't need to sit. But my husband is tired. He has trouble breathing." With an arm stretch I indicate to Clyde that he must sit, just as he is seized with a fit of coughing which makes me explain what we went through with Clyde's illness and treatment.

The Customs girl is very sympathetic and so are the two young African girls in starched Customs uniforms who have offered their assistance and are now looking into the computer. One of the girls is the boss and wears a more important uniform.

As we shake hands, she says, "My name is Tsoroshai."

"That is a beautiful name. What does it mean?" I ask.

"It means *Give Us Rest*," Tsoroshai explains.

I imagine that she is one of many brothers and sisters and she probably started as a secretary and worked herself up the ladder. She takes over the computer search, while Clyde goes outside to sit on a bench below the trailer window, intensely watching the crane transporting the big containers and lifting them up in a grip, as if they have no weight.

Inside Customs I have started telling them the full story of the tragedy surrounding the Mercedes Benz and I do not disguise the fact that Clyde and myself have no personal interest in the outcome, but like in Africa we have the same system, we must help our extended family and we feel indebted to the old man who has passed away. For his soul to rest we must help his heir to the farm. Under no circumstances can we just leave it to the shipping agents, or he would end up paying more in duty for the vehicle than the cost of buying it from new in England.

The Customs girls are trying to be very helpful and work even more keenly, when I describe to them this young, handsome Danish widower, who was left with three small boys, when the wife passed away. Their eyes become so big that I can see the white under their eyeballs and I recognize this universal feminine reaction to the possibility of meeting such a catch. By now they have gone into another website for secondhand cars online and the prices are going down and down.

"I can see you are on to the British secondhand cars," I ascertain, whilst leaning over the computer with one hand on the desk. "What about trying Germany, because that is where the car originates from. It was made in Germany and the prices are lower there for secondhand cars, as they all drive new cars."

Tsoroshai has now completely taken over the control of the computer and explains, "That is not our policy to go back to the manufacturing country, if the car was purchased somewhere else. I cannot deviate from our policy."

I continue smiling and glance over to the computer. It is my experience that there is nothing you can do when an African wants to follow policies. They will carry through the instructions like a robot and show no flexibility for the individual situation. They are extremely keen to follow the law or the rule, exactly as they read it and there is no attempt to make various interpretations of the same, nor would they try to look for another rule. It is like when they have chosen one path to walk on in the bush, and even when it is full of water, they will continue walking on that path regardless, because they have always done it. They are stubborn like the elephants on Lake Kariba, crossing over to Zambia on the same old path they had walked in slow-motion for generations through the deep valley. After the dam was built and their pathway ended in the deep waters on the bottom of the lake, they persistently continued to walk the same migration route as their ancestors and although some of them managed to swim to the other shore, many of the elephants drowned in the process.

"Shame with the new rule. When I used to sell diplomatic cars to CMED, we *had* to always go back to the manufacturing country." I definitely need to keep them on my side and it is a balancing act that takes tremendous self-control. Inside you are fuming and feel like screaming, but on the outside you show nothing, just keep that friendly conversation going, even if it goes nowhere. My own smile, with that bright new red Yves St. Laurent Lipstick No. 23, that Clyde bought for me in London Airport, makes my mouth turn into a wide African smile with white teeth and big lips. I feel my own transcendence into this form of sisterhood that is so hard to explain. I become the role. I become the person that I am pretending to be.

Suddenly, the girls see a good price from the English secondhand car list. They take a photocopy and show it to me. It is only 12,000 US dollars. I am nodding approvingly and for the sake of it I ask, "Father Ryan says then you can calculate with the zimdollar rate to get a lower figure. Correct?"

Tsoroshai exclaims, "Father Ryan says that? What else did Father Ryan tell you?"

"Just that," I say dangling my black high-heeled slippers in the air, as I am still sitting on the desk. "He says in that way you can get a lower figure because the Convent cannot afford to import cars if the duty is too high."

"How many kilometres has the car on it?" asks Nomsa. She has now taken back the case, as the major problem has been solved and only trivial matters remain. Tsoroshai does not perform menial tasks, she is in charge only. She has taken off her navy jacket, as it is getting very hot in the trailer office.

"It is more in kilometres, because the car was made for miles," I offer helpfully. "The car is not that new anymore."

"How do you calculate that?" they ask me.

"You multiply by seven," I say confidently. "In my young days I lived in Oxford in England and that one I remember clearly." I feel on very safe ground now and start seeing results.

"OK, Bodie," says Nomsa, "now you wait outside till we have finished the document."

I join Clyde on the bench under the trailer window. It has no back rest. He is completely fascinated by the capabilities of the cranes, but says in a very low voice, "I was listening through the window. You got it totally wrong, Bodie. You do not multiply with seven. It is one point four or something like that."

"Really! Are you sure?" I am slightly baffled. "So perhaps it was one point seven. What do I know after so many years? But seven is better, right?" I turn my head towards him with tongue in cheek. He does not quite follow me when I do these silly card tricks. I follow his hazel eyes under the cap of the baseball hat.

"Amazing that there are so many containers arriving. I would have thought most trade with Zimbabwe had stopped."

I try to change the subject.

"No, the sanctions are only there as a political symbol against the leaders. All other business is the same as usual," says Clyde and continues, "It is always a joke with these sanctions. They will just use the neighbouring countries and their friends."

Tsoroshai comes out of the trailer-office and opens the trunk to her brand new Peugeot car placing some wine bottles there that she has received as Christmas bonus from customers. Then she goes back into the trailer office and calls us inside. I admire her hair, which stays despite the humidity in the air and the slight wind. It has grown to a maximum length of 12 cm because of a straightening perm and it looks so much more natural than the glued-on dreadlocks. She hands us the final statement. All included we must pay $18,000 American dollars in duty. She has crossed out the extra tires and spare parts on the list.

"Thank you, Tsoroshai. Thank you, Nomsa, and all of you for having spent so much time on this case." I shake hands with them vigorously, twisting and turning around in the Shona manner. Clyde does the same.

"Don't forget our Christmas bonus," says Nomsa. "We have worked overtime for your sake."

"I promise you. You will not be forgotten," and waving my hand in a final salute I leave the premises.

It takes Clyde a long time, but finally he says, "You did a good job."

I look straight ahead and say, "It is what I used to do, but am I glad I don't have to do it anymore." And I mean it. This type of work is so exhausting.

"Now we have to pay the 18,000 dollars at the head office and then clear it through the police," says Clyde. "First they contact Interpol to make sure that the car wasn't stolen and all that, but the worst is over. What is left for us to do does not take very long, now that we have a stamp on the document."

I turn to look at his face and I notice how tired he looks. He has hollow eyes and I fight to control the panic inside me.

THAT EVENING BROTHER PAUL PASSES by for a glass of red wine. He is again dressed in his traditional brown monk's frock with the sinister monkshood pulled over the head. It is like going back in time to the 13th century when the Franciscan Order started. These days the old formal costumes are worn more often because of the security situation. He is in open sandals and I catch a glimpse of his blue jeans as he walks. He is completely desperate for cash, as he cannot get money in the banks. Clyde gives him the last brick from the small safe. Now we have nothing for ourselves and nothing to buy food with. Hopefully, the swipe machines will work in some of the shops. Brother Paul's frock is typically made for men, who walk with their hands free, full of pockets inside, just like a man's suit. A man is a man, is a man. They do not carry handbags. Whether you are a monk, a businessman or a gofer, you always wear garments full of inside pockets.

Roy Orbison's soft voice is singing *Running Scared.*

Brother Paul has just returned from Ireland and he tells us that his father is now in a home for the elderly. It had been difficult for the family to take this decision, but he was completely senile, so they had to do it.

"But he seems happy there, he actually thinks he works there," says Brother Paul. "He says to my mother, *I really must go now, I don't want to lose my job.* In between he is so senile that he can't even recognize our family home and he says, *Where are you taking me?"* Brother Paul looks around the room recalling all the traumatic events and continues, "Then we have to make a detour to distract him."

On the way out to his rusty white Toyota parked outside our little townhouse, Brother Paul leans forward and says to me, "You know, Bodie, all your neighbours will think you are such a devoted Catholic!" Then he gives me a hug and laughs.

A COUPLE OF DAYS LATER Clyde has that familiar grim look on his face.

"What is the matter?" I ask.

"My caddie stole two golf balls. They are about 40 million each. That same caddie was OK the first time at Wingate Sports Club. But this time at Royal, he just had to do it."

"It is frustrating, I know. I also get so tired of seeing Salome helping herself with my creams and the whole wheat flour and all the other items that are in short supply," I sympathize with him and continue, "We never had that problem with Friday. He was a real African gentleman."

"Not only that. They are also stealing at the factory: plastic sheeting. They squeeze themselves in through the water hole going under the durawall. The hole is so narrow, Hilton says he would get totally claustrophobic and afraid of getting stuck in there. There are several guys in it, the guard too!"

Because of the dangerous situation we are in, we decide no longer to employ Salome as a part-time maid. It is too risky if she knows everybody coming and going, and will find out where we keep the money. Better accept a bit of dust and grime. Although I know that she gets a salary from the German next door, I will continue to pay her a lump sum under the pretext that I want to reserve her for better times when we have electricity again. She is probably only paid peanuts with an absent employer.

SHORTLY THEREAFTER I SEE SISTER Esseldrida, and I tell her about all the trouble we had with Customs. She has been grilled through the same process many times.

"For everything I have to find documents, even for powdered milk," she says, "and they go on and on: *Is it from a goat or is it from a cow?*" Esseldrida shakes her head and says in the same tone as she used at Customs, "Does it matter? It is probably from a pig!"

CHAPTER 17

FRUSTRATIONS

Clyde shows me some new documents from the Canadian government concerning my application for a residence permit. If the conditions worsen, it may be necessary to leave Zimbabwe in the dead of night. Or even better, should we suddenly win the lottery and receive an offshore payment, we must be ready to run. We live on borrowed time and the sands are running out; only in between, time is at a standstill.

"They want to have extracts from the police record to make sure you have no previous convictions," Clyde points at a special document, which has to be brought to the Zimbabwe Police and stamped. How ironic that Canada trusts a crime report from a country that is blacklisted, but the rules are nonetheless followed to the letter.

"I am going to show you where to go and if you take your own car and follow me, you will see the line-up," instructs Clyde. It is quite an ordeal to follow Clyde, as he drives zigzag along the road and at the highest speed despite the terrible road conditions. Today it does not worry me, as I know where I am going. I used to frequent the police pub in the good old days, when they had many experts sent out from the Manchester Police to teach them how to do fingerprints, methods of interrogation and forensic science after independence.

I arrive a few minutes later than Clyde and see him leave his vehicle. He points inside the gate towards a long line of people that leads up to a shanty house with a window on one side. We are all standing like children outside an ice-cream parlour in the baking sun waiting for our turn. All clients are served by a plainclothes man. Having waved goodbye to Clyde, I stand in line for ages in the sweltering heat.

Finally, it is my turn and I hand over the document from Canada as well as a copy of my Zimbabwean residence permit.

"Would you like to have it stamped, Madam?"

"Yes, thank you, it is only a formality. And please give me a receipt."

I get a receipt and am told to return the next day at 11 o'clock.

NEXT MORNING I AM THERE promptly, but again I have to wait in line and the sun hits me like an open flame. As my misery comes to an end, I hand my receipt to Constable Mandehvu, who asks me to wait. During the dreary period of waiting I notice it is only me and another gentleman who do not receive our papers. All the many Africans leave with their papers in hand. I am regularly told to keep waiting, but as they work in shifts and are now changing the whole workforce, I begin to suspect mischief.

At 1 o'clock, I begin to question the constable on duty. He is not wearing any police uniform, but is dressed in brown pants and a bright yellow shirt.

"We are unable to find the papers," he declares. "That is why we must have new fingerprints."

As Clyde has warned me not to lose my temper, I remain very calm and friendly.

"That is no problem, you are welcome to take new fingerprints now now." I follow him into a proper office building with columns and shady places all around. He leads me to the office of Assistant Inspector Shurd and introduces me to him in English. Then he explains my case in the local Shona language.

"I am very sorry, but we cannot take your fingerprints today. First, we must find out what has happened to your application. We must trace it and find out how it has disappeared. It could be anywhere, perhaps even in Bulawayo!" informs the assistant inspector. He is fat and dressed in a thin suit that looks as if it has been washed many times, but at least his shirt has a more official look.

"Very well. Perhaps you can return my receipt for handing in my papers?" I ask Mr. Shurd in a voice full of authority.

"Sorry, Madam. The receipt is for us to keep, until you are served, when we are dealing with your case. You cannot have it back."

On my way out of the office building I make a slight detour

and study all the nameplates in the colonnade. The highest title is a Senior Inspector Mutamba. I write it down for Clyde to approach him directly.

Later Clyde explains that all my difficulties are due to the native Africans' unwillingness to allow us all to leave Zimbabwe. They have become extremely worried about the exodus of the white population and now they are trying to put a spoke in our wheels, to stop it.

"But, I really don't understand. Mugabe wants all the whites out," I say.

"It looks like that," explains Clyde, "but in reality it is not the case. We are only a pawn on his chessboard. If he can use us to win the election, he will do it. He is a master of tactics."

JUST BEFORE DAWN I WAKE up from a nightmare. A pack of wolves had come to the town where I was. In a trancelike state I saw them attacking and killing a young woman, the next instant they raced towards a young mother, whose bursting belly told that she was near her time. The animals tore her apart and pulled out the baby, while the mother screamed and bled to death. Just before her final moment she tried to hold her abdomen together and I saw her desperate gestures, as she was surrounded by the beasts. At that point I wake up and hear the barking of dogs outside. Then there are heart-rending cries from little puppies. The noise is coming from behind the high durawalls and it occurs to me that my friend Smila has warned me about this. She thinks that the Chinese are now breeding dogs because of the food shortages.

Despite the nightmare I start daily routines and exercises, first doing some floor exercises including arm swinging, leg lifts, some yoga transitions with the right breathing, undulation and hip moves from Rachishaka belly dance. I finish off with a few quick jumping jacks. I have done the same programme for many years and I have always been an early riser. A little later Clyde starts his programme, which is more manly and rough, containing more weight and muscle lifts, as most of his work-out takes place on the exercise machine. Even when Clyde was sick and had treatment at the Glynwood Hospital in Johannesburg, he managed to carry out some of the exercises and I supported him – he must do it to stay fit. "You can always do the bicycle exercises in bed, if nothing else," I said. I was probably somewhat bossy, because I knew that if he just gave in and rested all the time, the poisonous chemo would remain in the body. For that same reason he had to drink three litres of water daily, and to protect the mucous membranes he had to consume lots of whey and an arsenal of vegetables and fruit. No wonder, they have named me *The General* in Africa among the natives, but secretly they have confided in me that they believe in my treatment cures. Builder Gabriel has sworn that only the wife can save a man, when he is on the brink of the precipice.

Sometimes my thoughts go back to that terrible time, when we lived like gypsies from one place to another: from Harare to Johannesburg, then to New York and on to Victoria in British Columbia.

CLYDE EATS ALL HIS MEALS at home to live healthy, but every day it becomes harder for me to find fresh veggies and fruit. The options are getting more limited every day and I have to drive around and find other sources many kilometres away.

As I turn around the corner on Isobels Lane, I meet a whole army of black crows. They fly up high when they hear the noise of the car engine. Somehow, there is something sinister about them, their black colour and their flock instinct, making them look powerful and making you feel as if you are just fodder. They sit there waiting for us to go rotten after we have died. Or will they, like the vultures, watch us getting weaker and go for the kill before we have expired? When they get disturbed, they fly up with high rusty screeches and then find a new place in a row or in a flock just a little bit away. Funny, how their feathers are always so clean and fine and with that white collar at the front, they look as if they are wearing *black tie* for a formal dinner. They never smell badly, perhaps because they leave nothing behind. Like vultures they wash themselves every day and spread out their wings to dry.

Clyde comes home early for lunch that day and is clearly upset because he was harassed by the police on the Beatrice Road, which has now been built into a four-lane highway. There were two policemen, a man and a woman, and they claimed that Clyde had been speeding and it was so serious that he had to go to court.

"How fast did you drive?" I ask.

"Eighty-eight kilometres and there were no road signs telling me you couldn't. Besides, with the new four-lane highway, it couldn't possibly be too fast," says Clyde.

"Could you not have paid a fine on the spot?" I ask, in order to understand why the case has to go to court. But Clyde explains that they were neither to be led nor driven, and even though a police vehicle had been driving right in front of him with the same speed, and there were neither pedestrians nor bicyclists, he now had to go to Mbare Court. In that case I suggest that I go with him and that we bring along Clyde's clinical report, just in case it might be any help.

The drive takes us out to the industrial area and we leave the Beatrice Road, which was the original name it had in the old days, but some years after independence, its name was changed like most towns and streets and it is now called *Simon Mazorodze Road*. When I first came to Zimbabwe, all the streets still had the old British names, but when they eventually changed, it was difficult to remember the new long names typically honouring African freedom fighters. Besides it took many years to produce the road signs and yet longer to produce new maps, and you end up being totally schizophrenic about the new names. Harare used to be Salisbury, but somehow we all like the name Harare and it is a nice short name. The city is also not very big and usually you find your destination easily. Far worse with the changes in South Africa, where they started changing Petersburg to *Polokwame*, but now the city of Johannesburg with millions of people is next on the list and so are other big cities with all its streets and alleys.

It is a complete waste of money, because the same will happen in South Africa, just like Zimbabwe when all the signs have been changed. The population will be so poor that they too will begin to steal the signs and melt them into other products. I find it ironic that you want to take over a colonial city with all its pomp and circumstance and then change the name, because it is hurtful to keep a name that reminds you of suppression. Why not instead build a new town area and assert your own Pan-African identity and perhaps make the old part into a kind of museum? But mankind's urge to plunder and take over another man's work is the strongest force. And the memory is short, when you look at advanced agriculture with modern agricultural machinery and irrigation. There are acres of fertile land surrounding the modern farm building with the latest in interior décor for the kitchen and the bath and swimming pool in the garden, and one tends to forget that perhaps that same family started only one generation back on an ox-driven cart driving north towards Zambia and building a house with their bare hands. They had no pre-fabricated materials of any sort and built everything from scratch, and the roofing was made out of grass. Despite all the odds, they advanced quickly, working hard every season and now they look rich. For that reason the African wants to take it from them, because he says it is his land. Mugabe told them so. But what the native African wants is not the land; it is the luxury lifestyle of these rich farmers. Like children playing grown-ups. And they want it now. Even President Mugabe has acknowledged that Zimbabwe has a "get-rich-quickly syndrome," but he forgets that he created this false illusion and let himself and his cronies take everything on display as they saw fit, using primitive war veterans and criminal elements of society to attack defenseless families on their lonely farms. Despite the fact that many of these farmers were trained both under UDI and in Africa's wild bush, most of them did not resist because they did not want another war. Instead, they chose to fight the injustice through the legal system or the agricultural association over many years, but it was a bitter fight doomed to failure in most cases. There is a black sheep in every flock and both systems were infiltrated with people of devious character. There was a lot of betrayal among them, as they were all out to save their own skin.

Since the farm invasions you have seen many small bakkies loaded to breaking point with the few belongings that a whole family takes with them, when they have to cut a long life short. But some of them were even worse off, they were forced to leave without a cent and leave everything they owned. The Western world kept silent and continued the diplomacy, because development aid had become a very important industry and big political interests were at stake. Business was more important than a minority population of white people without any connection to global corporate interests. Perhaps if we had oil, the West would have paid us more attention. The Western governments saw prospects in training and helping the looters to repair past injustices. The university world and the legislative assemblies started a new rhetoric, where human rights only related to people of colour; black or other exotic races were under their protection, white people were not even in their dictionary. They turned a blind eye to the suffering of young defenceless white farmers with small children; it was the blind eye of the West. Even old white folks in their seventies, who lived isolated on small farms surrounded by wild stretches of swaying savannah grasses, were targeted, and many of them were killed or maimed. The Africans came singing and chanting, armed with axes and rocks, with a ridiculous figure in their midst wearing a grass-hat on his head. His name is Chinotimba, and if it had not turned so violent and tragic, it would have been almost laughable, watching his face split open with two front teeth missing in the eternal African grin. But the chanting turned eerie and became threatening and the songs were replaced by shouting and screaming. Chinotimba is a self-made war veteran with a past as a watchman, but he sure knows how to create terror and violence, and he has been found very useful to the existing government. Many of the farmers' pets, like their faithful Ridgeback dogs and their devoted Labradors were chopped into pieces with machetes, and toy poodles were thrown into the fire they had lit to burn the outbuildings.

When the farms were invaded and claimed as the blacks' settlement, the cattle started suffering tremendously, lacking water and feeding, because the new settlers had no experience in the caretaking of livestock. For the same reason, because they were ignorant about normal procedures with regard to slaughtering methods and storing meat in deep freezers, they chopped off the legs of the cows, successively joint by joint. They call it to *hamstring* them, which in reality means that they cut through the large tendon on the back of the hock and cripple the animal at first, cauterizing the arteries thereby securing the necessary blood supply for the cow to continue living until the next joint is needed. These violent acts are never mentioned in the Western media, as it could upset the native leaders and present them as primitive and cruel, with the danger of creating detestation for development assistance. This lack of confrontation and exaggerated comprehension of cultural understanding due to political correctness and cowardice has resulted in tremendous suffering in the whole region.

My thoughts fly high and low like a flock of birds and are abruptly stopped when Clyde turns onto a small road. All over there is washing hanging on the clotheslines around the primitive houses, looking like a shanty town. The huts and buildings look neglected with peeled-off paint and broken windows, and the weeds have overgrown the maize plants. But all in all, the whole picture looks green and lush because of the heavy rains that have fallen during the last months.

"It is the police and their families who live here," explains Clyde and adds with serene contempt, "The houses are all falling apart, because they have done nothing to maintain them since they took them over from the whites."

After Clyde has parked the car, we enter the door to Mbare Court. At the reception desk the officers on duty stare curiously at us. Clyde is dressed in a decent shirt, but with his Nomads tie in the attaché case, in case he has to present himself to the Judge. Since we moved, we have been unable to find any of his ties, so the Nomads golf tie is the only one he can wear when he has to look formal. You are not supposed to use it for other occasions than golf events and golf celebrations, but as Clyde says, "I am not going to invest in more ties, when I am on my way out!" My navy blue pinstriped jacket with matching slacks has the desired effect. Like a uniform the suit demands respect and my diamond rings sparkle in the sun. Despite my Nordic looks I have adopted many Latin and exotic habits, and I speak with my hands continuously, jangling the bangles.

"We cannot see there is any case against you. You will have to continue to the traffic police office at the end of the road," explains the officer on duty.

Clyde reverses the big Mercedes out and drives down the narrow road, until he comes to another group of buildings, identical with badly maintained housing for big families. Again the many clothes-lines stand out, filled with all sorts of garments from underpants to uniformed shirts, and muddy pathways leading to different police offices. Suddenly, through an open door Clyde sees the same policeman who had stopped him on the four-lane highway, when he was together with a policewoman. Now the woman is no longer with him.

"I never thought you would come," says the constable with obvious admiration in his voice and continues, "You must be an honest man." Next to him is one of his colleagues, sitting on an old metal chair picking his nose. The chair is badly needing upholstery repair and crumbling foam is sticking out.

"These are my chairs!" explains Clyde and adds in a low voice to me, "That was when I had that crook Muwuto as a partner in the foam plant."

As the constable is told that the chairs are made by Clyde, he says, "So instead of paying a fine, perhaps you should repair our chairs."

"No way," says Clyde arrogantly. "The fabric alone costs more than going to court."

As I find out that they are really friendly, I volunteer, "We also make all your signs, *POLICE AHEAD*."

The constable looks very impressed and addresses Clyde with a lot of respect. He then writes out a fine for 40,000 Zimbabwe dollars, which is such a ridiculously small sum today that it is almost impossible to pay for. Fortunately, I still carry in my handbag a few dirty 10,000 dollar notes, which we never expected to use after the new notes were introduced, but Clyde has a habit of passing over to me all his old small notes. I carry them in a pink cosmetic purse with a zipper, more suitable than a wallet. I open the zipper and take out four notes and keep the rest in my handbag. The constable is smiling broadly, as he types with two fingers on his black museum piece of a typewriter, but in actual fact it is far more appropriate with all the power cuts. By hand he fills in another form, which is a very thick bundle with blue carbon paper in between each sheet – something I have not seen since the seventies.

THAT SAME EVENING WE WATCH *Hard Talk*, which is a BBC programme. The British zoologist and author Desmond Morris is being interviewed by Stephen Sackur. Morris believes that we must go back to times of origin, when the men were out in the fields hunting and fishing and the women took care of the socio-economic life. "Men are too big risk-takers," he says and explains how they risk everything, including their house, home and family because of their savagery, which can only be tamed by going back to the roots. I am fascinated by the programme, but Clyde has fallen asleep in the recliner.

Shortly after we prepare for bed, I quickly fall asleep in the king-size bed despite the barking of dogs and pistol shots, and I sleep right up to the wolf hour, when my deep sleep is interrupted by a nightmare. I dream of a young girl working for a big international corporate company. She is a competent company secretary, but her many hours of overtime made her neglect her dear horse. To compensate, she began riding during lunch hours, but the directors began to complain that she was absent too long and they also started noticing that she smelled of horse. The horse began to get frustrated and nervous and she ended in a fall. In my dream a journalist is making inquiries, "Was that why she fell off the horse?" Some of her colleagues explain that it started like that and the horse had been destroyed after she was admitted to hospital.

"But why did they amputate her leg? Could they not have saved it?" asks the journalist.

"Because it was written in her contract that the company would pay for all health expenses, and in the end it proved cheaper to amputate the leg instead of saving it. It was more expensive to treat the damage," explains one of the young girls in the company. The journalist began to look shocked, "Do you mean that they could actually have saved her leg?"

The girl nodded and continued, "Yes, what actually happened was that they put her under anaesthesia and cut off that part of the leg, even though it was not even fractured. She just screamed and screamed when she woke up and found out what had happened. They wanted to teach her a lesson."

"What do you mean, they wanted to teach her a lesson?" asks the journalist.

"She had not shown proper respect for the company. Her workplace was supposed to be her priority No.1, but her horse was more important to her," said the young girl, who was just an intern in the company, "she tried to sue them, but they were far too powerful and even the Judge said that she did not have a leg to stand on – yes, that was actually the expression he used and he refused to let her demonstrate in court how they had crippled her, as it was irrelevant to the case, which only concerned her contract."

"You cannot mean that she lost the suit?" asks the journalist dumbfounded.

"That is what happened and that was why she took her own life," answered the intern with tears in her eyes.

Although I am now completely awake, the dream has filled my body and soul with morbid fear, so strong that I cannot tell Clyde about it even if I can feel he is awake. Several days after, the details of my dream are vivid and still strong in colour, as the rhythmical aggravation of the situation was so intense that it all seems real and even in the daytime I have an uneasy feeling.

THE ROUND DINING TABLE IS set for six persons. Just as I am inspecting it, Clyde gets a message on his cell phone that Dr. Vick is on his way from Masvingo to St. Theresa Mission in Harare. I squeeze in an extra plate; with a little less elbow space we can sit seven at the table. There is no power cut and I have a tender filet roast in the oven and an Indian *Ghana aloo* on the stove. It is made beforehand and I just have to heat it up and serve with brown rice and ratatouille. At the last minute I will mix the green salad to serve it fresh. There is a thick white tablecloth on the table and big white cotton napkins and wine and water glasses in crystal by each setting. Clyde lights the candles. Besides the Indian *rotis*, which I heat up in the microwave, I also serve some slices of Tut's homemade health bread that she brought along. Good bottles of South African wine are stored in the garage and the minute this endangered species is served, a most convivial atmosphere is secured.

Dr. Vick tells about a wretched affair with a donkey which suddenly turned away from the herd and ran right out in front of his car resulting in a small collision. The donkey must not have been seriously injured because it continued at full speed afterwards. The impact had a more serious effect on the car, as the radiator was broken, resulting in fluid leaking and too much heat coming on. That was the reason for Clyde sending Hilton to Masvingo to assist Dr. Vick, who is now driving Clyde's Mercedes until his Twincab is repaired. During dinner I realize that I will be without any transport, as Clyde will need my Mercedes while his own is lent to Dr. Vick. What a mess! Perhaps I can drive the bakkie.

Dr. Vick's wife Dolores has gone to America and I fully realize the impact of this, as I look at his unshaven face, his growth having already turned beyond designer stubble. His look is intent as he continues, "I am too old to be alone for two months." Already he has been three times to Harare. Since his wife left he is certainly not at his best, and has lost the look of the prim missionary doctor we are used to seeing on his occasional visits to the capital. Without the female, manners and customs go and there is a decline of morale.

CHAPTER 18

THE LEGEND

Clyde meets Johnny Katsande in the street and invites him and Vania for dinner at our townhouse. Half an hour later than their expected arrival they still have not appeared. I suggest to Clyde, "Should you not call them in case he has forgotten? You remember the last time when we had dinner for the Nigerian General Peter Haruna and his wife Elisabeth, and Smila was dancing Flamenco?"

And quite right, it was deleted in Johnny's memory file, but he says, "We leave home now now. From the factory in Ruwa."

The menu is sadza and mushroom sauce plus filet steak and potato curry.

Close to 8 o'clock the intercom system rings and we open for Johnny. Out of his Twincab climb not two, but four people, for his 12-year-old son Philip and daughter Anne are also in the car. The children live permanently in London. If I had only known that, I would have made more sadza and gravy and made a bigger portion of potato curry. There is plenty of beef filet. Johnny presents a bottle of red wine. The youngsters are hungry and nothing is left behind. We have a cozy atmosphere at the round table and true enough, where there is room in the heart, there is room in the house and food enough. It is a wonderful evening and they are like our family. Johnny has a special sense of humour and Vania is always interesting to be with, as she has a wealth of knowledge. In the old days she used to work for the Ministry of Finance, but now she helps Johnny in running the factory at Ruwa. Apart from coffins, he also produces handcarved furniture imitating the Louis XIV style. Vice President Joyce Mujuru has already filled her whole house with these copies which are incredibly beautiful, and Johnny once gave me a parliamentary chair as a present.

During the evening I ask Johnny about this phenomenon of double rainbows seen when the moon is full at Victoria Falls. This is what I am told with a big broad African smile:

178

"Bow in our local Shona language is *uta*. *Utawadonde* means rainbow. History has it that this guy called Dande – yes, he is *invisible* – he owns the bow, *MaUta*. He shoots up in the sky and tries to hit the angels. Normally, you get rain when you see a rainbow. So Dande says to the people working in the fields: *You must finish work!* Because Dande has stopped the rain and says: *As long as you see the rainbow, Utawadonde, you are safe.* So the people carry on digging in the field, even when the rain starts falling, because Dande told them to do it!"

"*Utano*, Johnny, thank you for the story," I say laughing and raising my glass towards his.

"*Utano*," replies Johnny, who is a brilliant storyteller as is typical of the Shona tribe. Some years ago Johnny and I invented a Shona-word for *cheers*, because he said they had no word for it. We turned around many ideas, but only when I asked what the Shona word for *health* was, did we come to the right conclusion. Since then we have always used *utano* when we clink the glasses and it has actually spread and become almost official! Had the times been better, Johnny and I would have marketed our own utano-juice and utano-sandwiches made like some sort of maize-pancakes, of course, and then there was utano-beer! Although Johnny is totally fluent in the English language, he always says *ma* in front of many nouns as a definite article, as do many Africans.

Johnny also knows many stories about life in the bush and savannah, because his father was a good teacher. The young Africans today are between two extremes; on one hand they have lost what they had and it has been replaced with technological knowledge, which they can easily operate. But they have no deeper understanding of the gadgets because they have jumped from the Middle Ages into the computer age. Johnny recalls how they, as children, could not find water, but their father knew from which tree they could suck the bark and avoid dehydration. For snake bite they peeled bark from another tree, which they rolled into a stick shape after removing the outer layer. Then the stick was rolled back and forth many times across the skin until the poison came out.

Clyde now remembers his own childhood in Canada and he narrates how he as a small boy-scout learned a lot about survival in Canada's trackless forests. This is one rhyme they recited:

Green or red will make you dead,

Black or blue will see you through.

With this advice in mind, they always knew, even as children, which berries they could eat in the wilderness.

THE NEXT DAY I WAIT for the nuns, but Sweet Rit calls me at the last minute and tells me she is not coming.

"But why not, is everything OK?" I ask.

"Do you know why a banana is crooked?" she answers my question with another question. I think about it for a long time and even consider something naughty, but I leave that one out. Although Sweet Rit has a propensity to certain masculine entertainment like football, for example, she will hardly share their masculine jokes. Instead I say, "I have no idea why a banana is crooked."

"Exactly," says Sweet Rit. "You don't know why it is crooked, and I don't know why I am not coming."

Later Sister Nancy phones and tells me five people were arrested at the Emerald Hill Children's Home and they will remain in prison overnight. Tomorrow she will see what she can do. The local African nuns were tempted beyond their power of resistance when Mother Superior left for several weeks. During an inspection it was found there was an overdraft of several billions on the bank account, and this overdraft would cost the Home an interest of 700 per cent. Apart from that, computers and other valuables had also been taken.

I DECIDE TO DRIVE OVER to Green Park in Umwinsidale. This is a lovely new vegetable market under a thatched roof that opened while Clyde and I were away. They have more veggies and fruit and they even have meat and other groceries. Due to the heavy rainfall, the selection is not as big as expected. I enjoy walking around under the high thatched ceiling, which in typical African style reveals the actual straw on the inside and is held up by huge beams. It provides a magnificent height and coolness and reminds me of our lovely lodge at Mazvikadei Lake. Strings are wrapped around the beams, making it look somewhat rustic, even though it has been thatched with precision and flair like crochet work, because a big part of the thatching job was carried out by the local women.

My mood is lifted like a hanging cloud dissipating in the rising sun when I set my eyes on a shelf with washing powder for the automatic washing machine at a price of 62 million dollars. It is a bit expensive, but never mind, the swipe machine is working. As a bonus I get three plastic bags for the goods. This is almost unheard of now, but, by golly, is it ever useful for containing the garbage. We no longer get plastic bags in Harare. Most people with big yards have given up waiting for collection of garbage by the municipality; instead they ask their gardener to dig a hole in the back garden and burn the rubbish there. The hole is filled with all kinds of waste: empty JIK containers, toilet cleaner bottles and Handy Andy. Then it is all turned over in the burning hole. Nobody has any thought for CO_2 emission or the like, and how many thousands of years it takes to dissolve in the soil. We have enough other problems on our mind just surviving from day to day.

On my way home I forget to turn right in the new complicated round-about without any signs and suddenly I am on my way to the city centre. It is chaotic at most crossings, as the traffic lights are not working and some of them are manned by police. I turn off at Seventh Street to avoid getting closer to town.

Suddenly, two policemen are waving me down about two hundred metres ahead and, as I am already in the inner lane, I stop as it might be the President's escort coming. I wait in vain for the motorcade of blinking lights and noisy sirens, all the motorbikes, the ambulance and military vehicles with soldiers turning their AK47 and other weapons towards all the road users. Mugabe is escorted like that every time he leaves his palace. But nothing happens, except the two policemen approach my car. Not expecting any problems, I smile at them and open my car window.

"You passed a red light!" says one of the policemen.

"None of the lights in any of the crossings were working," I answer, still smiling, and explain in a friendly manner that it was not even my intention to come this way, but with the new round-about without any signs, I got lost.

"Where are you going?"

"Belgravia," I answer and expect to be waved off. The police guy wearing a brown uniform has acted friendly, but the other one, dressed in a bluish uniform that does not look genuine, takes over command and directs me to show my driving license and ID.

"It is only a photocopy," he states.

"Yes, of course it is. With the conditions we have here, who would drive around with their original documents?" I ask him.

"You are under arrest, you have committed an offence," says the guy in the dubious bluish uniform and he says these words as if he is licking a lollipop. Exactly at that instant my personality is taken over by No. 5 in the nuns' book of personalities, and I can almost hear Sweet Rit saying that *it is the devil peeping out!*

"For me it is now clear that you are on another mission. This is not about traffic safety and traffic control. You just want all whites out and that is why you are harassing me. Use your eyes and see all the potholes and the thieves stealing all the road signs and the metal from the traffic lights." My bombastic speech is full of contempt.

"Are you saying we are racists?" asks this neophyte of a policeman in his homemade blue uniform.

"Absolutely," I confirm and continue, "Besides I find that you are a dangerous guy. You are different than your colleague." I point my index finger at him and then look at the other guy, who has a single star on his brown uniform. "You were friendly, no problem, but your colleague is harassing me, even though I have done nothing wrong."

Like a boxer I am just beginning to warm up, and continue with a sound of surprise in my voice. "Perhaps now we are at it, what kind of uniform is it, anyway, he is wearing? He does not even have any stars. To me it looks like he has falsified the police uniform."

Suddenly, I run out to the middle of the road and flag down approaching cars. A Portuguese-looking driver stops and I shout at the top of my voice, "HELP! HELP! I am being harassed by the police and I have done nothing wrong."

"They do that all the time now. How can I help you?" asks the driver with one arm hanging out the window of the car.

"Could you please call my husband on his cell phone 011 601 916 and ask him to come immediately?" I ask. He immediately punches in the numbers and luckily Clyde answers back right away, because he cannot stand for very long the metallic melody on his new Chinese cell phone sounding like he is in a Chinese Opera, but as Clyde says, "Even in the factory you cannot miss it. It cuts right through all the noise of the machines."

"Your husband will be here within a few minutes, he is not far away," says the Portuguese. "Do you want me to stay and wait?"

"Thank you, but that is not necessary," I say and warn Mr. Blueshirt-without-stars, "Don't try any tricks. Don't even come near me!"

As soon as Clyde gets out of the car, I explain to him quickly in German that the light was not working and that I only stopped because I thought it was the President's motorcade passing by. In the meantime Clyde has his friend, the Commissioner of Police, on the phone. Unfortunately, there is no way around it. We have to come to the Main Police Station.

"I don't want to drive when I am upset," I say to Clyde. I then drive my green Mercedes behind Clyde's car into Morris Depot. Having parked the car I take the back seat in Clyde's car and the policeman without stars sits in front in the passenger seat. The other policeman in the brown uniform has mysteriously disappeared.

As we pass the traffic light which has caused me all this trouble, Clyde remarks that it does not work, but he continues driving towards our destination. It is a copycat experience of Clyde's own problem with the police.

Before entering the Main Police Station, Clyde warns me, "You just sign the fine without any argument like I did, so we can leave quickly!"

This I promise to do, so although the constable on duty is very primitive and speaks to me in an interrogating voice, I just willingly give him the correct explanation of the incidence with the police, but he cuts me completely off. That lets out the wolf in me and I ask him this question while leaning slightly over his desk: "Are you interested in my account, or is it irrelevant?"

"Sorry, Madam. You can continue. Would you like to sit down?"

"No, thank you," I say with heavy eyelids having inspected the broken chairs and continue, "I deny any wrongdoing."

"Is it correct that you called us racists?" asks the constable on duty.

"It is correct that I had that impression of that one there. This gentleman in his somewhat strange uniform seems to have a problem with white ladies or ladies my age." I identify the youngster by pointing at him and continue, "The other policeman in a correct brown uniform with one star had no complaint against me, but he disappeared mysteriously."

Clyde has taken a seat on the hard bench against the wall and I hear him asking, "Now how do we solve this between us?"

The constable on duty appears to enjoy a little drama and sketches problems. "But if she is accusing us of being racist, it must go to court."

Clyde punches in some numbers on his cell phone and talks to the Commissioner of Police. "Would you prefer the Commissioner of Police to come down here?" he asks, handing out the mobile towards the constable.

"No, let us try to solve it among ourselves." The constable directs a policeman on the other side of the room to fill in the forms.

"When did you arrive in Zimbabwe?" the assistant policeman asks.

"In September 1986," I reply.

"On which date?" he asks.

"I think it was on the 11th."

"Did you come over land or over water? Was it Harare International Airport?" I realize he is using some document that does not really cover this land-locked country.

"It was the old airport," I reply, bringing out a storm of laughter from all bystanders, a mixture of offenders and members of the police force.

"What is your position?"

"Housewife," I reply.

The constable on duty breaks in. "What was your position before that?"

"I was a diplomat and chargé d'affaires and often met the President of Zimbabwe," I answer a little coolly.

The fine is 40,000 Zimbabwe dollars, exactly like Clyde's. I start studying the form they have filled in.

"Just sign!" says Clyde in his commanding voice.

"But it says here I passed *red*, and I did not!" I argue, after which the constable grabs the document, reads it through and then ticks in *amber* instead. After that I just shake my head and sign. Apparently, they are completely unwilling to put in print that none of the lights are working in the whole area.

The Main Police Station is more formal than Mbare, but still very neglected. As we prepare to leave, Clyde meets a high-ranking policewoman near the entrance. They greet each other like they are family.

"Hi, Gloria," says Clyde warmly and introduces me: "This is my wife, Bodie."

Despite the heat she is wearing nylon pantyhose and on her short hair she is wearing a kind of helmet looking like the English Bobbies.

"What brings you here, my friend? Any problems?" asks Gloria.

Clyde explains and adds, "… and as I went past the light myself, I know that it is not working!"

"Shame! Did you get a big fine?" asks Gloria, inclining her head sideways.

"No, not at all. That is what I find so funny. I could have paid him right there and it would have been all over."

"That is no longer allowed. Every fine now has to be paid at the police station," explains Gloria.

After having waved goodbye and when we are safely out of earshot, Clyde says, "If only Gloria had turned up at the start, when we entered with this green bomber in his home-knitted uniform. You see, they have been forced to take on all these illiterates and train them in the police force, even though they are not even war veterans; just criminal greenhorns. But they are dangerous, because they like to show off and as soon as they get a weapon in their hands, they become trigger-happy and start shooting around. You were lucky that he did not carry any weapons – he just wanted a lift to the police station. Nobody stops to pick up police hitchhiking anymore, so they have to flag down people to get a lift to town. That is why they invent these fines."

FORTUNATELY, MY TELEPHONE IS WORKING when I return to the townhouse in Belgravia and I decide to chat with my two girl friends: first Smila, the Portuguese flamenco-dancer, and then my Hindustani girlfriend, Diya. Smila is happy to hear that it was a Portuguese who stopped, but she warns me, "You must never say they are racists, even when it is true. I have big problems in this connection, although that is with the Chinese." She has had a long case with the authorities and it has gone to court, because Smila claimed that the Chinese ate dogs and cats. As she has a passionate relationship with animals, she collects them in streets and alleys and takes them home to a self-established pet orphanage in Vainona, where she is running a big house with staff, trained to look after and feed all the animals. At the moment she has 10 dogs and 30 cats all given beautiful names. What happened when Clyde and I were away was that Smila, who is a pure vegetarian, had reported to the SPCA, the local organization for animal protection, that the Chinese eat dogs and cats, but a local African working for the animal protection agency had warned the Chinese about her complaints. This led to Smila being sued for 5 billion Zimbabwe dollars and her being totally out of balance. It affected her so much that she could no longer produce her usual quantity of herbal teas from the Nyanga Mountains and her orphanage started suffering when she was constantly absent spying on the Chinese houses. With camera in hand she was on constant patrol collecting evidence for the court case. From the beginning Clyde had warned Smila and said that she must mind her own business because the Chinese have a powerful mafia in Zimbabwe. I remember all Clyde's warnings and repeat, "Smila, they can kill you!"

"I know, and my father says the same. But think of all these defenceless little puppies. Have you noticed how many puppies there are in the Chinese houses? There is a reason for that. They come in the middle of the night and take them away to slaughter them." Despite the bad telephone connection with a lot of noise, I can hear there are tears in her voice.

Perhaps she is right. Just on the other side of the wall, where I often hear little baby screams from puppies, there are Chinese living in that house and the whole neighbourhood is full of Chinese citizens and Chinese restaurants. Whenever I have visited Chinese residences with Clyde, they have always been full of puppies, and Clyde has mentioned that many of the Chinese, who come here are very primitive like the Africans, because they come from the worst poverty-stricken areas in China and they do not even speak English. There is a huge gulf between them and the elegant people coming from Hong Kong and our own Chinese vet, Karen, who was born in Zimbabwe.

Luckily, Smila knows a Portuguese lawyer who is her friend and does not send her invoices for dealing with her case, and now he has succeeded in reaching a compromise with the Chinese. If they dropped the case, Smila was obliged to apologize in all the newspapers. Reluctantly, Smila agreed to do this, but already the Chinese have lost so many customers because over the Internet it spread like wildfire that dogmeat was served in these secret rooms of the restaurant, and that Alsatian puppies were stored in the deep freeze. That took away the appetite from even the most hardened Rhodies.

"I am still collecting evidence," says Smila. "One day it must come out to the world."

Despite the fact that my ear has become very sore from speaking so long to Smila, I phone up Diya. The first time we met was when we decorated the stage for Egyptian belly dance. Diya had a natural talent for decorating and the results were always very exotic. She had finished off by throwing rose petals on the floor. When she first meets a person, she draws immediate attention with the following declaration: "I am the only Hindu woman in Harare who has divorced her husband after 30 years of marriage!"

Now she says to me, "Sister, why talk on the phone? Why you not come over here? I missed you too much."

It is decided to wait till the next day, when Clyde is on the golf

course and he does not need any lunch. She lives in the area of
Highlands near our old residence on Montgomery Road. The main
building is rented out. Diya lives in a small guest cottage surrounded by gaudy flowers and graceful figurines, and both her front and
back yard are loaded with herbs and vegetables that she grows herself. Leaving my green Mercedes I see a rat disappearing behind the
wall, as Diya comes running towards me with open arms. Already the
sound of her crisp happy voice flitting between soprano and tenor,
sounding like little bells, lifts me up and lightens my spirit.

"Hello, my darling. I am so happy to see you!"

We hug each other warmly and let go of all sorrow and grief with
little Scampi jumping around us with his Chongololo tail and Chinese
looks. He whines happily and curls up by my feet.

"Scampi! Go away!" commands Diya towards this mini-version
of a Pug.

"It is all right," I say.

"No, it is not. She is full of fleas and they will bite your ankles.
None of us can afford flea tablets these days." True enough, and I
am actually allergic to flea bites. I get wounds from them growing
into huge craters that won't heal for months. Normally, they only
heal when the dry season starts and then the scars eventually disappear. Out from her living room, Diya's music by *Kabli Kushie Kablie
Gham* starts competing with the birdsong.

"First we have tea with *batteria* snack and then we have lunch. We
have so much to talk about," Diya chatters in her colourful *Punjab*.
Her long thick black hair is rolled in a pigtail and twisted, then held
together with a comb filled with rhinestones. She puts her hair up
when she is busy making *samosas* for resale.

Diya leads me into a backyard containing an impressive organic
garden. There are storks and toads in clay or stone around the garden
and we are completely surrounded by hollyhocks.

"See these purple leaves? That is for our *batteria*, which you will
try for tea. If you like, you can grow them in your townhouse. They
grow like weeds." She stumbles slightly on her bad foot, but never
complains. She picks up some leaves from the bushes with lemongrass and mint and I follow her into the kitchen. She walks through

the pearly curtains to the kitchen and immediately starts flaking the lemongrass and mint leaves into finger-long sticks. Then she puts the whole lot in an old metal pot without handles, already filled with water and she adds a teaspoon of ordinary tea and turns on the gas stove to let it boil. After one minute of boiling, the tea is ready. It is the most delightful and stimulating tea that picks you up better than a glass of wine.

Diya tells me that she is now making the *batteria.* "You take the purple leaves and put a paste inside as follows: 1 cup mealie-meal, 1 cup plain flour, 1/2 cup rice flour and 1/2 cup peaflour. Then you add fresh or homemade ginger, garlic and sesame seeds. Green chili also, garam masala and 1 teaspoon curry, 1 teaspoon salt, little turmeric, little sugar and tamarin."

"What if I don't find tamarin?" I ask.

"No problem, my darling, just use lemon juice or lacto. But if you do have tamarin, let it first soak in hot water. Take a handful, use juice only, squeeze it, add the water, just enough so it is a wet paste."

Diya is a head shorter than me and stands on a footstool to reach the top cupboard containing a large variety of Indian serving dishes. "Look here, Honey, each leaf take off the stem, wash it, dry it, then put paste on the leaf or two lots and roll like sausage, add more leaves, fold the second over, put in the steamer pot for half hour. Make it cold and put in plastic and throw in the fridge."

Diya is demonstrating the one we are having now, already defrosted and ready. She slices it like you do a cake. Then she pours a little oil into the frypan and adds red chili pepper, a few mustard seeds and when the seeds pop, she puts in onions and curry leaves. She stirs it around and takes a portion of sesame seeds in her fine little hand, so for me that would be *half* a handful, my hand is so much bigger. All slices of *batteria* are put in the frypan and when they are all heated up, we eat this delicacy, which is the filling inside a *roti* bread. The homemade tea is served with it and we sit on the open veranda with the white pillars shaped like raw twine, talking for hours. There are stacks of firewood next to the *braii*, as we call the grill, as one must expect power cuts any time.

We have a lengthy discussion about the desperate political situation. The rate has now jumped from 8 to 11 in relation to the US dollar. That means to buy 1 American dollar, you need 11 million Zimbabwe dollars! Everywhere people are exchanging at exorbitant prices for our daily needs. Everybody is trying to take advantage of the situation.

"But remember, my Darling, whatever you've got, be happy and share it. The more you give, the more you get. Now they are all going crazy over Laksmi, you know?" Diya is referring to one of the Indian gods.

"I know the Goddess Laksmi from India," I say proudly.

"Laksmi can drive you really crazy and in our Hindu culture she can come and go, whenever she feels like it. One minute she can shower you with the money and next minute, if she is not happy with you, she will leave you a beggar. It is like dirt on your hands, you can wash them and it is gone. All that with money is just greed and the more money you have, the more greedy you become. Same with class, you know all about the system in India and the caste system. True class is not the money. Class is to give love and care for other people. Not the caste or the money." Deep within her sombre eyes, Diya has revealed a vulnerable spot and it is quite unlike her to be that serious; she is always so cheerful and feisty.

"I totally agree with you, but you know we are not that different in other cultures of the world; the way you grew up and the way in the West. Both places they put you into a box and value you accordingly. Just look at the unions. Is that fair? Is it not another caste system? And the Old Boys' Club from their elite boarding schools, if you have not entered that club from the beginning, it is much harder to make it in life. Just look at the system here. It is an exact copy of the old British system. No, I don't think that the caste system in India is so different after all."

"Perhaps, my dear Bodie-bin, but somewhere along the line, one day I will tell you more. You see we were sisters for 10,000 years ago. Can you not feel it? Only a few are sent back to Earth. Not today, but another day I will explain it to you and you will understand."

"Sometimes I dream about a certain place, where I have never been. There are years between that dream, but it keeps coming back,"

I explain. The afternoon is well advanced and the sun is lowering its soft rays and making shadows in the garden. Being together with Diya is like ointment on an open wound, but time passes by so quickly.

"Bodi-bin," says Diya using the word sister after my name, "did I tell you that Brother Paul came by to be taught how to make *samosas*?"

"He called me to tell me about it. He really enjoyed that day. He also mentioned that Erik came by."

"Yes, that is right, but unfortunately, I had a power cut so I could not finish off the samosas," says Diya in a sad voice. She used to make one tray after the other selling *samosas* and other snacks to caterers and other private customers, but that business is impossible to run, when you cannot freeze your goods due to frequent power cuts. Therefore, she can only do small orders for parties, and they have to be picked up the same day. Everything is crumbling for everybody and our livelihoods are being taken away.

CHAPTER 19

PRIESTS AND POLITICS

Avis and Zeb invite us for pasta as they are preparing for their departure to Cape Town. We bring along a bottle of wine. Drinks are served in the mini-bar in the lounge and as usual I order a very thin whisky with lots of water. We have so many pleasant memories to share as our friendship spans over many years. We all miss our friend Gert and take a trip down Memory Lane and turn over lots of events since we first met in Cape Town, when Clyde and I bought a holiday home in the same complex they lived in. They introduced us to *the girls*, as Zeb calls the nuns, and over the years all of our friends became intertwined and grew into a big circle of friends, almost like a clan. In fact the girls were supposed to have been here tonight, but they could not make it as they had a farewell party for Father Ryan. Avis tells us all about the robbery at the Emerald Hill Children Home, how Mother Superior, Perpetua that is, had to go to Germany because of a sick relative and in her absence the indigenous nuns had taken full advantage.

"Did you hear that Mandela is now building a mansion for 20 million Rand for his sweetheart Graca in Mozambique?" asks Avis from her seat in the light grey velour sofa, where she is sitting next to Clyde, but there is hardly space for him with all the cushions. She is crossing her legs elegantly wearing open slippers, while Max, their Schnauzer dog in the same grey colour as the sofa, sits by her feet. No, we have not heard about Mandela's palace.

"It is being said that all the donations for the poor and the many suffering from AIDS, go to his private bank account in Switzerland," says the host from the bar, where he is busy mixing drinks. When he has finished the task, he moves to another subject, namely the American election.

"You know, I rather like that fellow Obama," he says to our surprise, as his Jewish heritage is very strong and one would not expect him to be sympathetic towards a candidate with an Arabic name and a connection to indigenous people in Kenya. He continues, "I find he is a man of dignity and he would do well as President. He behaves like a statesman. Maybe he can make peace between the Arabs and the Israelis."

"If he does not get shot when he is elected," comments Clyde cynically.

"You mean like the Kennedys? And members of the Kennedy clan have given him their full support. Even Schwarzenegger's wife, who is also a Kennedy, even though her husband is a Republican," I remark, feeling good in this party.

The good atmosphere continues during dinner, when we are served a very tasty pasta dish full of garlic. For dessert they have spent a fortune in eggs, because it is a Portuguese specialty, *Malatoff*, that requires numerous egg whites.

"Bodie, do you know that Arlene has moved to the Avenues?" Avis is asking.

"Yes, and I have even seen the apartment – fantastic views, and well protected among all the machine guns," I comment ironically, because of the close proximity to the Presidential Palace.

"Harvey doesn't like to live there and Arlene is mostly in Cape Town now," Avis tells me.

"They also had so much trouble renting out their big house to the Red Cross," I say quietly and can see in Avis's face that she knows all about it, and she continues my sentence and supports her friends.

"You are telling me! Poor Harvey, they were so mean to him, because the servants' quarters had not been newly painted; in these times, when nobody can get paint. They actually spoke down to him as if he was a terrible racist not caring for his staff."

"So typical with these organizations," says Clyde, who had also heard about Harvey's difficulties in connection with renting out. "They come here and pretend they are *so good* towards the blacks and treat us as if we are barbarians. But it is easy to be good if you collect the money at your workplace and have no responsibility for the budget. I would have told them where to go!"

"Yes, and when you get a salary in foreign currency, you have the same privileges as diplomats and other expats with imported cars and other tax free goods," says Zeb.

"Nobody treats their staff better than Harvey and Arlene," says Avis. "They kept their old housekeeper until the very end. He even died at the kitchen sink. We were actually there that fatal night. We waited and waited, but Arlene kept saying, he needs to take his time, now that he is old. Finally, Harvey went to the kitchen, and there he was, standing stone dead by the kitchen sink."

Clyde knows the story and does not like to speak about death, so he changes the subject. "Are you going to drive all the way to South Africa?"

"As usual we drive through Botswana to Johannesburg," explains the host, "then we get on the Premiere-class train *Tsotseloshe* from Joburg to Cape Town. We love the trip through the Karoo Desert lasting 24 hours. Besides all the staff on the train know us by now, so they give us V.I.P. treatment all the way." As is the custom here, Zeb uses the nickname Joburg instead of its full name Johannesburg.

Both Clyde and I decline to have coffee afterwards; we have to get up early the next day. The dog Max barks in protest as we get up to leave.

FATHER RYAN COMES BY OUR house in Belgravia Mews, because he is preparing to go away for some months and he brings Father Richard and two unknown fathers, but they can only stay for a short while as there is a lot to organize before his departure. I open a bottle of South African red wine and find the crystal glasses in the kitchen cupboard. Father Ryan is a very special friend and he was a great support when Clyde began to change character and became very aggressive about a year before his diagnosis. If only then we had known what we know now, that a huge tumour was growing inside his lung, and for every month it grew bigger, it gave more pressure on his ribs and other organs.

For many years Father Ryan has acted as a professional marriage counselor, which made me feel very safe, because I was aware of the fact that Catholics did not divorce. One day when shopping on Fifth Avenue, I found in the bookshop two books about how to recreate the harmony in your marriage and they were written by a Christian black preacher who respected the institution of marriage, so I bought both books. Wrongly I thought that even Clyde would find his books full of humour, because the writer was treating the problem surrounding unfaithfulness very thoroughly and he seemed to think that it was a problem you would always run into! As Clyde and I did not have such a problem I felt completely at ease reading that paragraph aloud for him, but when I went to the next paragraph, which was closer to our problems, Clyde asked, after a couple of minutes of listening, "Can I see it?"

"Of course," I said and handed him the book that I was reading from, after which he tore it apart with an incredible strength. The beautiful shiny front cover had been cut as precisely as if it had been done with a sword.

Father Ryan laughed so much when I told him about this unfortunate incident, and as he started to grow very interested in these Christian books, I ended up giving them to him, even the one that had been under the sword blade. Actually, it made me feel much safer with the books gone.

Today, Father Ryan and I know that it was not just the excessive consumption of alcohol, or the stress at work that had an effect on Clyde's behaviour, but it was a disease that came sneaking up on you like a thief in the night. It was a silent beast growing inside his body and it almost turned him mad.

"How is he now?" asks Father Ryan looking very relaxed on the golden velour sofa with one arm stretched over the backrest and his clerical collar undone.

"He is much better now, Father Ryan, but he is too ambitious with the scotch cart project and does not consider his condition. Besides they have stopped paying."

"You mean the Reserve Bank?" asks Father Ryan and explains to the other clerics about the big project.

"Not just Reserve Bank, but also the African partner. He does not stick to the contract. I say to Clyde that it is not that important, one day I will get a pension from Denmark and we will make it. But Clyde is afraid of being poor, because he grew up very poor in Canada." As I tell them this, they are all nodding with understanding and one of the Irish priests says, "It is a fear you always carry inside you."

"I also understand him," Father Ryan assures me.

"Sister Nancy once said that it is a fear that never leaves you and that is why some people cannot throw anything away," I say.

That same moment Clyde enters the room and joins the party. He looks glowing, perhaps because he can feel the good atmosphere meeting him. All the priests are commenting how good he looks and Clyde answers, "That is because she is always nagging!"

Precisely when all the Catholic priests are on their way out, Father John arrives. Although they do know each other they are not that close because they belong to different church orders. Like Brother Paul, Father John is of the Franciscan Order. It is a very strict order with less pomp and circumstance and their sole aim is to reach the poor. Father John is a very accomplished pianist and I ask him to play the *Lagenzeit Suite*, which he himself has composed. Clyde has never heard Father John play the piano.

"It is about the division in Belfast," says the Catholic father, while he looks at Clyde over his reading glasses. He places his long limbs on the piano bench and strikes the first key.

"This is where the river flows, right next to the street," he explains almost in a singing voice, while his hands glide over the keys. "Now the children are dancing." Both the river and the dance of the children you can feel in his music.

"The soldiers arrive," this information comes from me, as I hear the change of atmosphere and I know the piece. But ever so gently Father John's long fingers move away from the danger.

"You walk by the chapel in the evening and now the doors open... this is from an old chanting of the mass... *tanto mergo. Sakramentum.*" Father John plays it so beautifully and starts repeating the original music, "We are back at the river... the children are dancing...."

Clyde has tears in his eyes, the music spoke to him. We both applaud when the sound dies away and the room has turned quiet.

"Oh, Father, thank you!" I say and explain to Clyde, "Father John is becoming a member of our music club. I have already arranged it with Keiko and Dawn."

"Why did you not think of that before?" asks Clyde and walks into the kitchen to fetch a wine glass for Father John.

"I would love to see Ireland and Belfast one day," I say with enthusiasm, while Clyde is pouring wine into the glass.

"Me too," says Clyde and adds, "I hear they have fine golf courses."

AT EVERY PARTY THEY DISCUSS the election on March 29th in Zimbabwe. Most ambassadors and envoys from the West have confidence in the new party, which has been started by Simba Makoni, a previous finance minister, who was in disagreement with President Mugabe concerning the currency exchange and left office after that. However, he continued being a faithful servant inside the ruling Zanu-PF party. The Swedish Ambassador Sten Rylander has a lot of respect for Makoni, whom he has known for 25 years. I also have the opportunity of meeting the last Danish ambassador to Harare, Erik Fiil, who has been to a seminar in Juliasdale in the eastern part of the highlands of Zimbabwe. He shares the same opinion as his Nordic colleague and is hopeful towards a change in the situation, if Simba Makoni is elected.

Clyde says, "He is just a front, made by Zanu-PF, so that the world can't come and say that Zimbabwe does not have an opposition party." The governing party feared actually that Morgan Tsvangirai, who is Mugabe's most dangerous opponent, might refuse to take part in the election with his MDC party. By the way, it was a Dane, who *discovered* union leader Morgan Tsvangirai. It happened when ILO sent Georg Lemke to Harare. I always called him Jeff, since we knew each other from the young days when he worked in the Foreign Office. He was a prototype of an ambassador, very elegant and charming, but he left the service when he was elected mayor of the little town of Dragør near Copenhagen Airport.

"Morgan is a born leader," Jeff had said and supported him in continuing the anti-violent position that we Danes like. But perhaps indirectly that stance was the reason for Morgan not acting fast enough and not using the opportunity with his victory, for he could have fixed mass demonstrations, instead of letting Mugabe run off as the victor. When Morgan chose many years of legal battles, he had already lost. Jeff became very popular in Zimbabwe and had lavish parties with interesting people. He was most popular among the ladies, who saw him as a tall good-looking man, and they admired his knowledge about art and culture. Once he composed a Danish Grand-pris song, which was presented by the famous Dario Campeotto, and that year it won the prize. At the beginning of his stay in Zimbabwe, he received many visits from a good-looking French career woman who lived in Geneva, and they were very intimate. Once she told me that when she had breast cancer Jeff was always by her side. One summer she came with her two children from a broken marriage and Clyde and I invited them together with Jeff and his two sons up on the houseboat *Timela*. Jeff's sons had inherited their father's musical talent.

What happened to that French woman from Geneva I am not so sure about, but Jeff later met Sheila at the Avondale Coffee Shop and shortly after they became a pair, actually until he was forced to leave Zimbabwe. In between he had a whole army of women running after him, even the blacks. One of them was my girlfriend Maggie, an old war veteran. Once Maggie told me that Jeff had invited her to dine at the exclusive Barker's Lodge Restaurant, but it had offended her when he had brought along two tealights and lit them at the table, which already had candles in high candelabras.

"Is it because I am black that he only wants to see me in low lights?" she asked me. But I assured Maggie that it had nothing to do with that; Jeff was just a romantic fellow and Danes have a very special relationship with candles and soft lights.

When the situation became dangerous for Jeff, and the local intelligence CIO began to pursue him, it was Maggie who came to his rescue. The rulers of Zimbabwe had become very suspicious about the support Morgan Tsvangirai got from Jeff, especially because he was a legal expert and had worked many years as a lawyer. Maggie asked me to meet her at the Greek restaurant in Strathaven, where she went straight to the point and openly declared, "Bodie, you and I have the same back ground and we both know that these things happen. That is why Georg must immediately leave Zimbabwe. His life is in danger."

That very same evening I called Jeff and asked him to come for

drinks at Montgomery Road. He arrived with beautiful Sheila. Clyde was behind the bar mixing drinks.

"You must get out now, Jeff. Maggie has given you a warning through Bodie."

Jeff became very quiet, but he immediately understood the danger and he did not even finish his drink, but went straight home to pack a few things. We never saw him again. He bought a small house in the village of Fayence in the South of France, near the famous perfume town Grasse and the gourmet town of Dragnignan, and he began to divide his life between Denmark and the South of France. Sheila visited him once in Denmark.

Suddenly, we heard that Jeff got married and immediately thereafter we received the news that he had had a stroke and passed away. In the beginning he sent us letters, but he never wrote to us about the new relationship, which led to a new marriage. When he was buried in Denmark in the autumn of 2004, two sad widows followed his coffin: one was a Frenchwoman who owned a fashion boutique in Fayence, but she was originally born Danish and it was her that he had married. The other widow was his ex-wife Dorthe, with whom he had two sons.

AS THE UPRISING NEVER HAPPENED in 2002, President Mugabe said, "You will never catch us napping again!" In this sentence he acknowledged that if the opposition had pushed more, the situation might have changed. Mugabe strengthened his power through the military, the police and the war veterans and soon thereafter the revenge came against the white farmers, who had supported Tsvangirai.

Now Morgan Tsvangirai's MDC party has lost its magnetism and nobody sees them as a leading party anymore, not even with a new wing steered by Welchmann Ncube and Arthur Mutambare. Over the last years since the millennium we have been on a roller-coaster, sometimes a little bit up, but mostly down. Now it only goes down. This last year the melt-down in Zimbabwe has been so obvious and the tragedy so undisguised that even the most incurable optimists have stopped saying, *Let us pray.*

CHAPTER 20

MILLIONS, BILLIONS & TRILLIONS

C lyde is not himself; something has upset him and he is irrational and irritated. Either he snaps at me or he is completely quiet. Although I am aware that I married a man of few words, this is different. He is silent as the grave and the silence is becoming oppressive. Each day brings us more hardship and day by day we find it hard to survive. The rate has jumped from 11 million to 30 million during the night, because the Old Mutual insurance company in London rated their shares at 40 million and this was reported in the financial pink gazette. But the paper forgot to explain that it was in English pounds and here in Zimbabwe we only think in terms of the American dollar. The consequence of this was the rate went up to double that and it now keeps going up. Clyde has serious problems with the Reserve Bank, because they have stopped paying all manufacturers of agricultural machinery, and that includes also the African farmers.

For the start of production we only got paid half to cover purchases of raw materials, and instead of binding us to a quick delivery of 2,000 scotch carts, the Baron made a new deal with the Reserve Bank to the effect that only 300 scotch carts were delivered at a time and then subsequently the rate was adjusted after delivery. Therefore, the status is that Clyde has made 1,000 scotch carts with some prepayment, but for the last 300 nothing has been paid in advance. The dramatic rate of exchange also meant that the last scotch carts should be sold for a far lower price in US dollars, only 573 per scotch cart, compared with the old rate which earned over 1,000 US dollars per cart.

"What are you hiding from me?" I ask while polishing Clyde's Hush Puppies, which he likes wearing to the factory, because they are light and comfortable.

"It is the Baron. He does not live up to his promises. All the time he gives priority to other projects and forgets the contract with us," says Clyde, looking completely exhausted.

"But we did reach 425 billion, right? I know, it was supposed to be higher and paid before the 15th of November," I ask carefully with a searching glance.

"Yes, first he paid 425 billion, but then he made me pay for the other things, and as we got some of the payments outside and he at the same time persuaded me to pay for the welding rods and other things for the project, the amount went down from 425 to 342 billion." Clyde is now showing that he had been dealt a bad hand and he actually turns it as if he is in a poker game.

"Let us write it down on paper," I suggest as a typical civil servant. Clyde nods and explains as I write down, "The first payment from the British High Commission for 7,500 British pounds went to South Africa and the Baron paid in Zimbabwe dollars to us. The next payment for the same amount, and also in British pounds, went to South Africa and was spent on procuring welding wire and welding rods for the scotch cart production. The Baron never paid our company. Another payment for 800 million from another embassy went to England and the Baron never paid us that amount.

"But all these Embassy orders had nothing to do with the scotch cart joint-venture with the Baron, am I right?" I see Clyde nodding and continue, "That is our own production and has nothing to do with him, correct?" Clyde nods again and says firmly, "That is correct."

After a little while Clyde starts to ease up and continues, "You have to understand that there are many things. His sister Miriam was involved because of the car tires. There was paid 2 billion into my account in London from another order, and Miriam was paid 1.8 billion for the tires, leaving a balance of 1 billion. He started paying off the 19 billion, but stopped when he came to 11 billion. The rest he has never paid. Besides all the cash that the Baron gave us for changing currency and which should have been writing off his debt to buy the company, that was instead used to finance the project, pay for goods in South Africa and to buy angle iron locally with the result that we get nothing."

Clyde takes a deep breath. "Instead of paying 30 billion to us, the amount was used to buy tires for scotch carts, even though that was supposed to be financed by him. More and more it seems he is not financing anything and he is not producing his part of the deal. Also he has stopped paying towards buying the company. Apparently, Alex is owed 20 billion and du Brain 10 billion. This 60 billion would bring the total to 485 billion. But the fact remains that he has not even paid that amount, when we consider the hyper inflation and the erosion of the currency. Besides, most of it is what we have earned ourselves. The joint-venture has not given us what it should."

Clyde punches in some figures on the calculating machine. "750 million plus 800 million was not paid to the company at the parallel market rate. The other 750 million, which was paid to Products Division, was used to bring in welding rods. That further reduces the amount by 23 billion, so you see we have never reached our goal."

I breathe in slowly. It is like being attacked by a shark. Or like the ironic twist in Hans Christian Andersen's fairy tale about the husband who started off with a horse and ended up with rotten apples. "What the old man does, is always right."

"I thought it was to our advantage if I helped him along with other projects, so partly it is my own fault. I let myself be carried away trusting he would fulfill the agreement if I made it easier for him. I was able to find tires for his sister's project, which had nothing to do with us. Together we were able to move plastic raw materials to the aid of Rotwic. Our project did not move quite satisfactorily for the first 1,000 scotch carts, but it got worse when all the difficulties hit us from Reserve Bank, also because he could not deliver the rims on time and then you know the rest when nobody could get any cash from Reserve Bank."

It does him good to get it all off his chest. He gets up from the chair and fetches two whiskey glasses and pours a tot of Chivas Regal in each. "He also promised to pay wages and labour as we agreed, but he never did."

He places a drink by my chair and takes a sip from his own glass and sits down on the recliner. He presses the button on the side and leans back. "Then we delivered 1-kg tubs of peanut butter and 2-litre bottles, but he did not pay and it is really putting a strain on the whole company. The major slowdown for the second thousand scotch-carts has been axles for which we do not have the money to buy the steel rims for, but I hope that is now being corrected. The gum poles we paid for, it was 3,000 in November or before that and only 1,380 was refunded to the company. Where is the balance of 1,600 which we have paid for?"

Clyde is slightly raising his voice, but continues, "Likewise, 5 billion dollars worth of angle iron has never been delivered since November, although we paid for it. What they delivered was that old rubbish, all rusty, which they tried to paint over and that slowed down the production process. It is as if nobody cares about the outstanding 5 trillion dollars. Nobody cares about delivery of gum poles coupled with the fact that 5 cubes of saligna wood was purchased by Products Division and it never arrived although we paid up front. All these frustrations have been holding back the production, you see."

I take a big gulp of my whiskey-flavoured water and concentrate, as Clyde continues, "There was also the fuel. All the fuel was purchased for the project, but the fuel kept being used for other things by the Baron. Even when we ran out of fuel and Products bought 2,000 litres more, out of that 1,400 litres disappeared for his other projects. Then the thinners. We purchased six 200-litre drums and they were side-tracked to the Baron's company for their use in cleaning and spraying rims, which were sold to other people, so the project is short of four drums of thinners. Minor items such as very expensive rope from Products – you know, Bodie, we use it to tie around the packing when we deliver furniture. That has also disappeared, making it hard for us to deliver."

I feel I must make a comment. "I get the impression he is just looting the company and making us work for him instead of using the chance to buy us out."

"Exactly. He makes us work for his projects and his company and he does not keep the agreement on the scotch cart production. We are now in a situation where we hardly have any working capital. Products paid to have 300 scotch carts welded by subcontractors, but for the last 10 days he had no angle iron to supply the components. This gives us a bad name and it is like we are doing all of the work and paying for everything, but we are getting nothing in financial return. He gets all these new ideas about new ventures and contracts and never finishes the scotch cart project and it is not benefitting us at all. It is killing us.

One of the last projects, when originally discussed, was supposed to bring in 2.3 trillion. However, when it came to the final figures, some of the money was used elsewhere, and Products was still paying for 40 billion in overdraft on the project and that does not benefit us. Also with all these projects, we take all the risks for no gain."

"It has got to stop, Clyde. I will write up a memorandum. Do not give him the slightest chance to stray away from the contract. It is the joint-venture on the scotch carts only and the profit should go towards paying us off. He does want to take over the company and all the production, or has that changed?"

"Perhaps he got cold feet about buying the company. Maybe it is too big a mouthful even if he gets it for nothing with us producing the capital through production."

I get up from my chair to give this man a big hug and a kiss. "You know what, Lovie, don't worry about it. We conquered cancer; that is all that matters. The other things are just money, and like sister Diya says, they all go crazy over goddess Laksmi. She can make you more and more crazy. Like dirt on the hands – when you wash them, the money has gone."

"You are right. My health can no longer take this and all the risks involved and the sleepless nights. It is totally reckless and I feel I am being used while trying to help *him* go forwards."

That evening we go to bed early after dinner and for the first time in weeks Clyde falls into a deep sleep and he does not hear the heartbreaking puppy screams a few houses away, over the durawall. I twist and I turn for several hours and finally I give in and go to the bathroom to take a valium. Sister Nancy, who is educated as a nurse, has given me a portion of these tranquilizers for situations like this, when the brain refuses to relax and it is necessary to switch off the mind.

EARLY NEXT MORNING I START at the computer while there is still power and I write a formal memorandum to the Baron. I hand it over to Clyde when he eats his breakfast and after having read it, he signs it and puts it in his black leather attaché case. On his way out of the door, he holds me ever so tightly and for a long time. As soon as he has started the car, he speeds off, accelerating quickly towards the sign CHILDREN DRIVE SLOWLY, which he himself has produced in the factory.

DESPITE THE FACT THAT WE are completely without power the next couple of days, my emotional ability is lifted up. That is because our little chat has brought colour to Clyde's cheeks. He tells me that the Baron was rather shocked when he received our Memorandum concerning his breach of contract and he had asked, "Shall I go and talk to her?" But Clyde had said, "She is not interested in talk. She is only interested in money!"

I think it is fair to say that Clyde and I have been a good team and know how to use one another. Perhaps in this capacity and because Clyde tends to present me as a rather tough lady, I was some years ago first nicknamed *The General* by General Zhinavashe's nephew, Lovemore, who often asks Clyde, "And how is the General?" The name stuck and was soon enough used by the workers in the factory. When I first came to Africa, I was soon to discover that they had more respect for the military than the diplomatic corps, especially after the farm invasions and Mugabe's violent campaigns, so when anybody asks about my previous career, I just say, *military*. If they only knew that I cannot even pull the breech back to make Clyde's .38 Special ready. But then again, my theatrical talent is as useful as any weapon. Hopefully the Baron is now shaking in his shoes, but I have to keep him at bay; I will not meet him. Better act like the Parliamentary Commissioner, the last resort!

On the television they repeat the programme with zoologist and author Desmond Morris, with its message to return to the ancient ways when women ran the community, while the men go fishing and hunting. With men's passion for risk-taking, they have turned banks, investment companies and production companies, even whole countries into casinos – placing themselves and their families in mortal danger.

SATURDAY AFTERNOON WE WAVE AT Ian in No. 10 and he comes in for a cup of caffeine-free coffee. He thinks it is about time the complex invests in a huge generator, which can run the whole lot. However, he is aware that it might be difficult to get consent from all house owners, many of whom rent out. Mrs. Hanon in No. 3 cannot afford such an expense, although it is cheaper buying one big generator instead of investing in individual generators. But if we are going that route, we must get a noiseless one and the petrol has to be kept under lock in a storeroom, where gardener Rafael has no access. It would be too much of a temptation for resale if he had a key, especially when you know how he is boozing during week-ends.

"He was drunk this morning, so he comes up and asks, *Can I s-s-wash your car?*" tells Ian imitating Rafael's drunken drivel.

Salome is sweeping the grass with our German neighbour's inside broom. She is in her maid's uniform and the matching cap is covering her kinky hair. "How is Madam?" she asks with a smile.

"I am well. And how are you?" It is important to exchange these greetings with the locals, as it is very rude in their language only to say *Hello*. Salome asks if I would like some spring onions and some spinach. She wants to give it to me. I know she will not accept payment for these small favours because I have continued to pay her a small salary.

"It is no good with that inflammation," says Salome with a grim face.

"What inflammation? Have you got an infection? You are not sick, Salome?" I look at her, feeling worried.

"I am not sick, Madam. But the prices, they go up, up," she says.

"Oh, you mean *inflation*!" I say.

"Yes, Madam. Why it happens, Amai Tsitsi?" asks Salome using my African name.

"It happens when the budget does not balance and the government is importing more than it exports. Then you run at a loss and then we become poor. When we no longer produce anything in Zimbabwe and buy everything in South Africa, then the money box is empty and we even begin to owe lots of money. The same if you use more than your salary, Salome, and buy lots on credit, so you owe money left, right and centre and you own nothing. Then all the creditors make you into their slave. But when the government does it, they just print more bearer cheques and when they print more than the values in the mines and the soil, then the money has lost its value. If you run such an economy, it is like a cancerous tumour that grows and grows and eats away all the healthy tissue and you become very sick."

"Yes, Madam. It is inflammation. Just like I said," Salome looks as if she understood all along.

JOHNNY KATSANDE IS PASSING BY with daughter Anne in the cool clammy morning. He wants Clyde to sign some papers as a witness, so that she can get her passport. She is soon returning to Britain, where her mother lives. I have just made fresh orange and beetroot juice and offer them a glass.

"This is delicious!" says Anne looking healthy but hungry, so I give her a piece of toast knowing full well that young people are always hungry and these days their pantry is probably empty. She is a determined young lady planning to become a Bobby in England and although she did not pass the first round, she knows you just try again. Johnny's children are very European, but their good manners and warm personality stem from Africa.

CHAPTER 21

CANADIAN EVACUATION

An important message is hand delivered by the driver of the Canadian High Commission. They are having a town hall meeting at the official Canadian residence and all Canadians and their spouses must come. The meeting has been arranged in a hurry due to the growing political instability and we now have to prepare for evacuation in case the situation goes beyond our control. The whole arrangement bears the thumbprint of Roxanne Dube, who is the Canadian Ambassador, and with her elegant style and efficient planning she has organized the meeting outside in huge open tents. Inside the tents are big round tables and plenty of chairs. A special unit has been appointed to look after the children near the tennis court. The residence is a famous old building that used to be the Governor's house in the old Rhodesia. Roxanne is a stunning French Canadian young woman, who has become Ambassador at the prime in her life. Here she is not called High Commissioner, because Zimbabwe was kicked out of the Commonwealth. She is wearing a smart light spring green trouser suit with a formal jacket and she smiles warmly as we greet her. She has good face bones like Jacqueline Kennedy had and also the same petite figure, but she is much lighter in complexion and so is her hair.

"Where are you sitting? I will join your table," she says to Clyde and me. I choose a big table at the end, as you never know how many old friends would like to join in as well. Good choice! First Carolyn and Chris Chitsanga join us and they are one good example of a perfect marriage between black and white. He is professor emeritus in biochemistry at the Zimbabwe University and always in the forefront when there are chances of promoting science and technology.

Next Ann and Allan Ellis join the table. Lately, they have spoken a lot about a house on Prince Edward Island belonging to Allan's family, but they are afraid of settling down there, if they cannot find any work with satellite dishes and installing television for people, as they do here. Probably easier to find work in South Africa, says Allan. I assure him that with his qualifications he will quickly catch up with the latest in Canada and be in great demand. A warden is taking a seat at our table together with a new couple I have yet to meet. Once Clyde was a warden, but now since he has been sick, he cannot be responsible for others. Roxanne's husband Germany walks over to greet us and I introduce him to everybody. He is from Congo and looks a lot older than Roxanne. His afro-hair is almost grey.

Roxanne is like a TV hostess on the microphone and she speaks very warmly, "This is YOUR home!" She is referring to the official residence, but emphasizes that of course we do not expect events to happen like in Kenya, but then again, we have to be prepared. She tells us the big heavyweights from the Canadian Army came out to evaluate the situation and straight away they had discarded Harare International Airport, as that would be the first to be closed. Instead we would have to arrange to drive in different convoys to neighbouring countries like Zambia and Mozambique.

Roxanne then introduces every person who is responsible as a warden in case of an emergency, and each warden stands up, one by one informing which area they are covering. I now understand that Clyde and I come under Emerald Hill or the Avenues. Clyde has received a portfolio with more details about what we can take with us and what essentials of food and medicine we need to bring. At some point we will arrive at a safe haven and I am relieved to find out that all these details are not in the portfolio, because then we might as well put an ad in the *Herald Daily* newspaper, the mouthpiece of Mugabe's government and the only paper allowed now. Previously, it was my impression that the Canadian High Commission left most decisions to be handled by local Africans, but the aggravation of the situation has changed this tendency and I note with satisfaction that Roxanne is at the helm. It is quite clear that she is Commander-in-Chief.

The professor is holding hands with his wife under the table cloth and he does not try to hide that he is very worried about Zimbabwe. The two brothers Michael and David are sitting at the next table with their mother, Micheline, who is French-Canadian. She was married to the then-Finance Minister Chidzero when I came to Zimbabwe in the middle of the eighties, and the sons I know very well. They became members of our *Club de Célibataires*, which I started together with a French diplomat. Michael is laughing as he tells his mother how we had parties in their residence when she and her husband were away on official duties. Clyde knows Micheline and introduces me to her. In my ear he whispers that she is an opera-singer, played the piano, and in her youth was a ballerina. Now, why did he never think of bringing us together before? Especially when she is a widow and feeling very lonely. We are hooked on each other because of mutual interests and culminate in singing *coloratura,* not exactly in a discreet manner, rather loudly I think, because people at the other tables start starring at us. Before we depart, I ask her if she would like to come as a guest in the Music Club and perhaps then later, she might want to join as a member.

"I would like that very much," she says and suddenly she looks young and light-footed like the ballerina she once was.

On our way home Clyde says, "I've got to find another buyer; can't see the Baron paying for the whole business. I can always pay him back that little sum of money he paid, but definitely not the part which we ourselves worked for, that is if I get the full payment from this other guy."

"Have you got any specific person in mind?" I ask curiously.

"We met him at the airport in London, but at that time I said to him that I was not ready to sell." Clyde suddenly turns the steering wheel to one side because of a big pothole.

"But would it not just be a repetition of what we now see with the Baron, Clyde?" I ask, holding on tightly to the strap in the car roof.

"I would only sign over the shares if he pays it all up front," says Clyde. "No *pechena, pechena*, and no working your own ass off for nothing." He sounds very determined and I can understand that he is sick and tired with little here and little there, as the Africans mean when they say *pechena.*

"Yes, if that happens, you actually don't owe anything to the Baron, because he never lived up to the obligations in the contract. But for the sake of avoiding an arms struggle, better give him a part back," I suggest, looking at Clyde's profile. He looks far better after we talked about all the problems.

Later that night we watch the BBC news and they show cuts from a movie about Anne Boleyn. Clyde and I start laughing when we at the same time remark that both female actresses have these fat lips that seem to be in fashion these days, as if they all want African lips.

"They must be full of Botox," I suggest.

"All the movie stars now have fat lips and big mouths," says Clyde and then says the punch line, "I think they exercise them talking too much."

"Oh, no, Clyde, not that again. The same old joke about women talking too much. It is not even funny," I say slightly bored, and yawn behind my hand as if I am bored. But Clyde continues behind a knowing smile, "Perhaps I will try that one on the Montreal Comedy Show. Somebody else might find it is funny."

Now I begin to laugh until the tears are running down my cheeks and I cannot stop. Clyde has really saved up for this one.

THE FIRST WEDNESDAY EVERY MONTH we meet in the Music Club. Today we are meeting at Kathy Murphy's house on No. 25 Alfred Road. The road is tortuous and winding and one surprise after the other, but the mere fact that I am back in my old area makes me feel I am in the right spot. A handsome young man arrives at the iron gate together with a black Labrador and a brown and white Jack Russell.

"Are you having the Music Club meeting here?" I enquire.

"No," he says and the dogs are wagging their tails.

"Is it not Alfred Road?" I now ask.

"No, this is Kennedy Road. Go back to the T-junction and turn left."

I follow his directions and quickly find the Murphy residence. She is rather new in the Music Club and we have never been to her house before. The house has a homemade sign with the name MURPHY on it. I follow a long gravel road with grass in the middle. It is a rather large plot and full of big trees, many of them pine trees. I am relieved that there is still parking space and that it will not betoo difficult to reverse out. Then you can leave when you want. A path leads up to the kitchen. A young white teenage girl is dressed in a pink hippie skirt hanging low on her small hips. Her navel is pierced with a diamond belly-button. She is very sweet and pretty and holding a piccanin by the hand. "This is Tapiwa," she says introducing the little black boy.

"Hi, Tapiwa," I say and look at him while shaking his little hand. He has big soft eyes like a gazelle. Then I look around the kitchen and admire what I am seeing. "This is like Tuscany or the south of France, I love it!"

"Thank you. Here is the lounge."

The people living in this house are obviously very artistic and living in a very bohemian style. I like that style, a bit hippie. Many houses in Zimbabwe are very boring and without personality, as people live more outdoors like the Africans and they cannot be bothered about the atmosphere inside. Not like us in the European countries having to spend so much time indoors – for that reason our homes hold a lot of prestige. On the mantel over the fireplace is an impressive collection of smoking pipes in all shapes and sizes and on a stone column in front of the fireplace is displayed one of these ancient black manual typewriters that one grew up with.

Most of the members of the Music Club are already there, even Dr. Auchterlonie, who is a spinal surgeon from Scotland.

"Oh, so I was the only one first going to Kennedy Road?" My question makes them all laugh and I greet all my old friends. We wait for a while longer for the Japanese pianist Keiko, who has not yet arrived.

Shortly thereafter she arrives carrying a cake in her hand and that reminds me that I brought some biscuits. I take them out of my handbag and pass them over to the hostess. We all contribute as and when we feel like it and that has worked out perfectly for many years without turning the club into committee meetings and administrative orgies. Dawn, who originally started the club 24 years ago, is also there.

Hostess Kathy explains that her husband is the collector. Perhaps she does not realize it, but her feminine touch is all over. She has just been given a piano and we are all keen to hear her play on it so we can hear the sound. She is a brilliant pianist and plays a difficult classical piece without even glancing at any music sheets.

Today we are about to see a documentary on DVD about the famous cellist Yo-Yo Ma, who was born in Paris in 1955 to Chinese parents. His family moved to New York when he was five years old and already he could play both the violin and the viola, although it was around that time that he settled on the cello. Today we are about to hear about his training with choreographer Mark Morris and 15 classical ballet dancers. Yo-Yo Ma is playing a famous dancing ballet by Bach and the movie shows how the dancers follow the music, not the other way around. He admits his music gets inspiration from the way the dancers move. There are six parts in the dance and I decide to write it down so that I can later find out more about the meaning of this piece of music:

First there is *Prelude,* then follows *Allemande,* after that *Courante, Sarabande, Bourre and Dique*. Or said more plainly, first they play *ludo*, then they dance the old-fashioned way, then follows some quick-step, followed by Spanish flamenco and then back to the good old-fashioned way.

Although the music and the dance are captivating, I find this special tune by Bach rather plaintive, and sounding more like a requiem. But Ruby Atwort, who sits next to me and who in her younger days was a famous pianist, assures me that it is really one of Bach's typical dance songs. Ruby is a soft person with infinite kindness, much like Miss Moss, but she is less reserved. She and husband Hillary win all hearts and they never complain even though times are hard. Two of my friends have left the club: first it was June Rule, who lost her husband to colon cancer, and then it was Buddy, who left for Australia when her husband passed away. It all happened while Clyde and I were away.

After the DVD has finished, we all have tea and cake and circulate around to chat with everybody. Nyomi is here. She lives on our old street Montgomery Road, but she has stopped playing the flute. Japanese Keiko announces that the next meeting will be at her house, but due to the election, the meeting will be postponed until April 9th. That's a significant date for a Dane, one you never forget. Although I was born after the war, we were always reminded about the day when the German occupation of Denmark ended. I ask Keiko if I can bring Micheline for that meeting and explain what a terrific multi-artist she is. Already Keiko has welcomed Father John and Arlene whom I have also brought to her house. Keiko and Arlene had much fun playing and laughing together and remembering the strict examinations at Harare College of Music. Some students were a bundle of nerves and to calm down before the exam they would swallow a couple of beta-blockers. At the moment Arlene cannot come for our meetings as her and Harvey's lives have been totally jeopardized. The political insta-bility is the cause of this and forced them to rent out their beloved home and move into an apartment in the Avenues.

"Of course you must bring Micheline. Already too many people have left and we need new members," says Keiko with enthusiasm.

As I drive through the gate in Belgravia, I see Salome weeding out the cobblestones. We wave at each other. For a while I sit in the beautiful backyard that is full of birdsong and I watch the colourful birds who remain on the branches because I am still and quiet as a mouse. From inside I have often studied them and looked them up in the bird dictionary: the yellow weaver, the blackbird, the Hugelin robin, and the Hooper. Sometimes there are also doves and humming birds. Today I see the silky blue bee-eaters with their long beaks.

The golden Joburg pine tree in the corner is getting its spring green colour after Rafael and Givemore have pruned it, as it was growing right into the electric fence on top of the wall. If I continue sitting very quietly, all the birds will come by. We forget how important that birdsong is. In Mozambique just after the war all the birds had disap-peared and they never heard birdsong or the buzzing of insects, as the war had driven them away. At least in Zimbabwe the birds are still singing. But for how long? If it comes to war, the warbling of birds will slowly decrease and in the end completely disappear. The lull be-fore the storm. Perhaps there is no striving against fate. As Diya says, "What will be will be. When the time is ripe, it will happen no matter what you do." But I cannot really believe that we are doomed to such fatality. If I observe those alarm bells ahead of time, I can take charge and change that fate; even when the dice is thrown, the game cannot just be over. We ought to leave, while the birds are still singing.

CHAPTER 22

ALL KINDS OF CROOKS

" B e ready by 6 o'clock tonight! We are going for prize-giving at Chapman's Golf Club, where they will serve all your favourite Indian snacks," says Clyde. As always I am ready ahead of time, but Clyde is late as always. When we arrive at the parking area, Clyde drives around in circles looking for a spot, until finally he finds one. Having climbed the wide staircase with soft carpets in green patterns, holding on to the railing, we see the whole room completely full. There are no chairs in sight; everybody at this Nomads event is standing, apart from a few lucky ones who arrived early. Even the high bar tables, which were supposed to have comfortable bar chairs upholstered in soft textile even on the back rest, have been placed as lonely soldiers along the wall and seem to be used for stacking plates, and a few people are resting their arms on the back behind the plates.

"There is another party downstairs and they have pinched our chairs," Clyde shrugs his shoulders while eyeing a couple of golf buddies. They stand by a square table and have a place for their drinks. We are invited to join them. I recognize one of the guys. *Je me souviens*, the sentence passes through my head, like that little warning they have put on the number plates on the cars in Quebec. There he is, that bastard jeweller who once invited us for a Christmas party, just because he thought he could make us spend a lot of money buying jewellery, because he was no friend of Clyde's. Among his other guests that day were Teri Schmith and his wife Ulla. They are close friends, thick as thieves. All over his living room the jeweller had exhibited pieces of his ugly and boring jewellery, inside huge glass vitrines, like they were some museum pieces. Through the glass you could see he had labeled them at inflated prices.

The little devil in me peeps out, as I ask, "You are the jeweller, correct?" which he confirms as if it is flattery.

I continue, "I just remember how your prices were completely ridiculous, so instead I went to Alaska. There I got what I wanted, at lower prices and much higher carat gold." A thunderous laughter comes from the guys in the circle, when I shake one hand full of bangles.

In an instant his confidence has disappeared, the boomerang returned long after my throw, when I had forgotten about it. Justice sometimes comes like that when you least expect it. One fine day that same arrow will shoot his friend Teri. Several years ago, Clyde helped Johannes to sell his coffin factory to Johnny Katsande. The latter was an honest man and paid with a cheque in the local currency. At that time the inflation had not yet sky-rocketed. The cheque was deposited into Teri Schmith's bank account and it was agreed that he immediately should transfer the equivalent amount in pound sterling to Johannes's account in England. For unknown reasons Johannes had left for South Africa never to return. Johnny had issued the cheque in Teri's name not knowing that he was a scumbag and a crook, but having met his wife with teeth like elephant tusks, I was not surprised. Clyde was never suspicious like me and neither was Johannes, because they all knew each other from the golf club. From the beginning I had disliked Teri, arriving one day in a show-off red sports car and looking like some *sugar daddy*. Later I was not surprised to hear that Teri just ran off with all the money instead of merely earning a currency commission for changing it into pound sterling.

About three years ago Clyde and Johnny tried to put Teri behind bars to force him to pay out the amount. They succeeded in finding an undercover police detective by the name of Zack. He drove around town in a grey Dodge without number plates and reputedly had a license-to-kill. One night he entered the Schmiths' home and put Teri in handcuffs, after which he was put into solitary confinement at Marlborough Police Station over the week-end. During his stay in police custody Barrister-at-Law Milton passed by and got a confession from him. He is a Shona lawyer and one of Clyde's trusted friends. In any case it would have been to no avail for Teri to deny the theft, because Johnny's two cheques had entered Teri's bank account.

However, the case never went to Court and Teri did not stay long in jail. Probably, somebody paid a bribe. Whether Teri is still driving his ugly red sports car, I cannot confirm, but to this day Johannes has never recovered his payment for 50,000 pounds sterling, and he lost the coffin factory.

Over the years I have met many of these fraudsters – many of them from the distinguished Nomads golf club association which Clyde belongs to, eager to be seen to play for charity events. They always behave like royalty on a red carpet with their fine speeches and distinguished bearing, black formal club jackets full of badges over their trousers with knife-edge creases. They are always married to small gentle women living in their shadow. All right, there is nothing wrong with the purpose of the club, and there is a black sheep in every flock I suppose and certainly there were among the distinguished club members. Rotten characters like Teri, yes, and then there was Mat Horn, who borrowed 50,000 US dollars from Clyde and only by vigorous arm-twisting from my side did he pay half of it back. The rest of it was never paid back, because Mat Horn knew that we would not dare to use the borrower's note which he had signed, and take him to court. Many take advantage of the situation and of the corrupt and useless legal system in Zimbabwe. Notably, the law prohibits us from having foreign currency.

Paul Shortly was another friend of Clyde who was tempted beyond his power of resistance. When he got the chance, he stole the winning ticket because suddenly he stood with large sums of money in his hands. As a lawyer, he was trusted by the old white folks, who had sold their houses in order to leave the country and they believed he would make the currency exchange and pay the equivalent amount on their overseas bank account. Instead he filled his own pockets, transferred all monies to his private account and immigrated to America.

I am returning from my dream world and find myself back in the restaurant at Chapman's Golf Club without chairs. A professional golf player named Stewart stands next to me and states, "I just swallowed a chicken bone or perhaps it was fish."

"Did it go down?" I ask, worried.

"No, it is still here." Stewart points to his jaw bone behind the ear.

"Take some lemon. That will dissolve the bone," suggests Clyde.

Stewart goes to the men's room and returns. "I can still feel it, but it does not prevent me from breathing," he says.

"Just don't get drunk and forget about it," I admonish. "The Lufthansa director living here, his wife swallowed a chicken bone and ignored it. It got stuck down in her chest and she died two months later. Freeda, the Swiss ambassador's wife, also swallowed a chicken bone and had to fly to Joburg as an emergency to get it out."

The big strong man with sandy-coloured hair is beginning to look worried. Stewart understands now that this is serious and he promises to seek medical advice. When he gets ready to leave, Clyde and I also leave. We only had a single glass of white wine each. Clyde carries his prize winnings, a set of three items from Nestle: Nesquick, Cerevita and two litres of fruity Fling Cream Soda Syrup.

"Give it to somebody," I suggest to Clyde. "It is all so unhealthy."

"Don't you dare complain," warns Clyde with his index finger pointed towards me and continues, "Ready to go?"

I loosen up my red cardigan tied around the waist as a belt over the blue Esprit designer jeans from Canada. The engine of the blue Mercedes starts immediately, as Clyde turns up the sound of the music. As he reverses out from the parking lot, he plays *Life in the Fast Lane* by the Eagles.

Back in Belgravia I open up a tin of mussels and toast two slices of bread. After the episode with yet another victim of swallowing a chicken bone, we lost the appetite for more Indian snacks. With all the hardship, there are no longer any caterers throwing anything away, and that is why some of the carcass is often inside the meat you are eating. You can easily swallow it without even noticing.

Clyde tells me that the jeweller, who was captain for Chapman's Golf Club, committed fraud and was fired when he was found out. He fiddled by paying the manager an equivalent amount in American dollars lent to the insurance company Old Mutual after the parallel rate, without the Board of Directors knowing anything about it. The manager was fired and had to leave the job. It was a black man who blew the whistle.

Suddenly, Clyde stops talking. He turns on the news, but decides to watch TV in the bedroom. Just as we have locked the heavy iron

gate to the bedroom, the telephone rings and we can only answer the
call in the lounge. Clyde starts rattling with his keys and opens the
security gate. Stewart's girlfriend Alex is on the phone. She got out
that piece of chicken bone under his jaw bone with a pair of tweezers.
When she looked down into his throat with a torch, she could see the
bone sticking out with about one centimetre, but as she pulled it out,
it was five centimetres long! We are both relieved and lie in bed back
to back touching each other. Clyde does not even turn on the TV, but
falls asleep quickly, while I listen for the first baby screams from the
little puppies.

IT IS SUNDAY AND CLYDE is playing golf. I go to see my Hindustani
girlfriend Diya, as it is her birthday. She has invited ten people and everybody has brought along a dish. I have brought a green salad. Only
one couple is drinking wine, the rest of us are drinking alchohol-free
drinks. I cannot drive and drink and I am just as happy and funny
without it. Besides some of the spicy Indian dishes actually taste better without wine and Diya's food can really take your breath away,
even from the more hardened curry-eaters. Typical for Diya she has
invited many new friends and although they are all warm and nice, I
just do not feel like making new friends. Besides, I want to get home
before darkness falls. The shadows are already long, and as I walk to
my Mercedes I hear the sound of drumbeats, a sound that is able to
travel very far. It is carried from the mountains behind Domboshawa.
The sound of the drums becomes more and more intense for each
sequence. I am hearing the voice of Africa. With the drum they send
news to one another. That drum will tell you everything from the
cradle to your deathbed and the important things that happen in between, be it trauma or accidents and happy events too. The drum will
deliver all the messages. From village to village they communicate in
this way, deftly beating on the stretched drumhead.

As I turn up the sound on the car radio I hear the ZBC news,
managed solely by the government, as the free press is gagged and
all you get now is this drivel of a propaganda machine. Speaking in
the Shona dialect the female announcer is broadcasting in English

that *President Mugabe has signed The Indigenization and Economic Empowerment Bill. The bill stipulates that indigenous Zimbabweans should hold at least 51% in all business institutions and all other economic activities in the country.* Of course we had all been warned, when in September the bill passed through the House of Assembly, but perhaps we all thought it had a long way to go, first through the Senate and then Mugabe had to sign. Perhaps it would never happen. I feel that the news has given me quite a turn, and inside I start feeling anger.

The sky is still light and as I enter the house I walk through the lounge to open the veranda door, but the bee-eater is sitting on the door handle looking into the glass as if it is a mirror. Instead of disturbing the creature I sit down at the round dining table and only when the bird has flown away do I enter that part of the lounge close to the veranda door. It is dark when I turn on the TV.

CNN has a text line under their news saying *"Mugabe's bill compulsory for take-over of all companies."* Now there is no going back; it is going to happen. How come we all thought that Mugabe had second thoughts? That he somehow wanted to appeal to the Western countries? But it is exactly this kind of psychological agonizing terror that he enjoys.

When Clyde comes home, I tell him about the bill, but he refuses to believe it.

"It is only foreign-owned companies like Barclay's Bank, the mines and the other bigwigs," he says in a brush-off manner as if I have not understood the whole issue.

"It is also on CNN," I say carefully, but he keeps denying that it has happened, does not even watch CNN and only the next day, when the government-controlled newspaper announces the bill with bold headlines, does he abandon his position.

"We all saw it coming," he says lamely and almost with relief, as you react when you have feared the worst for a long time. He continues with a sense of reality, "He does it just before the election to win votes. Then they have another free license to go on a rampage and kill and maim us all like they did to the farmers."

"Yes, we are the goat to be sacrificed. We are the bait as sure as the worm on the fishing hook. He enjoys this game of torment and tease. I can almost hear him saying, *Look around. All this I will give you; all you have to do is attack the whites!"* I shake my head and continue, "No, Clyde, I don't believe you anymore when you say that he is not a racist."

"Personally he is not a racist. For him it is about being pragmatic and winning the election. He does not care who is in his way. He just has to get rid of any obstacles, whether they are white or his own people. Just to stay in power. He will pay any price for staying in power." Clyde understands this man's tactic, because he had himself earned the nickname *coyote.*

EDGAR AND TUT'S TELEPHONE IS not working. Clyde promises to call the fault complaint service, but that number is also out of order. Finally, Clyde gets contact with another complaint service and, having investigated the matter thoroughly, he finds out that the reason for Edgar's phone not working is because it has been taken over by the South African Embassy. This has happened despite the fact that the account is not in arrears and Edgar has even paid 300 million in advance towards calls. Clyde advises him to take action quickly, or he will permanently lose his number. The problem is that there are not enough cables for new numbers, so if you lose your present number, you will never get a new one. The grid system is so overloaded that for a new customer to get a telephone, there is a long waiting list and it might take years before you get a telephone, if it ever happens.

That incident has made me suspicious concerning our own telephone, as we receive quite a number of wrong calls. The phone is ringing and the same happens.

"Can I speak to Tapatwa?" asks the voice, sounding like an indigenous person.

"Which number have you dialed?" I ask and am a little surprised to be given my own number. The woman on the other end of the line is a soft-spoken Shona.

"What company do you want?" I now ask.

"UTC," she says with the velvet voice.

"Then you have a wrong number. We are not UTC," I inform her.

That same morning I begin to make a list of all the mysterious telephone calls that I receive, where they actually state that they have the right number, but wish to speak to somebody else. Are we perhaps paying for somebody else, who is using our line? When I discuss this with Clyde, he says he is absolutely sure this is the case.

One hour later Dr. Vick arrives from Masvingo. He has come to Harare to collect the ambulance, which Clyde had arranged to get repaired. He wants to invite us out for dinner the same evening. His designer-stubble has now grown into a long beard and he has certainly lost his designer-look. After all, a long beard is easier to maintain when you have no power.

"Would you like some green tea? Or perhaps some breakfast?" I ask because we are still in the midst of our breakfast ritual.

"No, thank you. Just a slice of bread toasted," says Dr. Vick.

We talk about the dramatic crash of the economy that we have experienced since we last saw him and the sky-rocketing prices for our daily needs. Dr. Vick has worked out a calculation and come to the conclusion that if in fact we have price increases every two weeks, the true inflation rate is 6.8 billion per cent, because we all tend to forget that they (meaning the government) took away 3 zeroes more than a year ago.

"Mugabe came to see our mission," says the doctor and carries on, "but if he would only come more often, we would have better roads to drive on. You know they asphalted that stretch he had to pass on and it gave a lot of work in our district."

HALF AN HOUR LATER BROTHER Paul arrives together with an old priest, who has just been operated on for cataracts. Clyde wants to know everything about how he is feeling and the procedure itself, because he is himself suffering in one eye, so much that he can hardly see. The treatment Clyde had to go through with both chemo and radiation was a tough job on both body and soul, and resulted in a cataract on one eye. The priest tells Clyde openly about every detail of his surgery and says it was actually the famous eye doctor Dr.

Guramanturu in Harare who operated on him. The irony is that our local Dr. Guramanturu is a surgeon in very high esteem who happens to travel often to Edinburgh to operate there. He also goes into the wild African bush to operate on poor Africans without charge. It so happened that a friend of Clyde's had travelled to Scotland to be operated there, because he wanted to avoid being operated on by a black, but fate would have it that it was Dr. Guramanturu from Harare who carried out the procedure.

"I know him," I say. "Once he checked my eyes, when I felt a kind of pressure in one eye, but nothing was wrong. He even advised me never to be tempted to have that laser-surgery, because in my case it would only be a trade-off. Even if I would be able to drive a car without wearing glasses, instead I would end up having to wear glasses when I am reading."

"He is considered one of the best worldwide," says Brother Paul.

"And you know what? He does ballroom dancing internationally. He took part in Latin American rhythms in Argentina and elsewhere and he loves the tango. When I was in his consultation room, he asked me, *How you keep fit like this?* And I said to him that I dance Egyptian belly dance. That was how he told me about himself," I tell them enthusiastically.

"Not many doctors like him are left here," says Clyde.

When I serve the German coffee, which Sweet Rit has given us, Brother Paul inquires if the Reserve Bank has started paying for the scotch carts. But no, not yet, and now with the new black empowerment law that permits the looting of 51% of our shares, the whole situation is rather hopeless. Brother Paul has himself felt the pinch, because at the very beginning of February they transferred 20,000 pound sterling from Ireland to Reserve Bank Harare and now, 45 days later, they cannot find it. After having investigated, they said it had gone to Reserve Bank in South Africa, but nobody seemed able or willing to try and retrieve it.

DURING THE FOLLOWING DAYS OUR situation is worsening and I can no longer use my plastic card from Barclays in the supermarkets

TM, Bon Marché or OK. In all the places I get the same reply, "Our machine is not working!" Is this some kind of conspiracy? Are they all trying to force us to pay for everything in cash? Is it the banks, or is it the supermarkets? Clyde says it is the supermarkets. He thinks the managers and the staff are trying to fiddle, and that they can only do that when they are paid in cash. That is why they destroy the machines. Only TM Supermarket in Borrowdale allows me to write out a cheque, but they only have a few of the items on my shopping list.

"It is getting more and more desperate," I tell Clyde that evening. "The prices are horrific and the staff is getting more and more cheeky."

Clyde is in his own world and does not listen. Instead he says, "We get paid next Tuesday."

"By whom?" I ask.

"Reserve Bank. See this invoice from the Baron." I bend towards the document he is holding and quickly read the content.

"Is that the total sum?" I ask.

"Yes," says Clyde with shiny eyes, "and when we change that into US, it makes $200,000 to $300,000. Far below the cost price, of course, but I can't be bothered anymore, if only I get a little out of it. Do you know that one beer now costs 40 million? One beer!"

"Yes, or more," I say as I remember that in some shops they cost 80 million per bottle. Clyde measures price increases in beer or other masculine products. I measure price increases on daily goods such as veggies, toilet paper, chickens and eggs.

IN A WAY IT IS a relief that we are forced to eat out most of the time, because I am sick and tired of cooking under such conditions. We meet Mano and Zsa Zsa at the China Town Restaurant. Both of us bring along bottles of wine, which we ask the waiter to open, as then we only have to pay corkage for drinking our own wine. We are thrilled to be together and they tell us about their last stay in Lyon in France. The political subject is unavoidable, especially after Simba Makoni has entered the stage as a presidential candidate.

"What does he know?" asks Mano shaking his head, "He is not even an economist. He has a bachelor degree in chemistry only and during all those years, when he was a gang member, did he ever object to their policies?"

"But he is greatly favoured by most people in the West," I say to test him and I am very happy that Mano has the political maturity to look behind all the staging. Just like Clyde. That is why they are buddies.

"How is Muffin?" I ask Zsa Zsa referring to their Yorkshire Terrier and to change the delicate subject of politics.

"Fine, he loves to be back – he does not like Rome," says Zsa Zsa, laughing. "In Rome we only have a Philippine maid, so it becomes very boring for him. Here in Harare he has lots of staff to bark at. Besides, now we have found out what is wrong with him, why he did not put on weight."

"What was the diagnosis?" asks Clyde seemingly interested in the dog's welfare, but also because he was behind the adoption of Muffin.

"He got an ulcer from stress," explains Mano to help Zsa Zsa, as she is not as confident in the English language, "but now they are able to cure it with penicillin. This is quite a new treatment."

"I know all about it," says Clyde while pouring some more wine in our glasses. "It is not only the animals they can cure like that. An Australian doctor made this amazing discovery and during a medical conference in Europe he injected himself with the disease and then cured it afterwards with penicillin to prove the case. It caused quite a stir."

Into the restaurant walks quite a mismatched couple, but they know Clyde and me and wave to us. It is an older lady, who used to be a filing clerk at the embassy after I left. Her face looks very old from many years of boozing and smoking. I have not seen her for many years. She is in the company of a Dane, who used to visit Zimbabwe on a regular basis. He was once living here, as he was a truck driver for a Danish NGO.

"Who is he?" asks Zsa Zsa.

"Just some consular case I had to deal with after I left the embassy," I answer and briefly explain, "He ended up in jail and they asked if I could help with the court case. It should have been a simple matter, but instead of weeks it lasted over many months. It is a long story I must tell you about some other time. He is not a criminal, but he had bad luck falling in love with a local prostitute from Bulawayo and he believed she was a model. That love story really got him in deep trouble."

CLYDE TURNS ON THE TV as soon as we arrive at the townhouse. Pope Benedict is in the international news speaking about the seven sins and about the destruction and greed which the global economy is causing.

"What did I tell you?" I ask Clyde. "Just what I have said for several years. Now the Pope is saying the same."

Clyde does not react. He is in his own lonely world of despair and at a loss what to do. There is some sort of wall around him and nobody can encroach on his territory. The TV screen is just a focus point, which he stares at like the dancer does in order not to lose his balance.

NEXT DAY I PHONE SISTER Sweet Rit and ask her about the seven sins, as it was delivered ever so fast on the TV screen and I did not get all the points.

"There are seven deadly sins," explains Sweet Rit kindly. "The first one is *pride*, number 2 is *envy*, number 3 is *gluttony*, number 4 is *lust* and the fifth sin is *wrath*. Number 6 is *greed*. The last deadly sin is *sloth*, meaning laziness or avoidance."

"I never knew pride was a deadly sin," I tell Sweet Rit. "When I grew up they always said you must have pride."

"A little pride is necessary in life," admits Sweet Rit. "That is not wrong. It is the ugly pride, the one that is evil and arrogant, that is a deadly sin. It is the root of all other sins. You will need humility to fight it."

"I do not quite understand the word *gluttony*, do you know another word for that?"

"It means when you do something too much, like eating and drinking too much. But it also means overindulging in other things. Such people cannot draw the line, they constantly need to be stimulated one way or the other. When you don't know your limits, then you are wasteful," explains the wise old nun.

"I am also unsure about what *wrath* means," I confess.

"It simply means anger. Just remember *The Grapes of Wrath*. Some of us get more angry than others, and few of us are able to stifle anger completely. Sometimes we turn hostile instead of being angry, but it is basically the same thing. The worst sins are those of pride and envy, because they are spiritual sins. Lust, gluttony and sloth are also bad sins, but as they are weaknesses of the flesh, they are less bad." Sweet Rit has such a soft voice that I wonder if she ever gets cross.

CHAPTER 23

ELECTION

We are approaching Easter, but this year it is of no significance. The only important words passing our lips were *the coming election*. I have started to stock up, but hopefully we will not have lengthy power cuts or any frozen food will all be wasted and I will commit the third deadly sin! During the last month or so I have had a bit of luck. Having visited all the different supermarkets I have spent 1.8 billion. Gardener Rafael appears from behind the Acacia tree pushing the wheelbarrow. He stops to greet me.

"Rafael, how much do you and Givemore now earn?" I ask.

"Only one hundred million, Madam. There is no way we can live on that," he answers.

I feel ashamed and give him all the money I have in my cosmetic purse to share between him and Givemore, who is standing close by.

"God bless you, Madam," they chant.

When Clyde comes home I ask him if we can take up the issue of the gardeners' salaries with the chairman. Their salary is calculated according to the American dollar every month. Clyde agrees with me that it is too low, but says it is not our problem.

"Stay away, we are on our way out," he warns.

When I go through all my purchases I find only one luxury item, namely a bottle of Portuguese red wine for 450 million. The rest is longlife milk, fruit and vegetables, oats and one chicken. A chicken now costs 60 million. I have a small filet roast in the freezer and I take it out to defrost. Then I clean the mushrooms. We are having a small dinner party, just the four of us, as Tut and Edgar are coming over. The menu is stroganoff with onions and mushrooms, as it is a dish you can stretch a little and it is rather simple to start preparing and does not need a lot of work after the guests have arrived. We are having mashed potatoes with the stroganoff.

Tut brings along some delicious homemade snacks, which we enjoy with our *sundowner*. For dessert we have prune-and-apple pudding, even though it is not one of Clyde's favourite dishes. "It gives me the runs!" he warns.

EASTER MONDAY WE HAVE INVITED Mano and Zsa Zsa for lunch at the elegant Meikles Hotel's Pavillion Restaurant. We arrive five minutes early and as I find out that our table is not very good, despite the fact that it was booked ahead of time, I ask the waiters to turn it around so that all four can sit and enjoy the rose garden. The waiters are paying attention and working very hard. It looks as if they have been on a crash course in serving us. Normally, they just stand and wait.

In the wine bag we have a nice cool French Chablis, and Mano puts a bottle of Italian red wine on the table. The waiters immediately fetch wine glasses, as we order mineral water. No doubt they are specially trained for the election. The maître d' recommends that we do not wait too long to go to the buffet, as a big party is arriving. For that reason we dish up both the starter and the main course and walk with two plates each back to our table. Zsa Zsa has never tasted *sadza* before, that special maizemeal porridge which is the staple food in Zimbabwe. We tell her to eat it with brown sauce over it.

"Bodie, it tastes really good! Do you know how to make it? *Come si dice,* Mano, *sadza?*" asks Zsa Zsa thrilled.

"It is not even difficult," I say, "buy the rough maize meal, not the refined one, it is more healthy. Then take two cups of water and just before it boils, add half a cup of maize meal, stir it around and when it boils, put a lid on the pot and turn down the heat to simmer for 3 to 5 minutes. Do not stir during that time, but after 5 minutes you stir a lot and then you add a little more maize meal and keep stirring. That is all. It only takes 15 minutes to make. It tastes extra good if made over an open fire."

Everyone enjoys the well-prepared dishes and as we return for an extra bite, I notice how really elegant Zsa Zsa looks in her navy blue designer-suit from Italy, the discreet slit in her skirt showing off her shapely legs.

Just after we have fetched our dessert and the waiters have served the coffee, the large party arrives. It is a mixed group of men, women and their many children, all dressed up like they are going to some wedding. African men in pinstriped dark suits and the women's dresses in a variety of colours, but all of them are overweight and move around slowly because of their heaviness. The children run back and forth between the dining tables and the buffet table to hear the sound of their new shoes, and especially the girls enjoy clacking their heels on the tiles. Although most of them are only around eight years of age, they are wearing high-heeled shoes like their mothers. The party is taking in the atmosphere of calm harmony at the best hotel in Harare, and together with Zsa Zsa and Mano we laugh about the whole situation. It is just too obvious that the party consists of outside election observers and already they have given the governing party top grades. Even before the election has taken place, it has been named *the harmonized election*.

"Mano, I like Meikles Hotel. Why not stay here during election?" Zsa Zsa suggests and continues with a roguish twinkle in her eye, "What about the bridal suite, Mano?"

"I know that suite," I say, "once I rented the bridal suite as a wedding present for a good friend of mine, who wanted a special wedding in Africa and he asked me to host it. He was a TV producer in Denmark and became famous when they landed on the Moon."

"What was his name?" asks Mano.

"Joachim Jerrik," I tell them, but apparently he was only famous in Denmark, because they have never heard about him.

After coffee we leave the restaurant together and take the lift down to the underground parking to see Mano's new Mercedes sports car. It is coal-black inside and out and with left-hand drive as he is going to take it with him to Rome.

"Try and sit in it," says Zsa Zsa. "It is completely like an aeroplane. I am going crazy!" Her laughter is the sound of bells and very contagious, she is all kindness. As we drive away in separate cars, for a while we keep waving to one another in the city traffic until we go in opposite directions. The last thing I see is Zsa Zsa's thick dark curls, which do not even move the slightest, despite the wind in an open sports car.

WE HAVE ENTERED THE ELECTION week. Only on Tuesday March 25th do they allow me to pay with a cheque in Bon Marché and I am able to hoard for the election taking place on Saturday. That date is to become known to the world media, *the 29th of March, 2008*. Clyde and I do not vote, as we are guests in Africa and whether or not we are allowed to put a cross on that ballot list, we choose not to. It is better to stay away from politics and very dangerous to be opinionated and express your thoughts.

For the last couple of weeks I have tried to warn Clyde that it is unsafe to go out on election day and the days after the event, but he is provocative and says, "I go to the factory as usual!" Only when the Baron speaks to him and warns him to stay inside for two weeks after, does he listen and gives a reluctant consent and promises to *wait and see*. Oranges now cost 31 million a kilo, mangoes 33 million, avocadoes 18 million and a small filet roast weighing 800 grams only is priced at 164 million. The mushrooms are more than 18 million for 200 grams and the 3 tomatoes are 15 million. It is apparent that all the products are not meant for the peasants, even though the products are produced in Zimbabwe. Gardener Rafael walks to my garden gate and tells me that they just got their salary. It has gone up from 100 to 300 million per month.

CLYDE IS COUGHING AGAIN AND not just in the morning. It is all those signs that paralyze you and make your heart pound.

"It is that flu that is going around. They all have it," says Clyde.

The next days I am his private nurse and I serve him hot toddies with tea, lemon and honey. In between Clyde sneaks a little rum into the toddies. He takes echinacea supplements twice a day and stays in bed or floats on the peach leather recliner. When he wakes up at night I also automatically wake up. Sometimes he likes a toddy there and then to relieve his sore throat.

SUDDENLY THE FATAL ELECTION IS taking place and it is not being postponed. As Clyde is sick I do not have to restrict him; he stays at home voluntarily. That is until he begins to feel better. Sunday – the day after election – he drives over to one of his buddies to play poker. He comes home after 8 hours of the game and has won 600 million. I am cross and ready to blow my top, but instead of reacting I have gone to bed, putting his dinner under a microwave plate. Here you are looking after your man like he is an infant and then he is totally irresponsible with his health.

I take one of the valiums which Sister Nancy has given me. At least it will make me fall asleep so I do not have to look at that stupid husband of mine.

MONDAY AFTER ELECTION DAY, MORGAN Tsvangirai, the leader of the opposition party, is seen on the international TV channels and his spokesperson, Tendai Biti, announces that *Morgan Richard Tsvangirai has won the election.* Although the result has not yet been declared by the election committee, Biti tells us that it is no secret as the election results are hanging on the outside of buildings where the elections were held and he adds that the international media has heard and seen about the election results. Clyde and I have also on CNN seen these blue sheets with vote counts hanging on different buildings, such as schools and those round houses characteristic of the rural areas. By adding up all the results from every polling station, the opposition party has ascertained that the presidential election finished at 50.3 per cent to Tsvangirai and only 46 per cent to President Mugabe. There is a roaring laughter when Tendai Biti hints that perhaps the result of the election is to be found on the black market, as no official declaration from the election committee has been forthcoming.

The following days there is a pregnant silence and no comments from the governing ZANU-PF party or Mugabe. Is it really possible that after 28 years of dictatorship, a new President will take over? If you believe in miracles, then it is possible. The first spokesman of the government is Bright Matonga and he also speaks on behalf of their

ZANU-PF party. Soon we are to hear his voice repeatedly on the local and the international media and my gorge rises when his barefaced impudence and cheeky juvenile arrogance is broadcasted. He is assuring us that the results of the election are indeed very complicated, as we have had both parliamentary election, election to the senate and election of the President. According to the rules of the SADC – Southern African Development Community – you have six days to declare the official results.

During the first days you see the broad smiles on the African faces and a display of the open palm as a greeting, which means that they have voted for the opposition MDC party. Tuesday becomes Wednesday and Wednesday soon becomes Thursday, but still we have heard nothing from President Mugabe and we do not know whether he is still in the country. In the international media they are speculating that perhaps he has fled into exile, but we living here know better. He will never surrender power and he will always have absolute power. Thursday there are still no election results being declared officially, but we see more and more of Deputy Minister Bright Matonga from the Ministry of Information. His information shows clearly the intentions from the Politburo, a political broadside of 24 persons close to Mugabe, no longer even trying to hide the fact that they will use the power of the army to secure stability. Matonga warns the opposition that they have committed an offence by speaking publicly on the election before it has been officially announced and that is a betrayal against your country. ZANU-PF considers treason a very serious affair, he adds.

We wait till Friday, which is the last day for the election results, but nothing happens. Mugabe and his cronies are so confident in their position of power that they feel above the law, including their own laws and those of SADC, which they are a member of. In between we see the South African President Mbeki visiting Britain for a meeting about "good governance." In the press they warn us that the programme is tight due to other important points on their agenda, which results in a down-grading of Zimbabwe so that it receives no particular attention. On the other hand it is completely ridiculous that the West puts trust in Mbeki going against Mugabe. During all the years he has clearly demonstrated his diplomatic softness, just like all the other African SADC leaders who have already expressed their admiration for the newly-held harmonized election, despite the results which have been published and despite Mugabe's open threats about violence and terror against his own population.

My sister manages to get through on the telephone from Denmark and she tells me that in our home country there is hardly any news about our situation, but she is using an Internet link I gave her and in this way she is able to follow the development. I tell her how we are all anxiously awaiting the official election results, but we are afraid that the long delay indicates that they are trying to manipulate. Yet still we just hope for some miracle. There is no doubt in my mind that our ruler will never relinquish the reins of government to the opposition, not unless he loses the support of the army chiefs. That is very unlikely, as they would have too much to lose under a new government. The only problem the generals have is that they have not paid far enough down into the lower ranks, and they could face a major revolt. Up until now the people have only revolted at the ballot box, but feelings are running high and they have the attention of the world press.

The situation could easily escalate into a full-blown civil war, because it is a question of how much patience the populace has left with all the provocations from the rulers. The more suppressed they have become, the less they have to lose. According to the SADC rules, all the election results should be plastered on the outside buildings, I tell my sister. There are roughly 60 polling stations and if the opposition has been able to read all the results and add them all together, then there is no doubt that "the Archangel has lost." Many people refer to Mugabe as *the Archangel* because of his middle name Gabriel. However, none of us can imagine Mugabe ever admitting to defeat. He would rather start another war, I tell my sister. The Africans have not got the same logic as us and they have no system of double-checking election fraud, so the rulers may continue playing cat and mouse and create tension to trigger off some rebellion, which they can then quell.

One must admire that everybody has moved around without saying anything, without displaying their T-shirts with party symbols. Since the election day they have carried on with their daily lives as if nothing has happened. But it is a question of how long before their patience is exhausted.

Today it is Thursday and long past when the results should have been announced. Still we have no election results from the presidential election, only for the parliamentary election, but this negative election result only stimulates the anger of the rulers to force the masses to toe the line. According to the SADC rules, tomorrow is the last day for declaring the final election results. The world news media, from the American CNN to the British channels BBC and SKY, have made reports of election fraud, as it has been proved that dead people's names have been used on the registration lists to promote the governing party. They had even found the burial places of these people whose names were used to win the election.

The nuns have said that what we are experiencing is the *lull before the storm*, and if it gets serious, Clyde and I must come and stay at the Convent, as they are secured like all the embassies. We are all fearing an escalation like happened in Kenya. As more news is coming in from BBC and SKY, I end the telephone conversation with my sister. From the highest ranks they are threatening the people, and the military and the police are filling the streets. Still no results from the election committee and the opposition party has gone to the Supreme Court to force them to publish the result, but at the same time the governing party has sued the opposition party, accusing them of having bribed members of the election committee. All these court cases are totally useless, when you consider that all the Judges are appointed by the Archangel.

Morgan Tsvangirai has in the meantime requested help from the United Nations – another useless action when you take into consideration that they would need the approval of President Mugabe if they were to come here. Right from the start our international organizations are rendered powerless with bureaucratic rules hindering justice and virtually ensuring that blood will flow in our streets and in the villages. Besides, the Security Council of the United Nations will be on the side of the Zimbabwe government because China and Iran are Mugabe's close friends and appointed as election observers along with the surrounding African countries in the SADC-region. It is tragic that we in the West speak so much about human rights, when we make the rules in such a way that nothing can be done when innocent people – and that includes women and children – are to be attacked and brutalized.

CHAPTER 24

REVENGE OF THE VOTE

They start inflicting their cruel revenge. For the time being, six of the election counters have been put in jail, allegedly having omitted to count all the votes for the governing party. At the same time they have started a recount of the *actual* votes. Alas! No doubt, the recounting of all the votes will show a better result for the governing party.

The government has tightened its hold over the innocent population that only for a couple of days looked happy and hopeful and dared to greet us with the typical open palm, which is the sign of the opposition, like they did during the years from 2000 to 2002. Now their broad African smiles have gone, because they have learnt that without a new commander of the military, they have no chance of changing their lives. The 24 people in the Politburo tighten their grip over the people and rules by hook or by crook and make sure that *Medallah,* the old man, is not persuaded to surrender power, even if they were to grant him immunity at the Human Rights Convention in The Hague and let him disappear with a golden handshake. The rulers are just too afraid of losing their own fortunes and fear also for their safety as they became rich during Zimbabwe's participation in the war in the Congo, where they made fortunes dealing in blood diamonds and all the other atrocities they have committed together.

Sweet Rit passes by for a cup of coffee. She is on the verge of tears feeling so helpless. Her heart bleeds for the people of Zimbabwe. Both Sweet Rit and Nancy were here since the 1960s and know the country both in good times and bad. Right now, she is feeling very much alone, as Sister Nancy has gone to Ireland to visit family. We do not expect anything to come out of the court cases in the Supreme Court, the result of which will be known today or tomorrow. The judicial system is like everything else run with mediocre legal experts, and they have only been appointed the last few years to secure orders of the Court against the white farmers, who have started court cases against the compulsory acquisition of their farms.

Now the six farmers, who naively believed that they would be spared when so few are left, have been attacked. The scary part is the fact that the President runs the racist card and all his campaign was built on this issue, reinforced with a few heroic expressions from the liberation war. Ironically, it is now completely a new generation who never knew or took part in that war, and all they want is just to live in a modern world where they can find jobs, own a car and a house. Very few of them have dreams of becoming a farmer, especially not a small scale farmer, because that is all they become with that little parcel of land they are encouraged to till. From my own adolescence I remember how it was impossible to survive with so little land in Denmark, despite the honesty there surrounding co-ops in dairy and grain. Even farms with 20 acres or more had difficulties in feeding a family.

Therefore it is really tragic to watch the Africans trying to make a life for their extended families on only one or two acres of land. Clyde's ox-driven carts are of some help for their general transport and are also used as ambulances, for harvesting production and for freighting people in their wedding suits and dresses, and not to forget their funeral ceremonies. It is tragic that their agricultural production has failed, both because of the heavy rain in the rainy season, and also because they could not get any fertilizer. The African learnt early on to understand inflation, because when he had pinched and scraped together all that he had earned, there was not even enough to buy a bag of fertilizer. Although I am generally against the use of fertilizer, I also understand that in Zimbabwe there is a lack of knowledge, money and education to convert to organic farming, which needs different skills. Here their agricultural knowledge is centred around their hoe and badza for growing maize plants as their staple diet. They walk in a line in the fields barefooted and make two holes by turning the big toe in the soil. In each hole they drop a seed – *one for the bird and one for the planter*. Then the hole is covered and hopefully a maize plant will soon shoot up.

EVERY NIGHT CLYDE AND I sit glued to the television screen to hear about the election. The last five days we have become a world sensation, because our country is on the brink of a disaster, close to a civil war. Journalist Jim Clancy from CNN is standing on the South African side of the border reporting about our situation. He gazes towards the Limpopo River, which he cannot cross, as no foreign journalists have access to our land. Despite the fact that he is not allowed to enter Zimbabwe, he grasps something basic, which none of the other journalists were able to comprehend.

"It is just like baseball," he says, "it is all about the old boy's club and the selection process. To be a member you must have a background as a freedom fighter against the white regime. That is what drives them, that is the spirit behind the old African leaders in the region, which they call SADC. That gives them a special rank and eternal membership and they swear allegiance to one another. They have taken a vow of fidelity," explains Jim Clancy.

On the English news channel SKY we watch Stewart Ramsey, who has managed to enter Zimbabwe and he makes two good reports, but does not follow up and his news reporting quickly loses steam on the world stage, as he is unable to deliver more. Or perhaps he did not have the mandate to do so. The same is happening with BBC, where the South African journalist Emma Hurd is using old and monotonous slogans to describe our suffering. At least Stewart Ramsey has a couple of good photo shots of some of the poor creatures who were tortured. Yet despite the good close-up pictures, he does not make a description to go with it and we are left ignorant of what happened to these people.

But we here in Zimbabwe know that the young man with the terribly burnt and destroyed hands was attacked by criminal ZANU-PF members, these young bandits that were given a crash course in brutality and terror. They are called the green bombers and are often acting under narcotic drugs, and many of their victims die during their outrages. They are part of the gangs calling themselves war veterans, but they are so young that they were not even born during UDI. The youngster with the burnt hands is only 22 years old and comes from a village called Musaruro in Mudzi, close the northern border of Mozambique. They came at 9 o'clock in the morning to his little shop; they kicked the door in and pulled him out of the building. Then they shouted, "You are member of MDC!" They held him down and then they burnt his hands with grass. But that was not enough. Afterwards they smashed his two hands with barbed wire, until they became a swelling mass of burnt meat and skin. After this atrocity they proceeded to loot his shop of goods. At the Kotwa District Hospital he was given only two paracetamol.

More than 500 farm workers have become homeless; many of them had all their belongings burnt to the ground. Women and children have been beaten up and are left with broken ribs, broken limbs and deep skin lacerations and terrible fractures as a result of being beaten with wooden planks, barbed wire and iron rods. At some hospitals the wounded have been turned away, as the nursing staff is afraid of repercussion and suffering the same fate if they offer assistance. In other district hospitals and clinics there are simply no bandages, medicine or sterilized products. You can forget all about antibiotics and treatment for burns.

Tapiwa Mbawada, an MDC organising secretary for Hurungwe East, has been beaten to death on April 12th. His wife and brother were also severely beaten and it is unsure if they are going to make it. So many have been brutalized and had their front teeth knocked out. A school teacher in Mudzi was murdered and eight women were kidnapped. Several of these so-called war veterans ransacked all the belongings of the dwellers in the huts, and when they had had their pick, they set most of the huts on fire. Even chickens and goats were burnt alive.

In the district where President Mugabe is born, and many other places where he used to have a firm grip on the rural population, the same has happened with these brutal revenge attacks on the unoffending citizens. It has happened because the rulers are furious that their own kin and kind would dare to vote against them. They want to suppress the rebellion ruthlessly and make them fear and tremble, so that they will toe the line and vote ZANU-PF when they seek re-election.

At the Louisa Guidotti Hospital eight men arrived in a Mazda pick-up truck, carrying AK-47s, rifles and pistols. They walked between each hospital bed and pushed out the wounded, but some of them could not even walk. The nursing staff was driven away from the scene.

"This is your last chance!" the bandits threatened. "Next time you vote the right way or you will die."

They forced the wounded to sing party slogans and if they did not know the slogans, they were beaten.

In Gweru the opposition was attacked by soldiers, and in the rural areas and in the cities, the soldiers and the veterans came like vultures into beer halls and night clubs and without any remorse they attacked innocent people to show them that it is punishable not to vote for Mugabe and his cabin boys.

In the capital Harare many of the wounded received better treatment, as there were many unknown sponsors paying for their treatment.

"THEY ARE PREPARING FOR INDEPENDENCE Day," says Clyde, "on Friday the 18th of April it is 28 years since independence."

Our social life has been non-existent since the election and we are mostly inside our houses. For Clyde the resting is good for him. We watch the television and see the same pictures on the screen of the 24-member Politburo, who have voices oiled with flattery and they speak as if they are licking a lollipop, when they greet the almighty Mugabe. The nine-fingered Mutasa, who stood for the land reform and has been the speaker of Parliament and member of the security organization CIO, says in a twitter, "Oh, the dear old man!" All the time they repeat the new nickname, *Medallah*, when they speak of their maestro. There are only a few women who have become members of the Politburo, and they drop a curtsey to the ruler, as if he is the Emperor. Their faces are proud and callous.

CLYDE POINTS TOWARDS A COUPLE of big cardboard boxes and commands, "Count all the bricks!" He knows that I do not like this task.

Despite all the suffering of the masses, not much is spoken about the assaults; the conversation is more about the money. We are riding this merry-go-round and it never stops and you cannot jump off. They dance around the golden calf. If we do not hurry and change the new money, it loses value and then we cannot pay for the raw materials, which now to a greater extent are procured from South Africa, as the production in Zimbabwe is almost non-existent. We pull the heavy drapes on all the windows before we start stacking the bricks.

"Remember when I used pillow cases?" I ask, smiling and feeling that a sense of humour is always helpful. But Clyde does not reply. He is already concentrated on the task ahead.

"Soon we are back to where we started: the airport carrier on wheels, unless they take some zeroes away again. Or we may even end up using your scotch carts for transporting the money," I continue with amusement only to myself, as I do not expect my husband to change to a chatty mood. I am used to talking to myself and not expecting any reply from this inarticulate creature.

Finally, we have completed not only the counting of the money, but also the evening meal in profound silence. Clyde moves himself to the peach recliner and grabs the remote for the television. He checks on the poker games and the wrestling, his favourite recreation. I get up to find a book and another space.

"Do you want to see more news?" asks Clyde, apparently wanting me to stay.

"Yes, please!" Already the screen is focused on protests in Tibet, between items about the carriers of the Olympic torch, Afghanistan and Iraq. All the time the news is interrupted by advertising of global products, seemingly more important than the sports event.

"Here is something about Zimbabwe!" Clyde exclaims.

"Good," I say. "They are going to complain to the United Nations Security Council. Seems as if they are more vigorous now with the new boss after Kofi Anan, that Korean guy, what's his name?" I lean forward to read the text under the picture, "Ban Ki-moon. That's a difficult name to remember. What to compare it with? Hanky, panky or what?"

"Just think of *bank*," is Clyde's prompt answer. He can remember everything that has to do with money, banks or investment. He is a born capitalist.

"The rate is now 75 million," he mutters under his breath.

THAT NIGHT I CHANGE THE duvet and take out the warm goose-down from the cupboard, because the winter is upon us and tonight is a very cold night. Out in that freezing night there are many small children freezing to death, as they have lost their homes. Just like the Hans Christian Andersen fairytale *The Little Girl With The Matchsticks*.

THE CALENDAR IS STUDIED EAGERLY, as Clyde has put dates on it for our planned holidays overseas. Extra planning is needed, now that Clyde cannot fly anymore. Daily, our lives are becoming more and more desperate, and with the worsening conditions in the country, it is very likely that when we do leave, it will be for good. Clyde's health has deteriorated on the high plateau of the capital of Harare, where we are 1500 metres above sea level. Still, we tell everyone that it is not our intention to leave Africa – we have to play the game, or they will come and take the factory. Although it was the plan that the Baron should buy it, he has not even paid the first rate of payment, and the second rate of payment falls due on April 1st. I feel very worried about living in a country with no health care and with a husband who has presumably been cured of lung cancer, because what if the cancer returns?

A fighter plane is flying over our house and disturbs the silence, trying to break through the sound barrier. They are preparing for Independence Day, says Clyde. Against my normal routine I turn on the television, even though it is still morning. There is news about Zimbabwe, but it is like they are repeating the same old stuff. But then there is one news item that is very disturbing: In Durban Harbour on South Africa's East Coast a ship from China has arrived with 80 tons of weapons, destined for Zimbabwe. Furthermore, the newscaster informs that the ruling ZANU-PF party wants to have the votes recounted in 22 constituencies and they accuse the opposition party of election fraud. It is just so typical of them and has always been their tactic – to accuse the opponent of the crimes they themselves have committed. There are rising numbers of attacks on innocent people, and in response the opposition party MDC is announcing that there will be a strike on Tuesday. It is the height of folly, I think to myself, because then it will be obvious to everyone who is a member of the opposition, and easy for them to select which ones to beat up.

Time goes by and Tuesday Clyde comes home and says, "Only 10 workers did not come to work." He confirms more about the assaults and is also aware of the weapon freight in Durban Harbour. On board the Chinese ship *An Yue Jiang*, the cargo is 3 million rounds of AK-47 ammunition, 1500 rocket propeller grenades and more than 3000 mortars. At the same time an American Miami-based weapons dealer has been arrested for allegedly trying to sell 10 Russian military helicopters loaded with rifles, rockets and bombs – destination Zimbabwe's military junta!

In Durban Harbour there is a surprise reaction, because the workers are making protests. This cargo should not be allowed to go through South Africa and up to Zimbabwe and create suffering for the people there. The trade union COSATU supports the harbour workers and the case is presented to a Judge as a matter of urgency. No permit had been obtained beforehand from China and the cargo is of an illegal nature according to international conventions. The Judge tries to confiscate the cargo, but the Chinese vessel, which has been named *The Death Ship*, turns around in panic out into the open sea, hoping to find another harbour willing to receive its cargo. For several days we sit staring at images of this rusty crème-coloured freighter with its blood-red flag on its sternpost, and it is of some comfort to us that the incident has been covered in the international news media.

That night the rain falls incessantly. It is like the rainy season has returned, but it is an icy-cold winter rain and the temperature is dropping to below the freezing point. A few thousand people are now homeless since the systematic terror and over 500 houses and huts are burnt to the ground. One maid tells me that now they have no roof over their heads, because the bandits came and took their asbestos roof, the reason given: *that roof must have been given to you by MDC*.

Only a few are able to seek shelter in the big cities with family members. Most of them are sleeping in the open with their crying children in the cold night.

The morning after the heavy rain I walk outside to open the garden gate for the two gardeners, Rafael and Givemore. They immediately start watering the flowers in all the flower beds, in the big pots, and then they water the grass. I think to myself, *perhaps I should tell them that it is unnecessary after the rain,* but perhaps I'd better not. It might confuse them and then they might not water at all during the dry season, when we are away. Better let them keep their routine. Sometimes, I wonder if their lack of intuition is perhaps due to vitamin deficiency during their upbringing, but having lived here so many years, I find there are many reasons. Culturally, they never developed a diverse garden, they only grew their staple food. Besides, if they come from a poor kraal in the rural areas, their status remains the same through many generations. Perhaps they also marry and procreate too close to relatives and extended family, due to the lack of infrastructure and their polygamous nature. The more wealthy blacks grow up with a different mentality, more imagination and initiative; they travel and see the world and sometimes they marry into new blood. Unfortunately, the wealthy Africans tend to behave like feudal lords and lack empathy with the poor and often treat them as slaves. They forget to pay them salary for their work and they do not respect any rules concerning working hours and holidays.

To add to our despair, the inflation has gone up to 165,000 per cent according to the international media, but I believe it is higher, at least 200,000 per cent. On April 22, I note in my diary that the rate of exchange is 80 million, but already the following day I make a new note that it has gone up to 90 million. How strange to go back in time and remember that I paid Jester 180 Zimbabwe dollars each month in salary when I met Clyde in 1991, and at that time I could feed Jester and myself for a week for 20 dollars. Once Zimbabwe was the *Breadbasket of Africa,* and when I came to the country in 1986, the rate for Zimbabwe dollars was 1.5 to 1 US dollar.

During the week-end we have lunch at Panarotti's in Avondale. Dr. Vick and Dolores have driven to Harare from Masvingo, because

Dolores's sister has been visiting from America for five weeks, but she is leaving tomorrow. One of the nuns is with them, but I have never met her before. We order three different kinds of pizza and sit outside under one of the umbrellas next to the street. A beggar boy walks by our table and begs for food.

"Go away!" snaps Clyde and explains, "He will just sell it to somebody else."

It is a good evening and the atmosphere is warm. We all drink the local beer with the pizza. Although a smile hovers about my lips, it crosses my mind that *a day without wine is a day without sunshine!* We four women sit at one end of the table and Dr. Vick and Clyde sit at the other end next to each other. Funny, how English-speaking men prefer speaking to each other instead of speaking with the women. I could perhaps understand if the conversation is only about nappy talk, or looks and make-up, but that is not the case here. Right now we are having a serious discussion about health and healing. Like me, the nun has studied the subject for a number of years. She sits in a very thin blouse and I worry that she is feeling cold. The cold of the evening sneaks up on you. Dolores and her sister are wearing warmer clothes. They tell us that in America it has not gone unnoticed that there are thoughts about the existence of a one-world government. But who are the rulers? Dr. Vick and Clyde ought to be part of our exciting debates, yet the men do not even glance our way.

That same evening when we return home, Clyde tells me that the doctor and his wife are returning home due to the tense political situation. Especially in the area of Masvingo the unrest and the violence is worsening. The ambulance Dr. Vick was driving, when he had a little accident hitting the donkey, has still not been repaired in Harare, and Clyde has had a lot of trouble in this connection. When we open our e-mails on the computer, we receive this message from friends writing about the conditions in the region of Masvingo:

Hi folks,
Just to let you know that Chris was invaded yesterday by war vets.
I happened to be visiting Charmaine and Chris when a bakkie
load of about 23 war vets arrived. They made a lot of noise, as

they were singing war songs. Chris went out to them, but they told him to stay away, as he had to leave the farm, which they were taking over.

The police arrived about 45 minutes after the war vets and spent some time talking to them, with Chris remaining calm and reasoning with the chaps. The episode took about 2.5 hours with Charmaine, Laura and I watching anxiously in Charmaine's house. I was so worried that they might beat Chris up, as is so much their style. They left the property and have vowed to return today to "sort things out."

There was a carefully orchestrated war vet attack yesterday on the few remaining owned farms in Masvingo. The farms that I know were invaded were the Goddards and Connors, Borland, Richards and Sparrows. The whole Pa Nyanda Lodge was taken.

Graham & Cally were given an hour to leave their house. They did so with a few valuables, but didn't even have time to pack a suitcase.

The war vets have said that there are to be 2 dead white farmers in their province by Monday. Will update you later as to what happens.

Kerry

I find it ironic that when we write or talk on the phone, even when it might be our last communication, still we have to sound bright and make it a snappy dialogue, *hello there, hi folks, just passing by, but coming to think of it ... thought I would let you know that I won't be seeing you anymore. Hey you, they fixed me and I am bleeding to death. Also my pen is running out of ink, but you have a good time. So long, you old fart.*

IN THE TM SUPERMARKET I have a bit of luck, as the swipe-machine is working, but you have to wait for a long time, as the card has to be swiped through several times to be accepted. Meanwhile, I look around and study all the people in the queue. In front of me is an African couple. She has gold-rimmed glasses and is wearing an abstract-patterned skirt with offset layers in different lengths and mixed in orange and brown colours. I am pretty sure it is 100% polyester like her pinstriped brown jacket. The husband is wearing an olive green tailor-made suit, made extra wide over the shoulders. He has shaven off his hair like many do in the summertime, but now it is almost winter and we are close to the dry season. His bald head is showing deep frowns, and because he is fat, these two deep folds in his neck make the lower part of his skull look bloated. Both of them look well-nourished and wear sharply-pointed shoes, which are now so trendy with the toe of the shoe cut straight across into a ridiculous little square. It makes the shoes look extremely long, as you need at least eight centimetres of empty space in front of the toes. The couple is not talking to one another, as they are both on the cell phone while waiting.

Behind me is a young African man, who looks thin and hungry. He stands reading the weekly *The Zimbabwean* which is nowadays only printed abroad. On the front page are some frightening pictures and I ask him, "Where did you find that paper?"

"From the man by the bus," he replies trying to move his lips and giving me the ghost of a smile. There is deep sadness in his eyes.

As it is my turn at the till, the lady says to me, "We have to make it into two bills, as the amount is too big." That was because I found a bottle of olive oil for 1.2 billion.

Having returned the ramshackle trolley outside the supermarket, I jaywalk to the parking stand for the local Combi-taxis. These Combi-taxis are their only means of transport. The gutters are full of trash and many of the women stand with cardboard boxes or shopping bags balancing on their heads. So many times I have tried to learn this trick, but my hair is too slippery to carry anything. The African women have hair like a bird's nest and when they load something there, it stays there, even when they move around and walk. Being aware that the newspaper is only sold underground, I ask very innocently, "Where can I buy the small paper?"

The combi-driver looks at me and asks me if I know that horrible things are taking place now.

"Yes," I say, "that is why I want to buy that paper."

"It is expensive," he warns. "The price is 20 million." He knows it is a lot of money for a paper.

"OK," I say.

Then he sticks two fingers into his mouth against the eye teeth and turns his head towards a mate 10 metres away. The Africans are good at whistling. They make it into signals and make it sound like birdsong. Just like they are clever with the drums.

"Where do you come from?" he asks anxiously and follows me to his friend.

"Denmark," I say.

"Please tell them in Denmark what is happening here. Please tell the world about the cruelties. They beat us up, even our women and children. They kill us. What can we do?" His voice is broken with emotion.

While I open my handbag to take out two notes to pay to his friend, I see the grisly details on the front page and say almost in a whisper, "You must have the army on your side, so they can't use their weapons against you."

On my way back to the green Mercedes I start scratching my right arm. There are signs of two flea bites.

IN BON MARCHÉ I SEE that they have brown bread in baking pans. I ask the manager, "Is it whole wheat bread?"

"Yes, Madam," he says.

"Give me two," I say. He takes the one bread out of the pan and then I see to my disappointment that it is not whole wheat bread, so I quickly add, "Oh, one bread is actually enough, thank you."

Next to me an African woman is full of despair, "I wanted so much to have that bread, but he wouldn't sell it to me."

I wave at the manager back to me, "Please give my sister the other bread we put back in the pan."

She gives me a smile of gratitude and looks as if I have saved her from starvation.

Later, when I tell Clyde about the experience, he declares, "That is why they are so willing to beat up one another."

CHAPTER 25

BAD NEWS

"Should you not have an X-ray taken before we book our trip, Clyde?" I ask.

"Perhaps I should. I'd better go straight to the Diagnostic Centre, then I don't waste time going to the doctor first, only to get a referral."

That same morning he goes to the Diagnostic Center, but the result is not good. Despite the fact that there has been a lot of improvement with the healing of his right lung, which they burnt during radiation treatment in South Africa, a new growth has suddenly appeared in the left lung, which is his *good lung*. Clyde goes to Dr. Cunning's consultation room, but he is not there himself. Another doctor attends to him, studies his X-ray and reads in his medical file. Then he immediately organizes a CT-scanning, as the equipment is working at the moment. The result of the CT-scan is a crippling blow. Clyde is told that apparently there is a new cancer in the other lung.

Suddenly, the political situation and the sale of the factory are unimportant. Again, Clyde's life is threatened, by an inside monster reappearing and showing its ugly face. The ox-driven carts, the boxes full of money and the possibility of a life in luxury. How trivial all that is!

After a while I contact Mano and tell him the terrible news. Then I phone the nuns.

It is fate that we have planned on having dinner the next evening with the Italians and we have reserved a table at the Rainbow Towers in the elegant Le Chandelle Restaurant. Although Clyde has asked me not to ruin the atmosphere, I discreetly tell Mano everything about the result of the CT-scan and give him more details of his medical history.

"Bodie, please send me an e-mail about the progress of the disease and I will forward that to a friend of mine, who is a professor in Lyon," suggests Mano. "He is doing cancer research and is a professor in nuclear medicine. They do other things in Lyon than in the rest of the world and at the hospital, where my friend is, they have a lot of progress in cancer research."

All four of us are tonight dressed up in our best bib and tucker and we enjoy this moment of being together. Zsa Zsa gives me a small present from Italy. When I open the shiny black box, I see a stroke of genius and Zsa Zsa has already got one for herself: it is an elegant hook for a lady's handbag, which you can hang under the table anywhere, as it has a magnetic system.

"Wish I had made that invention," exclaims Clyde and with a little more wine in the glasses, Zsa Zsa's infectious laughter and the soft Italian accent, it is almost like for a while we forget the realm of shades.

DR. VICK AND DOLORES SEND us a message the next day that they are coming to Harare from Masvingo for the week-end. Apparently, they have heard the news from the nuns, because first Dr. Vick comes over to our townhouse alone to see for himself the X-rays and the result of the CT-scan. For a few minutes he is alone with me in the courtyard and he looks at me somberly and gives me a piercing glance.

"Bodie, this is very serious. You must realize that we can only do *so* much. You get to a point where you have to let it go."

Dr. Vick has put on the same statistic-voice as Dr. Cunning, but I am not going to waste my energy convincing him otherwise. Instead I say, "I know, Dr. Vick, but please do not take away his hope. Wonders never cease. Perhaps we are going to France."

He looks a bit skeptical as he continues, "Some people are unable to face the facts and they seek not just a second opinion, but travel from one specialist to another like people who cannot accept the verdict in a court case. Your refusal to accept Clyde's situation makes me worry that you might end in this category."

Clyde and I have arranged a lunch at the Pavillion at Meikles Hotel. Besides Dr. Vick and Dolores we have also invited our lawyer and his wife. Dr. Vick is bringing one of the nuns from the Convent and as Clyde is making the seating arrangement, I am pleased that he has put me next to Sister Rose Mary.

During the lunch we start talking about the Second World War and other things concerning Germany. The nun's father was a soldier and ended in a concentration camp in Russia. When he returned to Germany after the war had ended, he weighed only 75 pounds. He was so skinny and weak that that he could hardly walk and he crawled up to the door of the house of his younger brother, who had never gone to war as he was born with a weak heart. Upon opening the door and seeing an almost lifeless bundle lying on the doormat, he hardly recognized his own flesh and blood because there was nothing left of that feisty young man who had joined the troops for the front. That instant the younger brother's heart swelled and he became so strong that he put him on his back and carried him all the way over to Rose Mary's mother and the children. In the beginning they never understood why their mother had to look after this strange and sick man.

Sister Rose Mary has a gift as a storyteller and I can never get enough. Now she has moved on and she is telling about how she used to babysit for Dr. Vick and Dolores's children when they were small. Dolores adds some funny episodes and the lawyer's wife speaks across the table to be part of the girls' talk. The men as usual end up speaking nonsense.

DURING THIS HOPELESS SITUATION WE receive some good news. The professor in France will accept Clyde as a patient. His condition leaves hope that he may be cured. The next days I take an active part in booking our tickets, as our departure now has to be rushed. We no longer have the luxury of choosing a long trip without flying. This is it, it's kill or cure, the Devil or the deep blue sea. As I choose an early date for our flight, I suddenly realize that it might be the last week of our lives in Africa. The tickets are for business class from Johannesburg to Munich. From there onwards we will have to take a train to Lyon. For that reason we find a hotel room near the railway station in Munich. Sweet Rit tells us that the seats on South African Airways can be pulled out like a real bed, and when we fly in the night, Clyde can sleep all the way and start afresh when we land in Germany in the morning.

The nuns tell us about a number of assaults and terror attacks on unoffending citizens and we listen to some of the mediocre reports on the international channels, where it is confirmed that the West has only an insignificant interest in our tragedy.

"It is just so sad," says Sweet Rit. "They abduct the people, they torture them and leave them in the bush to die, their little children are left to fend for themselves and all the domestic animals killed, maimed or starved out on the farms countrywide. Bodie, these people have suffered so much over so many years and they are such good people. I try to remind myself that pain is an act of peace, but I feel they have suffered enough."

DR. SIMONE ARRIVES FROM THE Convent to speak to me. When I show her the X-rays, she holds them up in the light and studies each one carefully.

"I think that the new growth is completely isolated and easier to deal with than the first tumour. It looks to me as if it is a primary cancer."

Her words console me and I ask her if she would mind telling the same to Clyde. When he hears Dr. Simone's words, he looks immensely relieved and in his eyes I see a glimmer of hope.

Despite the positive news, I get this feeling again that I am like a tree that has been pulled up by the roots. Somehow I am never allowed to grow roots, now the same race is starting all over again, with correspondence and appointments and medical up and down periods. At the same time, Dr. Cunning has returned and he has had a serious conversation with Clyde.

When Clyde returns after the consultation, he looks as if his inner light has been switched off. It takes me two days to find out what the doctor has said, but it has hit Clyde like a ton of bricks. I have to combine fragments of conversation and it feels like picking up the scattered remains of something broken. There are hours between his monosyllabic words, but in the end I find enough debris in this wreckage of a man to understand what has gone wrong. Dr. Cunning does not believe it is a primary cancer, but a secondary, perhaps originating from the kidney, the thyroid gland or perhaps even the brain. I try to argue against Dr. Cunning's opinion by showing Clyde articles from a big stack of books and I also remind him about what Dr. Simone from the Convent has said.

"I can assure you that if your case was completely hopeless, they would not receive you in France," I assure him. But he is no longer the optimist he was before. His eyes are sunken and for the first time I see the colour of death in his face. It comes as a shock to me.

He is on his way out and as soon as I hear him starting the car and see him turning the corner, I dial Dr. Cunning's number. I recognize his deep voice on the receiver and he quickly starts repeating the same, as he has told Clyde.

"But everything you have said to my husband, is only based on statistics," I lecture him. "It is not scientific or a proven fact." To my astonishment I hear a click in my ear and realize that he has cut me off.

Bloody bastard, I think to myself as I redial but to him I say very warmly, "Isn't it just incredible how they cut us off all the time, just when we were having such a good conversation. Clyde is very fond of you as a doctor, you know. He likes you for your raw masculinity, because it makes you stand out from other doctors. Your accident on the motorbike only adds to that. But back to the diagnosis, no matter how close you feel you are to the truth, we just have to remember that without hope, none of us can go through life. You almost took away that hope. Because of his high respect for you, your words can have the effect of *voodoo* on him, so when you tell him that his chances are poor, then you actually kill him. If on the other hand you tell him that there is something positive, then he will shine and be able to go through the treatment in France."

"Are you going to France?" the voice on the other end sounds full of surprise.

"We are indeed. They are very advanced in the treatment of Clyde's disease and they are ready to receive him as a patient."

"You know what you just said, it reminds me of a patient I once had. He had brain cancer and I had to give him some very negative results, as there was nothing more to be done. You know, it is not right to give a glimmer of hope, when there is no basis for it, we have an obligation towards patients to be realistic and throw the dice. Well, I explained to him in detail and taking a realistic view of the situation I went through his prognosis, but he never grasped anything and said to me, *Thanks Doc, I am so happy that it is not that serious in my case!*" Dr. Cunning chuckles a bit recollecting his patient and continues, "But what do you want me to say to Clyde to give him his hope back?"

I imagine Dr. Cunning at the other end of the receiver in his thick sweater and sportswear as I have never seen him wearing the white coat and at that moment he reminds me of those men who really make an effort to find your G-spot and you are constantly directing the right of way, yes, a little to the right, now a little left, yes, you are close, *you are getting warm*! He has just been through a divorce and now after the motorbike accident, he is limping, dragging one leg and favouring the other.

"Perhaps if you say to him that you have studied the X-rays more closely and you are no longer so sure that it is not the primary cancer and that it looks isolated," I suggest a little hesitantly.

"I suppose that would not do any harm, if I were to say something like that," mumbles the doctor, but then he suddenly adds more passionately, "I promise I will call him in a couple of days and say something positive. And you know what? You are right about what you said about statistics."

After that conversation I feel a whole lot better and I am grateful that our dialogue did not offend the doctor. Actually, some kind of sympathy developed between us and there is no doubt that his words carry authority, even though he is not a cancer expert. Dr. Simone says, many of the doctors know less than me, who has studied so intensely since the disease broke out, and know much more about this individual case. Ordinary doctors and even specialists often reach a dead end, based only on routine delivery and test results. They do not seem to know the individual patient well enough, she says.

THREE DAYS BEFORE OUR DEPARTURE, Johnny and Vania pass by. I explain to them how I feel now, like I am pulled up by the root, like an exile or a fugitive, with that feeling of not belonging anymore.

"You are like one without a totem," says Vania, who was married to another African before she moved in with Johnny. "Do you remember when Mugabe used that expression?" she asks Johnny.

"Totem or no totem," I say, "if I was born today and I had influence on my own name, it is not just that I have no totem. Captain Longchase once said that Clyde and I had the zebra as a totem because that is both black and white, but it does not quite explain why I feel so lost. Then they called me Amai Tsitsi, the staff at the factory and at home, meaning that my heart reaches out. But right now that name is not how I feel because I am being forced to rush around all the time, never allowed to remain in one place, so how can I reach out to anybody? I feel like a plant that is prevented from growing strong: they keep digging me up and putting me in a new pot, one minute I am placed in the sun, the next in the shade. What name in Shona would I be given if I was born now because they would understand how I feel and name me accordingly?"

Johnny sits very quietly for a while and keeps nodding his head. In between he is writing things down on a piece of paper. Then he writes one long word: *Chinzvengamutsairu.*

"What does it mean?" I ask.

Johnny explains, "Your name would be *Chinzvengamutsairu.* *Mutsairu* is for the sweeper's broom. You feel like this: first you are sitting in the lounge and the sweeper is coming with his *mutsairo.* You start lifting the legs, but then you move away, in the end into the bedroom, but he comes after you. When you go into the kitchen to try and do something there, by George! He is now coming to sweep the kitchen floor. All the time you are trying to find a new place; that is why your name would be *Chinzvengamutsairu.*"

"You are absolutely right, Johnny. You are spot on. My name is *Chinzvengamutsairu.*" As I say my new name, I realize that it makes me feel better. Not that anything has changed, but just the fact that Johnny has understood how I feel, makes me feel that I will eventually come to some clarity of the situation.

"Johnny, come in here," shouts Clyde from the bedroom, "I want to show you something."

Immediately I know what it is. It is the highest gesture of friendship between two real men. He is giving him *Dirty Harry*, his .38 special, which has been his figurine on his bedside table since year 2000, and his 9 mm revolver which he has kept in the mini-safe. Through the doorway I can hear Clyde's voice, "You are my closest friend, Johnny, and you are the only person that I respect so much that I will pass over to you my weapons. You are the only person I can trust to use them properly."

Vania looks at me with an inquiring look and I whisper to her what is happening in the room next door. We nod our heads having shared this confidence, understanding the significance of this ritual. For thousands of years such ceremonial acts have been followed. Bonds of friendship have been sealed by the mingling of blood; entrusting one's sword or spear in the time of death; a solemn act from time immemorial, binding for eternity two hearts together in the mood of a moment. "Johnny, you will always be my friend," Clyde's voice is broken with emotion.

It is a great relief to know that the weapons now belong to Johnny and that he, in an emergency situation, will judge the situation and never do serious harm: only wound the attacker. His old .44 Magnum was so powerful that it could knock a man off his feet and blast him away like he had been in an explosion. Just the day before, Clyde confided in me that if he had not been so close to Johnny, he would have thrown both weapons down the mineshaft.

As the two men return to the lounge, they are both very quiet and it breaks my heart to see Clyde's glossy eyes, but he restrains himself and does not blink until they have dried out.

CHAPTER 26

THE FLIGHT

N ext morning the phone rings while we are having breakfast and Clyde gets up to answer it. I cannot hear what is being said on the other end, but after a while Clyde looks for a pencil and starts writing things down on his notepad. He finishes off saying, "I will keep you informed from France. And once again, thank you."

He returns to the round dining table and takes another piece of toast explaining, "That was Dr. Cunning. He has studied my X-rays more closely and he has now also come to the same conclusion as Dr. Simone, that it might actually still be the primary cancer which has spread to the other lung. If there were some microscopic cancer cells that survived the cancer treatment, they could have metastasized from the mediastinum. When he first saw the pictures, he was more focused on all the shadows stemming from when they burnt my lung, because it is very difficult to see what is infection and what is new growth, but he is now convinced that the new growth is totally isolated and in that case my situation is not nearly as serious."

Clyde suddenly looks like a different person and his sunken eyes, which were placed deep in the hollow spaces in his skull, are now more protruding and full of life. He pours a little more of the green tea that has been kept warm under the tea-cosy.

"I better go out to the factory so nobody suspects we are leaving," he says with renewed energy. As he is getting ready he continues, "Very few know we are on our way out. Johnny and Vania know, of course, and June and Dan Bailey. The nuns also know about it. Hilton and his wife Tippi will drive us to Johannesburg. Don't tell anyone else – it is better that they only find out after some months."

Shortly after Clyde has left, the telephone rings. June Bailey is asking how I am coping. The fact that she is asking about *my* well-being and not Clyde's, makes me fall apart.

"Bodie, I am coming over right away. I will be there in a sec because I am at the Gallery," she says.

She arrives moments later and gets out of the big SUV wearing very high stilettos. They are black like her skirt and she is wearing a very revealing red blouse showing a lot of cleavage. Her swelling bosom almost pops out as she moves around. She has olive skin like an Italian, as she grew up in the rural areas and she loves the bush and has always preferred to live surrounded by wild stretches of swaying savannah grass. Although she is a gourmet chef, her preference is a meal that has simmered for hours on an open fire and she can make *sadza* like a native. Now, she is working at the Gallery and she has created a very elegant business look. Despite the fact that we have no wind, she constantly brushes away a long strand of hair golden as the sun and thick as Zsa Zsa's.

We cover the whole ground and talk about politics, personal stuff and health and disease, sitting in the light wicker chairs on the veranda.

"You know, Bodie, that is how it is with cancer. Suddenly it pops up in a new place, but this time you have caught it in time," she says making the monster appear less formidable and showing some of her knowledge as a nurse.

"I just feel so sad about leaving Africa," I confess to June and continue, "I have never lived so many years in one place before and I am afraid that I will never come back. Here I have friends and I feel a sense of belonging. Of course I am aware that right now the situation is not very good, but still there are so many things that I love here and it is not the people's fault. They are much worse off than us." Then I tell her about my new name, *Chinzvengamutsairu.*

"They have a remarkable understanding of how we *feel*," says June pensively, "and just like they can be raw and brutal, the same way they can understand the finer strings. When I think about it, I realize how much we have learnt from them and we start seeing how bad we were. I remember when we called the scullery worker a black enamel dishwasher. That time we didn't understand how ugly it was. Looking at it today, I can see how much we have taken over from them and their African customs. If anybody has problems, they just move in and we don't even ask how long they are staying."

June has a way of becoming very intense and as she leans forward,

I fear all her attributes are falling out. "Bodie, I had a dream last night," she says, keeping her monuments in balance as she glances up at the Joburg Gold pine tree by the wall. "It was about President Mugabe. He was a giant lion high as an elephant, but now he was lying on the ground bleeding and wounded and he was no longer the giant he was. The natives poured water between his cracked lips because he was thirsty. And that is what they are like. They are very forgiving."

I nod in agreement, "You are right there. And you know what? I also have these crazy dreams. Sometimes I write them down and turn them into poetry."

"Read me one of your poetries," says June.

I get up from the wicker chair and walk inside to the small room, returning with a note book, and start to read aloud.

"You must meet Peter Godwin or his sister Georgina," says June eagerly. "They would be able to advise you about publishing it, and they know publishers in England."

She grabs her cell phone and dials a number, but then she changes her mind. Before she leaves, she squeezes me up against her soft bosom and although she is younger than me, her embrace is very maternal and makes me feel safe. It occurs to me that I was never embraced. I did not have a mother.

As June leaves I am aware that I will never hear from Peter Godwin or his sister Georgina, even though they are visiting because just like the natives, her purpose was to make me feel happy at this moment in time, to take my sadness away – not to make double-entry bookkeeping over what has been promised and what has been kept. As I see June steer towards the exit I wave goodbye to her, fully aware that her visit *did* make me feel better. After all, what is out there somewhere in the horizon, do not worry about it! Be happy today, live for today. Tomorrow is another day.

THAT EVENING ANISHA AND MUHAMED pass by. She is such a thoughtful person and has brought along some homemade *samosas*, and we sit in the cosy corner of the lounge and enjoy the snacks with a cup of tea, because they are Muslims and do not drink alcohol. I realize during the visit that Clyde has told Muhamed *everything* about our coming journey, but it does not mean so much. On the other hand Clyde has always trusted Muhamed, he is a close friend. The couple leaves early and we follow them out to the parking area.

"They are all praying for you in the mosque," says Muhamed, before he enters the driver's seat in Anisha's shiny new Volvo and turns the ignition key.

THE DAY COMES THAT SHALL be our last day. It is Saturday morning and I have made a cross on the calendar for the 10th May. We both wake up before the alarm clock. Clyde bends over me in the big king-size bed and gives me a lingering kiss on the lips.

"I had a dream last night," he says. "I was fishing on the Zambezi, and the river was full of crocodiles, but none of them had any teeth!"

"That was a good dream," I say. I put on the warm morning gown for winter and step onto the icy cold bathroom floor. Clyde stays under the warm duvet, while I take my shower. Today we are going to drive non-stop to South Africa, because Clyde has something within him that tells him not to stop at Bubi River like we normally do. He fears that something might go wrong the very last minute, that he might be put in jail for dealing on the black market because they offer rewards to whistle-blowers.

On Sunday we are taking a direct flight to Munich and we will stay overnight with Clyde's daughter in Johannesburg. All our luggage is placed on the tiles by the entrance and we have a total of 87 kg. Despite this heavy weight I have had to leave all my evening gowns, shoes and personal belongings behind. All I have packed is the most necessary wardrobe and *papers*, because Clyde wanted to bring his golf clubs. Since he talked to Dr. Cunning, he has regained his old energy and optimism and he only looks ahead. I dread the thought of travelling with all that stuff and with Clyde who cannot lift. We need no less than a miracle to get suitcases and sports equipment onto the train before the conductor blows his whistle. Hopefully, wonders will never cease.

The lounge looks rather empty since Hilton has picked up the German Hannover piano.

The mildness in the weather, which we experienced in April, has now turned into a harsh cold African winter, but later in the day when the sun shines from a cloudless sky, our temperature goes up. The winter is very beautiful in Zimbabwe and in the garden there are flowers in many colours. Outside, the birds are singing and we have sun and moon at the same time.

Hilton arrives in his silver-grey Mitsubishi with his wife Tippi. Despite the cold she is only wearing sandals on her bare feet. Hilton immediately starts putting the luggage into the car and Clyde locks the front door and passes the set of keys to Hilton, as he has to show the house when we are gone, so it can be sold. He then takes the passenger seat next to Hilton.

"Bodie, do you want to sit behind Hilton?" asks Tippi, shaking her trendy blonde bob. "We are so used to that with Hilton's parents. As they are deaf and only speak with their hands, they never sit behind each other, because then they can't talk with their hands." She speaks about their handicap with such an ease that I feel quite comfortable. A little later she says, "You can't imagine how much Sienna Rose enjoys playing the piano. She plays for hours, and *Gogo* can feel the beat in the floor. She is really talented and we must try and find her a piano teacher." Tippi uses the South African term *Gogo* for grandmother.

The city is almost dead so early in the morning, but as we drive out to the industrial area on Simon Mazorodzo Road, we see a number of people walking and carrying water, either on the head or by the hand. Clyde looks to the other side as we pass the side road to the factory. It is already like a past life; there is no turning back. As I have joined him on this pilgrimage, I leave a lot of unfinished business behind and many new friendships that would never have been had we not had so many hardships. Somehow we all ended up holding on to one another and ignoring all manmade barriers of race, religion and culture, and it widened our horizons. I just wish I had seen *the double rainbow at full moon*.

"Oh, look there is a *Medallah* on his bicycle," says Tippi glancing out of the window, where an old man is riding his bicycle. Only a few are on bicycles, most of them are walking. The cock crows and we hear the *cock-a-doodle-doo* from beyond the chickens. The car radio is playing African rock music as we pass Maniami River. In between they interrupt the music to let a newscaster announce, *"Your land is your prosperity, your prosperity is your land..."*

Tippi is using a lot of expressions from the native language when she speaks, but her chatter is relaxing and pleasant and takes away the feeling of unease.

"What means *Chivu?*" I ask her, as we drive through the well-known town.

"It means *the sharp corner,*" Tippi answers and it makes me laugh. We pass a flock of school children dressed in dusty shoes and stockings.

"Look at the sign on that house, Dr. Chiremba. It means Doctor Doctor, because already *Chiremba* means doctor and that is why so many African doctors are called Chiremba, but still they all put the English word for Doctor in front of their name," explains Tippi, while she is opening the lid on the water bottle and taking a gulp. "Are you thirsty?" she asks, but I shake my head.

Before we come even close to the *Balancing Rocks,* we see a cement truck that is overturned. A giraffe is crossing the road full of potholes. There is no longer a high fence to keep the wildlife inside the National Park, but then of course, his legs are so long that it would not matter as he could just step over it.

The Blue Mountains are in the background, but they are eclipsed by a crowd of policemen filling the road. As we come closer, they wave at us to move on. There is a single road sign left. It says *Masvingo 100 km.* We are close to Runde River. As I watch across to the passenger seat and see the silver streaks in Clyde's hair, I am relieved that he is not driving. He needs all the rest he can get, but it is the first time I see him for that long as a passenger and it feels rather peculiar.

Tippi opens the window when we hear drumbeat in the distance. Shortly after, she closes it again as the whole place stinks from a sulpho factory.

As we cross Sosonye River, we are stopped by the police. They insist on seeing Hilton's driving license. Close by I notice a flock of Franklings. They look a lot like crows, but they are more grey. Although not looking attractive for the hunters' bag, they are as tasty to eat as pheasant. Having scrutinized Hilton's driving license, the policeman hands it back to him and waves us to carry on.

A little further we pass *The Lion and Elephant*, a motel where we always used to stay overnight driving to South Africa. But not today, we take no chances. Clyde wants to cross the border as soon as possible. He does not even look out of the window, but I send a lingering look towards the thatched round rondavel guest cottages and wish there had been time to make just one last stop. I would have liked to sit under the healing sausage tree and pick some of its bark and leaves and later roll it onto Clyde's skin around the lungs.

Bubi River is completely dry. There is no trace of water from the rainy season. An African cowboy is herding 20 head of cattle over the road with a stick. He is only a small boy. There are a few stray huts with a grass roof, goats running around and a donkey eating from the hawthorn bush. The bird's nests are very conspicuous, as they stick out a mile in the dead trees that are having their winter sleep.

Surprisingly, there are only few potholes in the road and the asphalt is maintained on this section because we are driving on Zimbabwe's lifeline to South Africa. All the big trucks drive here and the small traders whose overloaded vehicles have long been ready for the scrapheap. On the left side we have the railway, but freight trains are only coming once a week. For passengers there is no transport. At the level crossing I can see two baobab trees. The third one I cannot find, but they always grow in a triangle. On the right hand side I can see a proper triangle of baobab trees and suddenly I see many triangles. There is a lot of superstition attached to the baobab tree, perhaps because it has such a devilish look to it, as if it has somehow been planted wrongly, with the crown down in the ground and the roots sticking up into the sky.

Evidently there is a lot of poverty. All looks desolate and dead. There are only a few people to be seen. A young man is riding his bicycle and a crowd of people is surrounding a car that has broken down. In the tall elephant grass along the road there are heaps of plastic garbage. Just then we pass the train crossing for West Nicolson and Bulawayo, which is Zimbabwe's second-largest city.

We are approaching Beitbridge which is the largest border crossing. Hilton steps on the brake and drives at a slow pace as we are getting close to the border post. On the left hand side is the Holiday Inn, but there are no cars outside. Many Africans are walking in the opposite direction that we are driving, with bags on their heads, bundles in their hands and babies strapped onto their backs. There is a more heavy police presence, but they do not try to stop us. It is on the way back that they check the travellers for smuggled goods. Cars are driving on their last drop of petrol, or they are being pushed. All the vehicles look as if they are ready for the scrapheap.

There is a new round-about and an ox-cart with four donkeys drives through it at full speed. Down below is the Limpopo River with lots of water in it and surrounded by jungle on both sides. In the narrow places, people try to swim across the Limpopo with babies strapped onto their backs. You sink or swim; there is no other choice than the Devil or the deep blue sea. Many of them manage to get to the other side, but sadly many lives are lost as the river is full of crocodiles.

The passport control on the Zimbabwean side is reasonably fast because we started early and we are not in the same queue as the traders.

A big sign announces that it is BEITBRIDGE and underneath is written, *You are entering a controlled area.* As the bridge ends, we are on South African soil.

"Do not look behind!" warns Clyde and grabs my hand and holds it tightly, "I do not want you to turn into a pillar of salt like Lot's wife."

We stand next to the tray with chemical agents in the water to prevent foot and mouth disease. When it is our turn, we step into the tray to dip our shoes so that we are free of the disease before we set foot on South African soil.

Clyde needs me more than ever before. Once he was a tough guy and had the tenacity of life. He was a strong man who created large-scale industries during his days of glory. He became one of Africa's latter-day pioneers when Zimbabwe was at its peak and known as the *Breadbasket of Africa*, but now there is only despair around: no jobs, no food and we are close to a civil war. In the hour of parting, Clyde is a broken man, bitter and sick with cancerous tumours, and our beloved country has also turned sick and wilted away.

We get back into Hilton's Mitsubishi and notice several long police busses with luminous blue stripes on the sides coming towards us from the other side. The busses are filled with border jumpers and are escorted by other police vehicles. They are forcing the poor people back to a country that has been destroyed because the South African election officers and the South African President Thabo Mbeki found the election that took place was free and fair. As the busses pass by, the passengers wave at us with the open palm. It is the emblem of the opposition party meaning *We have nothing to hide.* Even in the hour of despair they are proud of showing their open hands. Do not ever come and tell me that these people are cowards, that they have no courage! At least we are able to leave the country; nobody will force us back in shackles and burn our hands because we voted wrongly.

As we drive the last part of the bridge, five white doves fly by and a smile hovers about Clyde's lips as he watches them fly in a diagonal line over the roofs aiming for Zimbabwe.

The last time we leave the vehicle to enter the South African Passport and Immigration Control we hear some heavy drumbeats in the distance, but clearly from the Zimbabwean side. First it sounds merely like a monotonous drum solo but then the pattern develops and surges forward with other drummers joining, rivaling Ravel's *Bolero* where the music is intensified for each sequence and repeated with higher speed each time. You feel like you are rolled up and you reach the highest mountain peaks and the summits. The Africans are able to give that same experience with very simple instruments, and they have another ability which goes beyond that of the Western musicians: they can communicate with their drumbeat and the drum has a stronger voice than any election will ever give them.

In that moment it is like Tippi can read my inner thoughts as I whisper, "Goodbye, Zimbabwe. *Sarayi Zimbabwe.*"

She clutches my arm and says, "You can't just say *Sarayi Zimbabwe* on its own. There is not one brief phrase to express what you feel. They would never just say *Goodbye*. They would say something like, 'Until we meet again, farewell Zimbabwe. *Dakara tisanganazve, sarayi Zimbabwe'*." Suddenly, I am relieved to hear that in their language, they do not have an irrevocable farewell greeting with a single parting word.

Gradually, the drum song becomes more muffled as we disappear into the building and the day is already waning. Luckily, there is not a long line-up and waiting together with Clyde there is no more anxiety, as our stay in South Africa is only a formality and is over before it has even started. Our one night here is only like transit.

My pilgrimage has started towards a new unknown world, where they have summer when we have winter. There are two rivers: *Le Rhône* and *la Saône,* very close to one another. I will find a small place and build a nest there near the river sheltered at the foot of the mountains so Clyde can watch the ships go by. The small hiccups getting there, I can manage all that. Even if I have to carry Clyde on my back like Rose Mary's father was carried by his brother, holding a suitcase in one hand and waving a golf bag with the other.

"Did you see the white doves?" asks Clyde still with a smile on his face. "It is a sign of peace."

I nod and grasp his hand, although the thought just struck me that the white dove can also be a sign of death, when your gravestone is enriched with this precious bird in your final resting place. Hopefully, the doves will bring peace to Zimbabwe. After all, many of these symbols can have different meanings, just as many experts differ on diagnostics. Sometimes it is better not to understand the notorious facts, because they are usually unfavourable. In the end it is our own perception of the situation which is more important and makes us a winner or a loser.

EPILOGUE

B odie and Clyde arrived safely in Münich in the southern part of Germany. After arrival they hired a taxi to take them to a hotel. When the taxi-driver joked about the magnitude of the luggage, Bodie saw a chance to avoid a long journey by train. Realizing that this guy was a foreigner to Germany, she inquired about his origins. He came from Turkey a few years ago and his son worked at the airport. While Tyrolean music was streaming out of the car radio, a price for driving them all the way to France was negotiated. The taxi driver was ready to leave right away, but as Clyde needed a rest, it was decided to leave early the next morning.

The driver's name was Ibrahim and he arrived promptly at 8 o'clock looking very good in a white safari-suit emphasizing his black moustache. He greeted the couple cheerfully in French, *"Bonjour!"* It was the only French word he knew.

The morning had that special crispness of the European spring and it enveloped them as they carried the luggage outside and loaded it into the back of the taxi, which of course was a Mercedes like most taxis in Germany. Bodie asked, "Would you like to bring your wife to France so that you don't have to drive back alone?"

For a minute he thought about it and after having touched his moustache, he declared, "That is very kind of you. Perhaps I could bring my son, Hassan. You see, it is a holiday today in Germany so he is off duty."

That was how it came about that father and son got a holiday to France, going through Austria and Switzerland, countries they had never visited before; in fact they had not been to other countries since they came to Germany. Hassan was ready when the taxi arrived at the apartment block where the Turkish family lived. The mother stood waving her arms from the balcony as the taxi drove off.

The trip went over the Alps, passing idyllic chalets with flower-boxes under the windows. The cherry plum trees were in full bloom and covered with white flowers. Beech trees had that special light green colour which made Bodie long for her home-country Denmark. Happy Guernsey cows half white and light brown were lying in the grass chewing their cud.

Ibrahim never wasted time as he wanted to reach his destination on time, but Clyde said everyone needed to stretch the legs and have some lunch. He recognized many places from the years he was living in Switzerland and decided to invite the Turk and his son for a special treat in a restaurant near Geneva. They were almost embarrassed and chose the cheapest on the menu card.

When they entered France the landscape magically changed and the fields were full of cypress trees and grape vines. Realizing that Ibrahim had the same long journey back, Clyde suggested that they just be dropped at the nearest hotel when they came to the outskirts of Lyon. It so happened that the Kyriad was the nearest hotel and they had rooms available. Bodie felt very safe and welcome there and the friendly staff speaking in Arabic amongst themselves taught her new phrases in French: *Toute à l'heure! (Byebye), Alors (so?), Je t'en pris* and much more. The girls even explained to her how to order *balayage and slinger mer naturelle* at the hairdressing salon at Quai de la Pêcherie.

However, they were in the wrong end of town and far from the hospital and after a couple of days they moved to a hotel in St. Genis Laval. Eventually, they found a 1-bedroom apartment in the old part of Lyon at le quai Pierre-Scize belonging to a film producer who had once lived in Abidjan in Africa.

The building was over 300 years old and had many Roman features. There were still cobblestones in the yard below where they used to have stables for the horses pulling the carriages. Bodie and Clyde were actually on the *nobility level*, two floors above the yard. The elevator was tiny, because it had been added on recently to the building. When they stepped inside the apartment they saw very high ceilings with solid wood beams and a very comfortable living room with a dinette set. All the furniture was modern and from IKEA. Both rooms had French balconies and faced the winding Soâne. Clyde was completely dumbfounded over this miracle of accommodation and he never got tired of watching the ships passing by. Besides it was far cheaper than staying in a hotel. The market was across the bridge and Bodie would walk there with a wicker basket over her arm like all the French women did.

Old Lyon was like a small village, where it was easy to get to know people. Locals would walk their dogs and nobody picked up the excrements, yet the streets were very clean as the firemen came every morning with a pressure hose to wash the mess away. It was easy to take the train or a bus and go anywhere. When it rained it was nice to sit and have a coffee in Café Brioche and watch life go by – like the old drunkard wearing a black felt hat and singing Christmas songs in the middle of spring to a white dog sitting on his lap. One could take a bus all the way up the steep hill through the renaissance district and to the Basilica de Notre Dame de Fourvière. Inside the monastery angels were playing the harp; outside they were holding weapons. All the angels had rings around their heads. Those with red rings were the good angels, the bad ones wore blue rings. Blue was feared from the Roman times when the Barbarians used to paint their bodies blue to scare off the enemy. Red stood for life and strength, energy and dignity.

Many times the couple blended in with all the people on *Place Bellecour* indulging in ice cream with *coulis de framboise* or consuming *café allongé*. Once they were entertained by Tango-dancers, all dressed up in ballroom costumes in the middle of the afternoon. Parades came by as all the action centered around *Place Bellecour.* In the evening they would sit out in the streets and have dinner and the choices were endless: Les Enfants Terribles, Little Italy or a bistro in Rue Mercière. Once a month Clyde had treatments at the hospital and the week before he went for blood tests. On the day of treatment the nurses would warn him that he could not have any wine until after 5 p.m. One clearly got the impression in France that wine was as important as food and part of life! On special occasions Bodie and Clyde would dine at Les Muses, a restaurant unknown to most as it didn't advertise and relied on word of mouth recommendations, located on the 7th floor of the Opera House of Lyon with a panoramic view.

Clyde had to live without a TV in quai Pierre-Scize as he did not own the apartment and could not present proof of having paid utilities. That was necessary to get not only TV connection, but also Internet. In the end they managed without like many in France and soon found an internet-café on Quai Gailleton, which was on the other side of the bridge. The staff of the internet-café would arrive in the morning on *trottinettes,* riding these scooters very fast on the pavement among the pedestrians.

Soon Lyon became their home and Sister Nancy came once to visit. During that time they took her to the zoo through the majestic entrance admiring the impressive statue *Centauresse et Faune* depicting a horse that was half human. Then they hired a tricycle to show off the zoo, the two younger adults peddling and the nun grinning in the middle.

The idea of visiting the zoo originated from Zsa Zsa and Mano, who also came to visit on their way to Nice. "Have you been to the Zoo? Oh, you must go there!" she had told them during a brief meeting in a bar close to Place Bellecour. She had Muffin under the table in his doggy-bag and the minute she opened the zipper, he repeated his trick of shooting up like a rocket. Muffin appeared to understand the French language as well as Italian and English.

Tut and Edgar also came to visit Lyon to check on Clyde's progress. They drove from Zürich in Switzerland where they lived in the summertime. Never did they imagine that Lyon was such a charming place and the two couples chose one day to take a river cruise together.

Mostly, bad news came from Zimbabwe. Inflation continued to be rampant and from the time the notes were printed until they got into circulation, they had lost their value. The highest note in Zimbabwe and the last one printed was 100 trillion Zimbabwe dollars. One wondered if they called themselves *sextillionaires*? Since the government declared inflation illegal and froze all prices, many company directors were arrested for increasing prices and the country came to a standstill. In December 2008, the Reserve Bank of Zimbabwe under Governor Gideon Gono licensed around 1,000 shops to deal in foreign currency. This fix was like a drop in the ocean and finally, in

January 2009, the government accepted foreign currency as a legal tender on the market and you could now deal in U.S., Rand, British Pound, Euro and Suisse Francs. In April that same year the U.S. dollar eventually became the preferential currency.

For many, of course, it was already too late, because the price controls had drained their resources and they went broke. Also, the poor had no foreign currency and the rainfall the past season was not nearly enough. With no aid coming to the country, the people were starving. For several years they had not been able to buy seeds for growing their crops, and when finally this year, they could buy seeds again, all the germinated maize had dried up and withered because of the scarcity of rain. In many villages, all the rivers had dried up.

In the city of Harare, all the shelves were suddenly full of goods again and a few potholes on the main road were fixed. However, the general state of the infrastructure did not improve and people regarded basics such as electricity and water as a real luxury. Some had been living without running water for several years. The lucky ones with borehole-water were slightly better off, but they needed electricity to turn on the borehole and with no electricity, a generator was needed. The generator noise was unbearable, but there was no alternative.

As nobody trusted the stability in the country, the brain drain and money flight continued. Many foreigners living part-time in Zimbabwe suddenly found it had become expensive to have servants as they now had to pay them in U.S. dollars. The price of food and the cost of living had gone up drastically and they no longer felt like "the rich white man in Africa."

On the surface, Harare changed a lot with new places opening for evening entertainment, supermarkets offering fancy goods and a new mall opened opposite the main Post Office. You could suddenly buy anything your heart desired in U.S. dollars, but very few could afford it. Some of the local people never had the chance to get their hands on any foreign currency. The ugly truth was that the country started to look like other mismanaged states in Africa, with hardly any local production. The country could not even feed the people. The ones in the city and a few other areas with electricity would have power cuts five out of seven evenings and prepared themselves with little 'miner's lamps' strapped to their heads to have their hands free to carry things. Despite all the new restaurants, most people found it was a frightening experience to go by car at night, as there were no streetlights working in the city or the suburbs anymore. Rusty poles were left lying in many places after they had been hit by a vehicle. On a pitch dark night it was impossible to see all the dangers; potholes were so numerous and so deep that one had to drive on the wrong side of the road to pass them with traffic coming in the opposite direction threatening a head on collision.

Although the daily black market was replaced with a sense of Western consumer mentality, meaning you no longer had the hassle of keeping up with inflation, the flight of foreign currency continued and U.S. dollar notes in circulation were the same old notes getting dirtier every time they changed hands. The ruling elite, which were given productive farms taken from white farmers, had no farming experience and some of them hired back the previous white farmers that they had chased off, to run their farms as managers. Many of these whites started earning more than they ever did as owners.

Peasants driven to farm on land no bigger than a small garden in the city were doomed to remain in poverty as they could not even feed the family from the small crop they grew. Apart from struggling to survive with lack of infrastructure and no electricity and water, they had another worry far bigger for them. As a result of being relocated, they would not be able to join their ancestors when they died. They felt haunted by their ancestral spirits and knew they would be punished.

Large diamond fields always existed in Zimbabwe. In 2006, the Marange fields in eastern Zimbabwe were discovered containing one of the biggest diamond deposits in the world. Observers and watchdogs estimate that diamonds worth more than 2 billion U.S. dollars have been stolen by the President's inner circle in co-operation with international dealers and criminals. The proceeds never went through the state treasury, but the ruling elite from the military and politburo got rich.

Entering 2013, President Mugabe of Zimbabwe is again making a stir and calling for new elections. On the land question, his government announced in December 2012 that they would seize the last few white-owned farms protected under bilateral treaties. More than 4,000 whites were displaced and chased off their farms by the violent land reforms in 2000, but it was harder to expropriate the 153 farms which were protected by bilateral agreements; still the Zimbabwe government took 116 of them during the farm invasions. Now, the last 37 farmers are to suffer the same fate and although many of the cases are already with the International Court for Settlement of Investment Disputes (ICSID), there are leadership disputes in Zimbabwe concerning the liability to compensate the white farmers. President Mugabe vowed no payment for any land, but his land reform minister Herbert Murerwa seemed to disagree and promised the government would abide by the international court. However, the Zimbabwean leadership concluded that it was too broke to make any payouts.

Again, with a view to winning the coming elections in 2013, Mugabe has also alarmed factory owners as he has warned that the aim of his government is to transfer the remaining shareholding of 49% from whites to black factory workers. In other words, to win the next election he must unveil another reign of terror with a blood bath as he did in 2008.

B.A.K. SIM was born in Denmark, but has lived most of her adult life abroad. She has lived in 10 countries and was posted as a diplomat to Brazil, Venezuela, Saudi Arabia, India and Zimbabwe. She knew the foreign service inside and out as she was trained as a Chancellor. During her tenure of office she often acted as Chargé d'affaires a.i., and whilst in India she established diplomatic relations between Bhutan and Denmark.

The author is known as Dila to her many friends and colleagues spanning all walks of life. She has rubbed shoulders with ministers and politicians, international dignitaries, royalty and celebrities from television and broadcasting. Her closest friends run the gamut from old diplomatic and business colleagues to eccentric people in art and show business.

B.A.K. Sim lived in Zimbabwe for 22 years, and now lives in Victoria, on Vancouver Island in British Columbia, Canada, with her Canadian husband.